# Contents

# Tables, figures and boxes

## Tables

# Political marketing
# and British political parties

MANCHESTER
UNIVERSITY PRESS

**Political Analyses**

Series editors: Bill Jones and Michael Moran

# Political marketing and British political parties

## The party's just begun

Jennifer Lees-Marshment

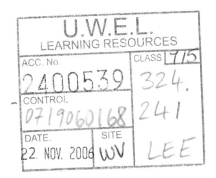
Manchester University Press
Manchester and New York
distributed exclusively in the USA by Palgrave

*Published by* Manchester University Press
Oxford Road, Manchester Ml 3 9NR, UK
*and* Room 400, 175 Fifth Avenue, New York, NY 10010, USA
http://www.manchesteruniversitypress.co.uk

*Distributed exclusively in the USA by*
Palgrave, 175 Fifth Avenue, New York, NY 10010, USA

*Distributed exclusively in Canada by*
UBC Press, University of British Columbia, 2029 West Mall,
Vancouver, BC, Canada V6T 1Z2


*British Library Cataloguing-in-Publication Data*
A catalogue record for this book is available from the British Library

*Library of Congress Cataloging-in-Publication Data applied for*


ISBN 0 7190 6016 8 *hardback*
     0 7190 6017 6 *paperback*

First published 2001

10 09 08 07 06 05 04     10 9 8 7 6 5 4 3 2

Typeset in Photina
by Action Publishing Technology Ltd, Gloucester
Printed in Great Britain
by CPI Bath

## Figures

## Boxes

To Tracey

# Series editors' foreword

The *Politics Today* series has been running successfully since the late 1970s, aimed mainly at an undergraduate audience. After over a decade in which a dozen or more titles had been produced, some of which have run to several new editions, MUP thought it time to launch a new politics series, aimed at a different audience and a different need.

The *Political Analyses* series was prompted by a relative dearth of research-based political science series which persists despite the fecund source of publication ideas provided by current political developments. In the UK we observe, for example: the rapid evolution of Labour politics as the party seeks to find a reliable electoral base; the continuing development of the post-Thatcher Conservative Party; the growth of pressure group activity and lobbying in modern British politics; and the irresistible moves towards constitutional reform of an arguably outdated state.

Abroad, there are even more themes upon which to draw, for example: the ending of the Thatcher–Reagan axis; the parallel collapse of communism in Europe and Russia; and the gradual retreat of socialism from the former heartlands in Western Europe.

The series seeks to explore some of these new ideas to a depth beyond the scope of the *Politics Today* series – while maintaining a similar direct and accessible style – and to serve an audience of academics, practitioners and the well-informed reader as well as undergraduates.

# Preface and acknowledgements

Acknowledgements are due to the organisations which provided the financial and institutional support that made this research possible. The ESRC funded my Master's Degree in the Department of Government at Manchester University between 1996 and 1997, and Keele University my Ph.D. through a Graduate Teaching Assistantship in the Department of Politics between 1997 and 1999. I am grateful for support from many people in all those departments, but particularly Matthew Wyman, my Ph.D. supervisor at Keele, who backed me throughout my doctorate, and David Farrell and Andrew Russell who helped me develop the idea of studying political marketing at Manchester. Outside these institutions, Dominic Wring acted as a 'surrogate supervisor', linking me into the UK political marketing group which offered invaluable encouragement, especially Phil Harris and Neil Collins. Allan Leonard gave feedback on conference papers and the book draft, as did Heather Savigny; she and Mick Temple supported the final push for publication. Roger Mortimore provided data from MORI. My involvement in the Political Studies Association, particularly the Graduate Network and serving on the Executive Committee, acted as a great source of motivation: in particular those such as Denis Krivosheev, Gabor Stojanovits, Dale Mineshima, Rachel Greenstein and Terri Collier within the graduate network. Outside of work I drew encouragement from my family in England and Australia with trips to Birmingham and Brisbane both providing most welcome breaks from academic theorising about Market-Oriented Parties. Flatmates Susie Bobbett and Caroline Whitehand provided a welcome retreat from the office; Peter Ingram, Anna Harrison and Mira Duric patiently listened to me going on about political marketing many times over coffee; away from Keele, Hayley, Asha and Jade provided a very welcome non-academic ear to my ramblings about parties acting like businesses and helped me to plough on in the Ph.D. battle.

Nonetheless, I believe that, after having thanked everyone who has helped so that they can share any credit, it is customary to make sure that one takes all the blame oneself. It was in the autumn of 1996 that I came up with the idea of what to study for my Ph.D. How political parties behave and represent the people has always been of interest to me. At that time, British party electoral politics was in a bizarre state. I knew traditional Labour supporters who were unhappy with the direction their party was taking under Tony Blair and Tories who were saying that for the first time in their life they were not going to vote Conservative at the next election. Both major parties were alienating their traditional supporters. Yet arguably this was at a time when parties were using marketing and offering voters what they wanted. This led me to study political marketing and write a book that reaches a somewhat controversial conclusion. At the turn of the century, parties are becoming more responsive to voters' needs and wants. They are not resting on support granted by socialisation, or a segregated social and class structure, but are trying to win and maintain support by identifying demands and then delivering them in government. The first half of the twentieth century was a positive start for party electoral relations, with the achievement of mass democracy in Britain. Towards the end, the story became a less happy one of party decline and rising voter dissatisfaction. As we start the twenty-first century, the prospects seem more positive. Parties may have a long way to go before the full potential of political marketing is realised: the current Labour Government has a difficult task to deliver all its pledges; but maybe it is at least on the right path. Others may consider this path to be a bad one. I respond by inviting them to say so and why. This book shows the road modern major parties have taken and although there may be a debate about whether this is a good one and where it will lead, at least it can now begin.

Jennifer Lees-Marshment

# Abbreviations

| | |
|---|---|
| BES | British Election Study |
| CCO | Conservative Central Office |
| CPM | Comprehensive Political Marketing |
| MOP | Market-Oriented Party |
| MPs | Members of Parliament |
| POP | Product-Oriented Party |
| SOP | Sales-Oriented Party |

# 1

# Political parties
# and political marketing:
# what is it all about?

British party behaviour has changed. Political parties no longer pursue grand ideologies, fervently arguing for what they believe in and trying to persuade the masses to follow them. They increasingly follow the people. This is because voters have changed. The majority of the people in this country will not simply vote for the party their parents supported. They are more critical of parties, expecting them to deliver what they want. To survive in this new electoral market, where voters act like consumers, parties are acting like businesses. Parties use modern technology and marketing techniques to understand what voters want. Moreover they adopt the market-oriented concept: they focus on satisfying voters' demands. Rather than relying on traditional ideology passed down through the family to secure them votes, parties concentrate on proving effective in improving people's lives through their action in government. They produce clearer pledges and, once in government, all attention is turned to delivery. When they go against this behaviour and focus on selling themselves (sales-oriented) or simply push their argument in the old-fashioned style of politics (product-oriented), they lose votes. They then try to become a Market-Oriented Party once again because this is the most likely way they will ever win a general election.

This raises questions for British democracy. If parties change, the whole system could be transformed as the focus moves from debating what politicians should do to implementing what the public wants. Is this what parties, politicians, our leaders and governors should do? Can parties ever really deliver? Or is it an improvement in democracy: as the people become demanding of their leaders, maybe only now, in the twenty-first century, will we see true democracy emerging where parties and government really serve the people. This is a debate that needs to begin now, but first we must understand how party behaviour has changed. This book will show clearly what has happened.

## The study of political marketing

Political marketing is a new area of academic research. It requires under-standing and integration of two disciplines: political science and management science. Marketing is a field within the latter. Political marketing attempts to be a field of both. It also calls for a brave scholar to do battle with both fields of academia because arguments for the rise and importance of political marketing always meet with opposition. Political marketing has been criticised for being simply about advertising, slogans, sound-bites and spin-doctors. This is part of marketing, part of the tech-niques, but the more fundamental difference comes with the *concepts* of marketing, most notably the market-oriented concept. These can be applied to the political product, not simply how it is sold or advertised. Political marketing can be applied comprehensively to all aspects of politi-cal behaviour. A party can use political marketing to determine its behaviour including policies, leader, and membership powers. It is not simply concerned with how it sells itself.

One of the reasons for misconceptions about political marketing is that academics have not demonstrated how broad its scope is. There has clearly been a sudden increase in conference papers, articles and even books on the topic produced since the 1990s, but the majority focus on campaigns and communication. The subject also remains somewhat limited in theo-retical understanding and scope. These limits are unsurprising given the youth of the field. But if political marketing is to reach its potential it needs to be pushed beyond the confines of political communication. Existing liter-ature in the field can be broken down into three groups. This book leads the field into a fourth stage of development: Comprehensive Political Marketing or CPM.

### *The founding fathers: management science and political science*

Both disciplines offer plentiful literature on the basics of marketing and politics. Management science, and within it marketing, discusses the goals of firms, their organisation, their approach (product-, sales- or market-oriented) and techniques (the 4Ps: product, price, place and promotion). Political science discusses the different political organisations: parties, interest groups, the media and other aspects such as election campaigns, voting behaviour and political communication. It also offers models of behaviour. The literature within both is immense and provides a solid foundation for political marketing which aims to bring the two areas together.

*The innovators: non-profit marketing*

The management science discipline/marketing field was the first to take marketing for business and apply it to non-profit areas, including charities, and hospitals, as well as political candidates and parties. In 1969, an article by Kotler and Levy argued that the domain of marketing should be expanded to include non-business organisations, persons and ideas. This aroused tremendous controversy within management science with criticisms including those from Tucker (1974: 32), Luck (1969), Carman (1973) and O'Leary and Iredale (1976: 153). Arndt (1978: 101) objected, on academic discipline grounds, that such 'a combined semantic and territorial expansion may threaten the conceptual integrity of marketing, add to the confusion in terminology, and widen the gulf between marketing theory and practice'. Nonetheless, theoretical and empirical research followed on the use of marketing in areas such as university recruitment, fundraising, transportation, public services and churches. The *Journal of Marketing* in July 1971 contained several articles on non-profit marketing. Lovelock and Weisberg (1977) produced a book of case-studies. Kotler (1969, 1972, 1979, 1991) authored and co-authored a number of other pieces of research, such as an article (1979) on how to introduce marketing into a non-profit organisation, with full appreciation of marketing theory for businesses, but also a consideration of the differences between business and non-profit organisations. His book (with Andreasen (1991)) was dedicated to the subject of marketing for non-profit organisations. Other examples include Rothschild (1979), Shapiro (1973), Scrivens and Witzel (1990), Cousins (1990), Gwin (1990), Von der Hart and Hein (1990), Lancaster and Massingham (1993), Evans and Berman (1994: 398) and Walsh (1994). Within management science today there is significant research and teaching on non-profit marketing. Its value, at least for understanding politics, is nonetheless limited because it somewhat inevitably neglects incorporating traditional literature in political science.

*The developers: political marketing communication*

The next stage in the development of the field was led by political science scholars who attempted to bring such marketing concepts and techniques and apply them to political communication. Works in this category include Farrell and Wortmann (1987), Franklin (1994), Kavanagh (1995) and Scammell (1995), Harrop (1990), Bowler and Farrell (eds) (1992), Webb (1992b: 43–62) and, in the USA, Shama (1976), Niffenegger (1989), Newman (1994, 1999), Newman (ed.) (1999), Wring (1994–95 etc.) and O'Shaughnessy (1990). This has key limitations:

- it focuses on political communication: on how politicians sell themselves, not how they behave;
- it does not use marketing theory.

Franklin (1994), Kavanagh (1995) and Scammell (1995), for example, provide valuable empirical observation of changes in political communication in Britain: how politicians sell their product. But they do not analyse how they determine the nature of that product in the first place. Research in this category also neglects a comprehensive or in some cases even simple utilisation of marketing theory. Scammell (1995), for example, has little discussion of what political marketing is, beyond a definition offered by the Academy of Marketing and a few sentences. It does not offer or use a theoretical framework and does not consider all the three marketing orientations (product, sales and market), choosing to take marketing as equating a market orientation only. In this regard, Wring (1994–95 etc.) is the exception. Wring applies all three orientations but, again, the focus is on communication: on party campaign organisation. Political communication is obviously an important area of research, and election campaigns an exciting area of study, and all political marketing work in this category is undoubtedly of value. But in the real world political marketing is not used simply to determine communication. It is applied much more widely to inform the design of policy, organisational structures and participation rights. Political marketing can enrich aspects of political studies far removed from election campaigns, such as local government, the media, interest groups and party behaviour. It is the fourth category of political marketing study that will do this.

### *The integrators: Comprehensive Political Marketing (CPM)*

This category takes the field of political marketing further in five distinct ways.

1 *CPM views marketing as more than simply political communication*
   Indeed, the main argument of this book is that the most significant influence political marketing has had on parties is to determine their behaviour, not simply how they advertise it.
2 *CPM applies marketing to the whole behaviour of a political organisation*
   In this book about parties, therefore, marketing is applied not just to how they campaign, but what they try to sell in that campaign – their product, not just how that product is advertised. Marketing is applied to a party's leader, policy, organisation, members, candidates, symbols, activities and staff. Analysis carries from the beginning through to the end of an electoral cycle (not just the election campaign).
3 *CPM uses marketing concepts, not just techniques: the product, sales and*

*market orientation as well as market intelligence, product design and promotion*
This book therefore produces different models of a Product-, Sales- and Market-Oriented Party and produces a marketing process for how each one would behave during an electoral cycle.
4 *CPM integrates political science literature into the analysis*
Marketing is integrated and adapted to suit the understanding gained from traditional study of parties. The party's 'product' is therefore defined to include all the aspects of parties we study.
5 *CPM adapts marketing theory to suit the differing nature of politics*
In this study, therefore, aspects of marketing are changed or adapted to suit what we already know about political parties. There is a synergy between the two disciplines. It does not simply take marketing and apply it as it is even where it does not make sense. Work produced strictly from a management science perspective will fail by trying to fit politics into marketing, when the empirical reality is the other way round. It uses marketing to deepen the understanding of politics, to add to that already gained by existing traditional political science.

This book falls into this category. Comprehensive political marketing requires a greater integration and mix of literatures than has previously been attempted and this study is the first to attempt such a goal. CPM could also be applied to other political organisations, such as the public services and local government. This is where the real potential of political marketing lies: to help understand different approaches to behaviour and how organisations respond to those they seek to serve. This book will show how political marketing helps us to analyse political parties: future books and research which work within this category will have important stories to tell us about other areas of political studies.

## Methodology

Political science in the USA and now Britain has become dominated by the empiricist, positivist, behaviouralist approach to studying politics. This favours hard data, statistics, in an attempt to 'prove' things that literary analysis – words – cannot. I sympathise with this approach and fully appreciate the arguments behind it: that it leads to greater objectivity; data which can be re-tested; and fulfils the desire of politics to be studied scientifically. Indeed, I was 'brought up' in this tradition, studying American politics as an undergraduate before I turned to Britain. However, this book, which researches party behaviour, attitude, management and how this affects the level of support that parties attract from members and voters, is not amenable to such a methodology. The topic is too broad and too complex to be amenable to statistical verification. I cannot prove that parties act as Market-oriented Parties – even if I had been able to interview all politicians within the two parties from 1979 to the present day, how could we trust their word? Or their understanding of a 'market orientation'? I also had no desire to repeat empirical accounts of 'what happened' that already exist. There is no point in repeating data gathering to achieve apparent originality, especially considering that interviews and impressions are often best conducted soon after the event rather than twenty years later. But I still wanted to do this research and was not going to be put off because it did not fit with a particular methodology and approach.

I have written this book because someone needs to say (and write down) what is happening in British party politics so that it can be discussed. Some people might say we already know how parties behave, but nowhere is it to be found written down in its entirety in a way that we can take its lesson and teach it to undergraduates as a way of updating the by-now-out-dated common material on first-year university politics courses. This book is about analysis. It contains thoughts about empirical behaviour using integrated theoretical concepts. It is about how parties behave and voters responded to them. It contends that analysis is not an academic crime. Although primary data gathering is important, secondary analysis that questions such information, explaining why and how, making connections, and discussing consequences, is equally as valid an academic activity.

The book draws on a wide range of literature. It takes material from marketing, political marketing and all relevant areas of political sciences: literature on political parties (organisation, functions, policy, members, leaders), voting behaviour, changes in society and political culture, the media, election campaigns, electoral studies and polling. Both primary and secondary sources are used, on both theoretical and empirical levels. It also includes party documents, accounts by party figures and statistical measures from polls and the British Election Study (BES). It integrates this literature theoretically and empirically. This synthesis, within a comprehensive political marketing framework, produces new analysis. It is not intended or designed to be 100 per cent original: to override all political science before this date would be nonsensical. But there is a need for a timely and topical re-assessment of party behaviour which captures what parties do, why and with what effect. This leaves the book open to criticism, of being full of assertion only – we cannot prove that a market orientation and nothing else won Labour the 1997 election. But we can analyse all the available evidence and argue that it did. If we limit political science to that which is only 'provable' we restrict the subjects that can be discussed and would miss debating extremely important phenomena.

This book is intended to ensure that we do not lose the opportunity to discuss the marketing of political parties.

### Structure of the book

The rest of this chapter will outline the theoretical framework. It will first outline the traditional views of political parties, and recent changes to the electoral market which have helped to encourage the rise of political marketing. It goes on to explain what political marketing is, and how parties can use it. This sets out the models of the Product-Oriented Party, Sales-Oriented Party and Market-Oriented Party.

This framework will then be used throughout the rest of the book to show how the party that adopted a market orientation was the one that won the election. At times, either Labour or the Conservatives would move away from this behaviour, focusing on trying to sell policies voters did not want (sales-oriented) or simply arguing their case and expecting voters to agree (product-oriented). As the book will show, this behaviour always lost support for the party.

Chapter 2 analyses the Conservative Party under Margaret Thatcher from 1979 to 1990. Parties in Britain throughout the last quarter of the twentieth century used political marketing. Not only did Thatcher use advertising professionals to try to influence her image as leader: the results of market intelligence informed Conservative policies. The case is an effective illustration of how political marketing influences not just the presentation but the nature of a party's product. The rest of the chapter explores the Conservative Party's ability to deliver and remain responsive to voters in government, between 1979 and 1987. Finally, it studies how problems emerged for Thatcher between 1987 and 1990 as the leader's increasing strength and control over her party made it difficult for her to maintain a market orientation. She neglected the more subtle organisational aspects of political marketing and took on a product orientation with regard to the party and indeed the country. Political marketing can be very successful, but problems emerge if a party or leader begins to neglect it.

Chapter 3 examines Product-Oriented Party behaviour. When parties simply do what they think is best, voters reject them. The Labour Party became increasingly product-oriented in government and subsequently lost the 1979 election. Between 1992 and 1997 the Conservative Government adopted similar behaviour and suffered heavy losses in the election. In 1983, Labour adopted a classic product orientation in opposition, pursuing its ideology above voters' demands. The party not only lost the election but experienced its lowest electoral fortunes. The market has changed: voters will no longer accept this approach to politics. Political conviction has died.

Chapter 4 shows the limits of sales-oriented marketing and why Labour did not win in 1987 and 1992. Sales-Oriented Party behaviour focuses on trying to sell the product more effectively. Although Labour adopted a sales orientation in 1987 and ran a professional election campaign, this did not yield electoral dividends. Changes to the actual product remained circumscribed even by 1992, and Labour remained in opposition. Voters want the product to change, not just its presentation.

It was only when Labour adopted a market orientation and began directly to design its behaviour to suit voters that its fortunes changed. Chapter 5 explores the most recent case in political marketing in detail: Blair and the New Labour design. Covering 1992–99, it shows how Labour was in many ways the classic Market-Oriented Party, but also shows the limits of Blair's marketing. It has caused many problems for the party at the beginning of the twenty-first century.

The overall conclusion in Chapter 6 is nonetheless that political marketing is here to stay. Labour is still focused on delivery in government and staying true to the Market-Oriented Party model. Since the 1997 election and their substantial losses the Tories have nevertheless turned round very quickly to try to adopt a market orientation. They have a long way to go but the changes made 'behind the scenes' under the Hague leadership have laid important foundations for future recovery. Overall, both British major parties are currently competing to be market-oriented. This is where the real competition will come, as both parties struggle not to convince the electorate of their ideological argument but that it is the best one to respond to what voters want, to deliver in government. The rest of the chapter discusses the consequences of this conclusion: considering political marketing and democracy, the problems and the potential for improving representative democracy. It also considers the political marketing revolution – how marketing can be applied to and used in other areas of politics, such as interest groups, media, local government and the public services. Political marketing will make the British system more responsive to the people. The party has just begun.

## Political parties: the traditional view

The study of political parties is a major area in political science: all major undergraduate textbooks on politics devote a section to party behaviour. They form the government and hold potential influence on policy outputs that affect people's everyday lives. They also fulfil a normative representative role. They have an important part to play in the political system as a whole. Existing literature on parties gives us a fairly clear idea of their basic nature: of their definition, status, functions, goals, market and characteristics.

## The basics

### Definition
In liberal democracies such as Britain, a political party is an organisation that seeks to compete in democratic elections in order to win elections to hold public office. It consists of a group of people, with common ideas, which puts up candidates for election and has a more or less permanent organisation. The desire to win elections renders it distinctive to pressure groups, who, although seeking to influence government, do not aim to form that government themselves and have a smaller, more specific interest to represent.

### Major/minor status
There are important differences between major and minor parties. Minor parties compete in elections but attract less electoral support. They do not realistically expect to control government, although they may form part of it with other parties. They tend to focus on a smaller range of issues or represent a smaller constituency. This research will focus on established major parties, because their role is much wider. Major parties are expected to win general elections and more questions are asked of them if they successively fail to do so. Challenges to parties are aimed more at established major parties, threatening their dominance as the major channel for demands and participation in the system. They have different goals and starting positions and will use political marketing differently to minor parties.

### Functions
Parties perform practical functions: they recruit elites, providing the country with leaders and office-holders at all levels. They organise and form government and facilitate co-operation between the executive and legislature. Great importance is traditionally attached to their role in the political system. Parties are the principle means of representation, serving to ensure that there is an effective link between citizens and the government. They also serve to aggregate and defend interests, bringing a variety of conflicting individual demands together, which aids governing. They formulate and implement goals through designing party manifestos, competing in elections and passing legislation in government. Parties also facilitate political socialisation and mobilisation, bringing people into the system. This helps create amongst voters a feeling of belonging and

connection with government, which increases diffuse support for the system as a whole.

*Goal*
Political parties have various goals arising from these functions. There is a debate in political science about what parties try to do. Traditionally, parties are viewed as pursuing a particular ideology. In the case of Labour that is Socialism and the Tories' Conservatism. From this they determine their policies and try to put these into practice to suit those who they represent. An alternative and dominant argument is that the main goal of major parties is long-term electoral success: they aim to win enough votes in general elections to win control of government and do whatever is necessary to achieve this (see Downs (1957: 28), Laver (1997: 111), Lock and Harris (1996: 25), Schlesinger (1984 and 1994) and Harmel and Janda (1994) for discussion).

*Market*
Major parties seek to serve various sections and sub-groups in society. The interests of these groups sometimes conflict and are influenced by institutional features, such as the party's organisational structure and the electoral system, as well as the political culture and concept of party in the particular country. Traditionally each major party in Britain has its own separate constituency based on class: Labour represented the working classes and the Conservative Party the higher classes.

If the dominant goal of a major party is electoral success, however, its prime market consists of the voters whose support it requires to achieve electoral success and this can vary. Superficially, then, it consists of those eligible to vote in a general election, limited to the section of it required to win office, taking into account electoral rules, boundaries and seat distribution. The party would also consider any other part of the population with influence upon this electorate. For example voters may also be influenced by the needs and wants of others in the population, such as their children. Voters make up the party's external supporters, but may be affected by a sub-set of members: the party's internal supporters. It has been argued by Seyd and Whiteley (1992) and Whiteley *et al.* (1994) in their study of the British Conservative and Labour Party memberships that loyal and active members generate votes. A party will therefore need to pay attention to members' demands because they can influence external supporters. Members may have different and conflicting goals themselves and thus want different things to voters at large. Political parties have to try to reconcile these differences or to ensure that the membership is representative of the electorate so that their goals and interests will be similar. Members can also help a party achieve its goal, as they too want electoral success. Another likely demand that members make is for participation, which need not be counter-productive to winning elections.

*Characteristics*

Political parties have many additional characteristics, although they vary between political systems and countries. In Britain a political party's behaviour encompasses many characteristics, is ongoing and offered at all times (not just elections), at all levels of the party. It thus includes the following aspects:

- *Leadership*: powers, image, character, support/appeal, relationship with the rest of the party organisation (advisers, cabinet, members, MPs), media relationship.
- *Members of Parliament* (existing or proposed): candidate nature, relationship with constituents etc.
- *Membership*: powers, recruitment, nature (ideological character, activity, loyalty, behaviour, relationship to leader).
- *Staff*: researchers, professionals, advisers etc. – their role, influence, office powers, relationship with other parts of the party organisation.
- *Symbols*: name, logo, anthem.
- *Constitution*: formal, official rules.
- *Activities*: party conferences, rallies, meetings.
- *Policies*: those proposed for when in office and those enacted once in office.

All of these components are important, not least because they can influence the support a party is able to attract from its market (even if some factors have more influence than others). It is not just a single candidate, its manifesto or campaign posters which is important in British general elections.

### Behaviour

Now that we have an idea of the basic make-up of parties, we can move to the next level of analysis and discuss how parties behave. Parties can take different approaches to how they determine their behaviour. This in turn affects their ability to achieve their goals and fulfil their role in the political system. Political science already has a number of models that attempt to portray the way parties behave: the Mass Party, Downs' economic rationality model, the Catch-All Party, the Electoral Professional Party and the Cartel Party.

*The Mass Party, Duverger (1954)*
The most long-standing model is the Mass Party (Duverger (1954)). This

argued that parties emerged from and to represent a group (or class) of people in society. Parties had strong roots in that section of society: providing channels by which people could be involved in politics, not just politically but also socially. Parties also pursued a distinct and particular ideology according to the 'stratification of society' (Duverger 1954: 419). Thus, the British Labour Party emerged to represented the working class and advanced a socialist ideology: the Conservatives came principally from the higher classes and sought to promote Conservatism. Each party offered competing views on 'production and the distribution of wealth, on the distribution of incomes, on the organisation and promotion of the elite'. Arguably, this ensured electoral choice and defence of different interests in society. Ideology also helped to generate strong, long-term support for the parties and thus the political system as a whole.

*Downs' economic rationality model (1957)*
The Mass Party was challenged by Downs (1957). Built on the foundations of economic rational choice and ideas originally put forward by Hotelling (1929), Downs argued that parties are rational actors and change their behaviour to capture the middle ground of electoral support in order to win elections. Therefore 'parties formulate policies in order to win elections, rather than win elections in order to formulate policies' (1957: 28).

*The Catch-all Party model, Kirchheimer (1966)*
Kirchheimer (1966) used the same rational choice basis, but provided more detail about how parties would behave as Downs suggested. He argued that Western liberal democracies had seen the rise of the Catch-all Party, which tries to attract the support of a broad majority in society: to 'catch-all'. The main characteristics of such a party are (see Kirchheimer (1966: 190)):

- drastic reduction of the party's ideological baggage;
- further strengthening of top leadership groups;
- downgrading of the role of the individual party member;
- de-emphasis of the specific social class in favour of recruiting voters among the population at large;
- securing access to a variety of interest groups.

*The Electoral-Professional Party, Panebianco (1988)*
Panebianco's (1988) Electoral-Professional Party followed the same line as Kirchheimer. This rests on the same basis as the Catch-all Party: that parties are changing who they appeal to. The Electoral-Professional Party appeals to the 'opinion-electorate' which votes according to its views, rather than a sense of belonging. The significant addition is that the

Electoral-Professional Party gives a central role to professionals within the organisation. Panebianco (1988: 264) thus explains that in 'the new type of party a much more important role is played by professionals (the so-called experts, technicians with special knowledge, they being more useful to the organisation than the traditional party bureaucrats), as the party's gravitational centre shifts from the members to the electorate'.

*Cartel Party model, Katz and Mair (1995)*
The most recent addition to the models of party behaviour is the Cartel model, by Katz and Mair (1995). This suggested that parties increasingly collude and act together, using the resources of the state to ensure their survival and resist challenges from new parties or movements. Rather than being 'brokers between civil society and the state, the parties now become absorbed by the state' (1995: 16). This is particularly true of 'countries in which state aid and support for parties is most pronounced' (1995: 17). Parties co-operate, using patronage appointments and offices, state resources such as party finance and regulation of the media.

If we tried to gain an understanding of party behaviour from these models, we might be a little confused as to which one is better or more accurate. One trend is distinctive: party behaviour has moved away from the Mass Party model because all subsequent models suggest a more rational basis for operation. It is not surprising that the first model might seem out of date. Party behaviour has altered over the last fifty years: parties need to respond to changes in society if they are to survive. At the turn of the twenty-first century, however, even the most recent models need updating, particularly for the study of parties in Britain. All the existing models can be criticised in some way which means that overall they do not provide a convincing explanation of current behaviour. For example, the Catch-all Party argued that parties were downgrading the role of the individual member but both parties in Britain, and indeed elsewhere, have sought to increase and expand their participation rights (see Katz and Mair (eds) (1994) and Seyd (1999)). Katz and Mair (1995: 25–6, footnote 4) themselves acknowledge the limited applicability of their Cartel Party model to Britain, because the political system or market-nature is different to other countries. Additionally, the models do not provide a complete picture as to how parties might act. For example, Downs argues that parties move towards the centre-ground and the median voter, but how do parties find out what the centre-ground is, how do they know what voters want? All models are subject to criticism. They are also likely to become time-bound, especially when the political environment has changed so substantially in Britain.

## Changes to the electoral market

A number of changes in the British electoral environment since the 1960s affect the way parties behave. This not only reduces the value of existing party models but provides an explanation for the rise of political marketing in Britain.

### Political factors

*Party identification* in Britain has fallen in terms of *overall level* but also the *strength of attachment*. The BES shows that although the overall number of respondents reporting identification remains high, those who report a very strong attachment has fallen: see Table 1.1.

**Table 1.1** *Party identification: strength of attachment, 1964–97*

*Question asked: [of those who express identification]: How strongly about [chosen party] do you generally feel – very strongly, fairly strongly or not very strongly?*

| Election study | % expressing very strong identification |
|---|---|
| 1964 | 42 |
| 1966 | 44 |
| 1970 | 41 |
| 1979 | 21 |
| 1983 | 20 |
| 1987 | 19 |
| 1992 | 19 |
| 1997 | 16 |

*Source:* BES except for 1970 which is from Norris (1997a: 101).
*Notes:* n = 1964: 936; 1966: 936; 1979: 1,893; 1983: 3,955; 1987: 3,826; 1992: 2,855; 1997: 3,615. 1970 not known.

*Party membership* levels have fallen: see Tables 1.2 and 1.3.

Furthermore, membership has also declined in terms of activity levels, as shown by studies of the Labour and Conservative Party by Seyd and Whiteley (1992) and Whiteley *et al.* (1994).

*New movements* challenge parties. Voters more readily turn to different forms of political participation, such as citizens' initiatives, new social movements, protest parties, anti-system parties and interest groups. These can provide more attractive and rewarding channels of action.

*Electoral volatility* has increased: see Table 1.4. Voters are less likely to vote for the same party over and over again.

**Table 1.2** *Party membership figures for the Labour Party, 1952–97*

|      | Estimated membership |
|------|----------------------|
| 1952 | 1,014,524 |
| 1957 | 912,987 |
| 1962 | 767,459 |
| 1964 | 830,116 |
| 1966 | 775,693 |
| 1967 | 733,032 |
| 1970 | 680,191 |
| 1972 | 703,030 |
| 1974 | 691,889 |
| 1977 | 659,737 |
| 1979 | 284,000 |
| 1982 | 273,803 |
| 1983 | 295,344 |
| 1987 | 288,829 |
| 1990 | 311,152 |
| 1991 | 261,000 |
| 1992 | 279,530 |
| 1993 | 280,000 |
| 1994 | 300,000 |
| 1995 | 345,840 |
| 1997 | 405,002 |

*Sources:* Seyd and Whiteley (1992: 16), Fielding (1995: 20), *Labour Weekly* (27 September 1979; quoted in Butler and Kavanagh (1980: 58)), Norris (1998a: 27), Seyd (1998: 65), Webb and Farrell (1999: 48) and *Daily Telegraph* report (14 May 1995).

**Table 1.3** *Party membership figures for the Conservative Party, 1953–97*

|      | Estimated membership |
|------|----------------------|
| 1953 | 2,800,000 |
| 1964 | 2,150,000 |
| 1966 | 2,150,000 |
| 1970 | 2,150,000 |
| 1974 | 1,500,000 |
| 1979 | 1,350,000 |
| 1983 | 1,200,000 |
| 1984 | 1,200,000 |
| 1987 | 1,000,000 |
| 1992 | 500,000 |
| 1997 | 400,000 |

*Source:* Norris (1997a: 105) and Webb and Farrell (1999: 48).

**Table 1.4** *Indications of electoral volatility in Britain, 1964–92*

| Year | Partisans voting for another party (%) | Decided in election campaign (%) |
|------|------|------|
| 1964 | 8 | 12 |
| 1966 | 9 | 11 |
| 1970 | 10 | 12 |
| 1974 (F) | 13 | 23 |
| 1974 (O) | 11 | 22 |
| 1979 | 11 | 28 |
| 1983 | 13 | 22 |
| 1987 | 14 | 21 |
| 1992 | 17 | 24 |

*Source:* Webb (1996: 372).
*Note:* F = February, O = October.

The support the major parties attract has declined. We can see this is various ways (data from Webb (1992a) and Norris (1997a: 38 and 47)):

- Their aggregate support has fallen:
  1959: 93.2 per cent
  1987: 73.1 per cent.
- Their share of parliamentary candidates has fallen:
  1945–70: 77 per cent
  1970–92: 55 per cent.
- The proportion of by-election seats which changed hands has increased:
  1945–70: 12.4 per cent
  1970–92: 30.4 per cent.

Voters also appear to be *anti-party*. They are more critical of politicians, parties and government. We can see this in various measures of voter satisfaction. For example, as Tables 1.5 and 1.6 suggest, satisfaction with the system of government and system efficacy have fallen.

**Table 1.5** *Satisfaction levels with the system of government*

*Question asked: Which of these statements best describes your opinion on the present system of governing Britain? – It works extremely well and could not be improved; it could be improved in small ways but it mainly works well; or it could be improved quite a lot/needs a great deal of improvement.*

| The system of governing Britain ... | 1973 (%) | 1977 (%) | 1991 (%) | 1994 (%) |
|------|------|------|------|------|
| 'could not be improved' or 'could be improved in small ways' | 48 | 34 | 33 | 29 |
| could be improved 'quite a lot' or 'a great deal' | 49 | 62 | 63 | 69 |

*Sources:* Curtice and Jowell (1995: 146) [for 1973, Crowther-Hunt and Peacock (1973); for 1977, Opinion Research Centre Survey; for 1991, MORI/Rowntree Trust State of the Nation Survey; for 1994, British Social Attitudes Survey].

**Table 1.6** *Trends in system efficacy*

| Those who strongly agree (%) | 1974 | 1986 | 1987 | 1991 | 1994 |
|---|---|---|---|---|---|
| Generally speaking, those we elect as MPs lose touch with people pretty quickly | 19 | 16 | 16 | 16 | 25 |
| Parties are only interested in people's votes, not in their opinions | 19 | 19 | 15 | 16 | 25 |
| It doesn't really matter which party is in power, in the end things go on much the same | – | – | – | 11 | 16 |

*Sources:* Curtice and Jowell (1995: 147–8) [for 1974, Political Action Study; for 1986, 1994; for 1994, British Social Attitudes Survey].
*Note:* Respondents were given a five-point scale (four-point in 1974), ranging from 'strongly agree' to 'strongly disagree'.

### Non-political changes

The challenge facing political parties is that there are underlying forces that contribute to these changes which, although influencing them, are outside their control. Such developments are subtle in nature, more like trends than actual concrete changes. A direct causal link is too complex to prove but there is still a strong argument that these social, economic and technological changes influence the political.

Before the advent of mass technology and its role in political communication, voters' engagement with partisan politics came via family members and other peers, reading newspapers, being members of a party, socialising at a party club and attending party meetings. From the party's point of view, these sources of political information were also sources of loyal, long-term support over which the party had some degree of control. People not only voted but supported a party according to a long-term, socio-psychological attachment created by family background, class and socialisation. Parties attracted support on the basis of something other than the satisfaction of policy-oriented demands which was sustainable even through short-term failure in party performance. A greater deference to leadership, lower levels of education and less fluid social structures helped to protect this support. Since the 1960s, socio-economic changes have undermined parties' ability to draw support from these traditional sources. Britain's society has changed significantly.

*Television has become the main source of information about politics for people in Britain.* Voters now receive their information:

• from a source over which parties have less control;

- about a greater number of issues;
- more of the time;
- and from different angles and perspectives.

People no longer need to rely on partisan sources of information such as newspapers in order to learn about politics. Television news-reporting is also more questioning of politicians and parties, making the television a critical force in the political environment.

*The availability of education has increased* substantially since the 1960s. An expanding number of institutions offer an ever-growing variety of courses, and greater numbers of people from diversifying backgrounds (in terms of age, gender, wealth and class) take up these opportunities. People leave school later, more go on to university, and greater numbers return to education in adult life. Table 1.7 shows that the percentage of the adult population achieving educational qualifications, particularly a degree, has increased. The proportion without qualifications has fallen.

**Table 1.7** *Qualifications of the adult population*

| Highest qualification | 1972 (%) | 1981 (%) | 1987 (%) |
|---|---|---|---|
| Degree | 3 | 7 | 10 |
| Higher education below degree | 5 | 9 | 12 |
| A-level or equivalent | 3 | 6 | 9 |
| O-level or equivalent | 10 | 13 | 20 |
| CSE, grades 2–5, etc. | 9 | 12 | 12 |
| Foreign and other | 3 | 4 | 3 |
| No qualification | 68 | 50 | 34 |

*Source:* Heath *et al.* (1991: 206), using the General Household Survey.
*Notes:* n = 1972: 23,163; 1981: 11,425; 1987: 15,637.

Higher educational levels arguably makes voters more critical and less attached to parties.

Other changes have occurred within the social structure. *Economic and geographical mobility has risen,* resulting in looser and less-controlled social organisation and interaction. Indeed, O'Shaughnessy (1990: 24) argues that political marketing arises when, amongst other things, 'geographically and socially mobile societies create a "value vacuum" and political territory is open with low pre-existing loyalties'. There has been *a decline in class and the salience of social cleavages* in Britain. The BES showed that the number of respondents who identified themselves as working class has fallen considerably since 1964: see Table 1.8.

**Table 1.8** *Self-identified class, 1964–92*

*Question asked (with minor variation): Do you ever think of yourself as belonging to any particular class? [If yes] Which class is that?*

|  | Working class (%) | Middle class (%) |
|---|---|---|
| 1964 | 74 | 25 |
| 1966 | 71 | 29 |
| 1974 | 57 | 36 |
| 1979 | 28 | 17 |
| 1987 | 30 | 16 |
| 1992 | 28 | 16 |

*Source:* BES.
*Notes:* n = 1964: 280; 1966: 892; 1974: 1,036; 1979: 1,983; 1987: 3,826; 1992: 2,855.

The needs, wants and demands made by people on government no longer stem from a cohesive and particular social group. In particular, the manual working class has declined: see Table 1.9.

**Table 1.9** *Decline of the manual working class, 1911–81*

|  | Total occupied population | Manual workers | Manual workers as % of occupied population |
|---|---|---|---|
| 1911 | 18,350,000 | 13,685,000 | 74.6 |
| 1921 | 19,332,000 | 13,920,000 | 72.0 |
| 1931 | 21,024,000 | 14,776,000 | 70.3 |
| 1951 | 22,515,000 | 14,022,000 | 64.2 |
| 1961 | 23,639,000 | 14,393,000 | 59.3 |
| 1971 | 25,021,000 | 13,949,000 | 55.7 |
| 1981 | 25,406,000 | 12,128,000 | 47.7 |
| 1987 | – | – | 44.5 |

*Source:* Fielding (1995: 23) except for 1987 which comes from the BES 1987.
*Notes:* BES n = 3,826. Figures shown are the percentage of the total population.

Studies such as the British Social Attitudes Survey show that more subtle changes have occurred within the class structure. Working-class communities that were once socially cohesive, based on one source of employment, have been eroded by the decline of heavy industrial employment (Heath and Topf (1987: 51)). There has been an increase in home ownership, share ownership, white-collar/service sector employment, part-time work and a shift of population from city to suburbs and countryside. For example, in 1961, 36 per cent of employees were in manufacturing, with 47 per cent in services; by 1991 those in manufacturing had declined to 22 per cent while the number employed in services had increased to 71 per cent (Denver (1994: 64)). There has therefore been a movement between the classes, especially upwards from lower to middle classes, and an increase in intergenerational social mobility. In the 1950s around a fifth of all manual workers were home-owners; by 1983 over 50 per cent were. Increasingly, households and families are mixed class.

*The family structure has changed.* Increases in the number of single parent families, divorce and re-marriage in society means that the potential composition of the immediate family can take many forms and is more likely to change. Furthermore, contact and communication between voters and their family (other than partners or spouses) has declined over time (see McGlone *et al.* (1996)). Political values are less likely to be passed down from one generation to another and individuals are more subject to influences outside the family.

Additionally, as Seyd and Whiteley (1992: 201) observed in their study of party activism in the British parties, *leisure opportunities had increased both quantitatively and qualitatively.* This has created competition for partisan socialisation and political participation. As Gallagher *et al.* (1995: 249) observed, a 'rise in living standards, a huge increase in leisure outlets, and the advent of television have all combined to reduce the appeal of spending evenings playing tennis in the local party hall'. Archie Norman (1998), appointed as the Conservative Party's Chief Executive after the 1997 general election, noted how:

> Membership attitudes today, particularly amongst young people, have evolved from the days when the Conservative Party was a form of social infrastructure. Today people want to feel they are involved in politics and that above all they have a right to be listened to – at the top.

### Consequences: how parties win elections

A new electoral market has emerged in Britain: societal changes have made voters more critical of party behaviour. They in turn undermine traditional models of voting behaviour. For example, the standard American Voter or Party Identification model contends that an individual acquires an identification with a party in childhood, stemming from the influence of the parents. This identification then strengthens through adulthood through socialisation centred around the family and people of the same views and is used as a basis for voting decisions throughout life. The non-political factors just outlined erode the foundations of this model. The family's role in socialisation and communication post-enfranchisement has now declined which will reduce the chance for political influence from these sources and make less likely the solidification of any party identification first built in childhood. The information voters receive about politics has changed in source and nature because of the rise of television and the educational level in society. Voters are exposed to different sides of an issue as well as given greater skills to critically assess any information they receive.

Societal changes also undermine the influence of class on voting behaviour. This is a matter of debate for psephologists, but several detailed studies of voting behaviour such as Franklin (1985), Rose and McAllister (1986 and 1990) and Denver (1994: 62) support this argument. Moreover, voters are increasingly in 'mixed-class' families or households and as Crewe (1992: 66) argued, 'subject to partisan cross-pressures'. Partisan political participation once acted as a force to support and strengthen party identification but, as already discussed, this is an increasingly less popular activity. Voters are less likely to offer support to one particular party simply because their parents did. Sanders (1998: 221) explains that if one analyses this in terms of the American Voter model's 'funnel of causality', it would appear that 'variables closer to the vote may now have a greater impact on party preferences than the sort of deepseated factors such as class and party identification that lie further back in the causal sequence'.

Indeed, voters are therefore more likely to choose on a rational basis and follow the issue voting-behaviour model. The BES asked voters what the main reason for their vote decision was: see Table 1.10. The majority of respondents claim they vote the way they do because it is the 'best party', not because they have always voted that way.

**Table 1.10** *Reason for vote decision, 1983–92*

*Question asked: Which one of the reasons on this card comes closest to the main reason you voted for the party you chose: I always vote that way; I thought it was the best party; I really preferred another party but it had no chance of winning in this constituency; Other?*

|  | *Always do (%)* | *Best party (%)* |
|---|---|---|
| 1983 | 20 | 55 |
| 1987 | 23 | 67 |
| 1992 | 21 | 56 |

*Source:* BES.
*Notes:* n = 1983: 3,955; 1987: 3,292; 1992: 2,855.

The electoral market has therefore changed and with it the way that parties must compete to win elections. The market is more open for voters and parties. Either major party can attract votes from the opposition's traditional voter constituency. However parties cannot assume support from voters simply because they hold identification with the party or are from a particular class. As Andrew Lansley MP indicated at the EPOP (Elections, Public Opinion and Parties) Conference in 1997, 'the I've always been a Conservative feeling amongst voters has gone: politics has moved into a new and transactional era of politics where parties have to engage voters in a discussion on why they should vote for them'. If a major party is to prove successful in attracting support, it therefore needs to change its behaviour in response to the demands of the voters. This is where political marketing is important. Parties have begun to respond to these challenges in their environment by utilising marketing techniques and concepts used originally in business. To analyse this, however, we first need to know what political marketing is all about.

### Political marketing

> Marketing is a pervasive societal activity that goes considerably beyond the selling of toothpaste, soap, and steel … every organisation performs marketing-like activities whether or not they are recognised as such. (Kotler and Levy (1969: 10–11))

### *Definitions*

Political marketing is about political organisations adapting business-marketing concepts and techniques to help them achieve their goals. Political parties, interest groups and local councils are amongst those entities that increasingly conduct market intelligence to identify citizen concerns, change their behaviour to meet those demands and communicate their 'product offering' more effectively. Because political marketing is a new field of academic research, we need to develop a new theoretical framework to explain what we mean by this. The rest of the chapter will do this.

Political marketing derives, unsurprisingly, from marketing. Marketing is a part of management science: the study of how business organisations manage their activity. Marketing:

- is about how businesses try to gain more custom, design their product and promote it;
- is about the relationship between a firm's products and resources and the response to it from consumers, or the market and all influences upon that relationship;
- aims to help an organisation compete with its rivals to obtain a limited amount of consumer spending;
- is concerned with all areas of a firm's behaviour, not just the sales department.

Although at first it appears quite alien to the political science scholar, marketing offers analytical frameworks and terminology that can be adapted to deepen our understanding of politics.

In defining political marketing, therefore, we should create a broad definition beyond the narrow focus on communication that characterises much of existing literature. Many people think marketing is the same as advertising or selling. Advertising is simply a technique that can be used by a wide variety of organisations without them utilising the concepts and ideas that marketing offers. Indeed, Drucker (1973: 64–5) makes the point that:

> *The aim of marketing is to make selling superfluous.* The aim of marketing is to know and understand the customer so well that the product or service fits him and sells itself. Ideally, marketing should result in a customer who is ready to buy. All that should be needed then is to make the product or service available. (My emphasis.)

Marketing is about much more than advertising. Political marketing is concerned with the demands of the market and political behaviour in a much broader sense. It is much more comprehensive, which is why we are using comprehensive political marketing as opposed to the more narrow type of approach.

Therefore, in the CPM tradition, as a field of research: political marketing studies the relationship between a political organisation's 'product' and the demands of its market. Such political organisations include parliaments, political parties, interest groups and bureaucracies; their product legislation, policies or meetings; their market the public, electorate, members, financial donors, tax-payers or benefit receivers.

As an activity: political marketing is about political organisations (such as political parties, parliaments and government departments) adapting techniques (such as market research and product design) and concepts (such as the desire to satisfy voter demands) originally used in the business world to help them achieve their goals (such as win elections or pass legislation).

### Orientations

Conceptually, marketing uses several orientations to explain business behaviour: product, sales and market orientations. A *product-oriented business* concentrates on producing the best product it can, as efficiently and cheaply as possible. It assumes that the good will then sell. If it does not, the business would argue that this is because the customer is ignorant and lacks appreciation of how good the product is. A *sales-oriented business* has the same attitude towards designing its product but puts much more effort into selling the good. The focus is on employing sales techniques such as advertising and direct mail to persuade buyers that they want the good the firm is offering. It tries to create the demand, rather than respond to it. A *market-oriented business* will design its product to provide consumer satisfaction to achieve its goals. It is continually altered in response to changing customer demands. A market orientation is much more likely to satisfy its customers and will stand a better chance of securing their long-term custom.

If we adapt this to politics, a *product-oriented organisation* would determine how to behave from its own skills, expertise and beliefs. It would then expect its users to respond. A *sales-oriented organisation* would focus on presenting their service in the most positive light in order to achieve positive evaluations from users. It would concentrate on communicating the benefits of its behaviour. In contrast, a *market-oriented organisation* would have creating user satisfaction as its goal. It would attempt to understand those it seeks to serve and deliver a product that reflects their needs and wants. It would be open to changing the way it behaves in order to obtain more support.

*Activities*

Within the marketing literature, in order to provide a fuller picture of how businesses could actually adopt a particular orientation, a number of activities which include market intelligence, product design, price-setting, promotion and distribution have been noted. They are portrayed as a marketing mix or marketing process but are commonly called the '4Ps'. The 4Ps for marketing businesses are:

1 Product: the product being sold.
2 Price: the price at which consumers buy the product.
3 Promotion: advertising the product.
4 Place: where the product is delivered.

These can be adapted for politics, although not all will be relevant. There are a number of differences between business and politics. Marketing literature itself has acknowledged that all non-profit-organisations are substantially different to business organisations in terms of goals, products and markets (see O'Leary and Iredale (1976: 153) and Evans and Berman (1994: 399)). Transferring marketing principles from business organisations to non-profit organisations is therefore a complex process (see Rothschild (1979: 11)), but this does not make it impossible. As Scrivens and Witzel (1990: 13) note, if non-profit organisations have differences, 'marketing approaches must be adapted'. Each time the traditional nature of the political organisation being studied, whether it is a party, interest group, or public service, must be taken into account. A broad framework for studying political marketing in various political organisations is, however, outlined in Figure 1.1.

**Figure 1.1** *Political marketing by political organisations: a conceptual framework for analysis*

A: *define the organisation, market and product*

| Step 1 | Step 2 | Step 3 |
|---|---|---|
| Define the organisation | Define the market | Define the product |

B: *analyse how the organisation goes through a marketing process*

| Stage 1 | Stage 2 | Stage 3 | Stage 4 | Stage 5 | Stage 6 |
|---|---|---|---|---|---|
| Market intelligence | Product design | Convey product | Market receives product | Product delivery | Solicit feedback |

For example, in Step 1, the organisation might be a party, Parliament, the NHS, the civil service, a local council. Research needs to define its nature: what it is like, how is it structured, what are its goals, who works in it and whether it has formal members. In Step 2, study needs to define the market for this organisation: who uses it, who supports it, whether anyone is a member or donates funds. This includes all the people the organisation is designed to represents but also those whose support it needs to survive. The third step is to define the 'product' that the organisation produces: with a Parliament, this can be the passing of legislation, a party, policies, NHS, health treatment.

Stage 1, market intelligence, is about discovering the needs and wants of the organisation's market. Stage 2 is where the organisation decides how to behave or what kind of product it will offer. Stage 3 is about communicating what is on offer. In Stage 4, the user takes the product: for example, the electorate votes a party into government, citizens use the health service, someone signs up for membership of an interest group. Stage 5 is delivery: parties deliver policy promises in government, a patient gets treated (and made better) at hospital, a member goes to a party meeting. Stage 6 is cyclical marketing: the organisation continues to solicit market intelligence from users to monitor how its product is being received. It then goes back to Stage 1 to begin the marketing process again. This framework would need to be adapted depending on the organisation being studied and its particular characteristics.

*Marketing political parties*

Marketing orientations and processes can now be applied to political parties in particular. As with all political marketing studies, this application has to be done carefully. The goal of a political party is different from a business and its performance is more difficult to measure. It may have several, possibly conflicting, markets, which are generally undefined and unknown. It is not a profit-making enterprise and is conventionally seen as having normative roles or functions to play in society. A party's 'product' is less tangible and is more complex to design, as well as envisage conceptually.

The framework set out here is the result of careful adaptation. The framework also goes further than the ideas previously provided by Niffenegger (1989), Wring (1994–95 and 1996a and b), Newman (1994: 12 and 32) which focus on campaign organisation, individuals and image building. This study applies marketing to party behaviour as a whole. It builds on previous work to advance the political marketing field.

The representations of the marketing process also differ significantly from marketing itself and previous studies of political marketing which do not always change marketing as extensively. The 4Ps are formed into a chronological process consisting of various stages a party will go through within one electoral cycle. They are significantly altered to create more appropriate activities, stages that are not relevant are discarded and terminology is changed where appropriate. For example, with regard to the pricing notion within the traditional marketing 4Ps, this has been altered considerably to 'product adjustment'. Wring (1997a) includes this in studying campaigns, building on Niffenegger (1989), but although it has some utility for campaigns (the cost of advertising, for example) it has less for party behaviour as a whole. Place is also discarded because although it is appropriate for the study of campaign organisation it makes less sense for party behaviour as a whole. Certain stages overlap with political studies. The use of polls by parties, for example, exemplified by the stage of market intelligence, has become a notable area of study in political science. The marketing process does not leave it in isolation, however, but connects it to the communication and design of behaviour.

Certain aspects of marketing language are nevertheless retained. Party behaviour is called 'product' to encourage parties (and scholars) to think about party behaviour as a 'product' to be given to voters. This is also true with product adjustment for a Market-Oriented Party. Stages 2 and 3 could be combined, but there is utility in keeping them separate and in that order – find out voters' demands first, before thinking about internal party concerns. Swap them around and you reduce the tendency of a party to look more fully at the electorate rather than internal members.

Nonetheless members must, at least in the British context, be considered, alongside the other components of Stage 3. Other aspects of the process are designed to integrate similar and/or equally valuable understanding from both marketing and political science, such as the implementation stage. The standard marketing process does not include this as an actual stage, but within marketing literature there is much discussion of how important it is that those working within a business organisation accept the idea of the desired orientation if it is to succeed. This is of particular relevance, if somewhat problematic, for a political organisation such as a party.

*A party's product, goals and market*
Before marketing is adapted, we need to know what a party's product, goal and market are because these will influence how it uses political marketing. Focusing on major parties in Britain, and using understanding derived from the traditional literature about parties, these can be defined as follows:

Product:

- is a party's behaviour;
- is continual, not just at election time;
- exists at all levels of the party, e.g. is not just the most senior party figures but includes behaviour at the local level;
- includes leadership, Members of Parliament, membership, staff, symbols, constitution, activities and policies.

Dominant goal:

- is to win long-term electoral success: thus, to win general elections and control of the Government over a long-term period.

Market:

- is the electorate, but within that members, and the general population as it influences both.

Parties use political marketing in order to increase their chances of achieving their goal: they thus consciously and sub-consciously alter aspects of their behaviour, including policy, membership, leadership and organisations to suit the nature and demands of the market. As Kotler (1979: 40) argued, the 'interesting thing about marketing is that all organisations do it whether they know it or not'. Thus, parties may in fact use marketing without intending to. Marketing can also be used in different ways: organisations can adopt different orientations to their behaviour, depending upon their goals and the nature of the market.

*The three types of party and their marketing process*
The product, sales and market orientation can be applied to parties, for they too behave in various ways and take different attitudes to how to achieve their goals. Furthermore, a marketing process can be created for each party.

## The Product-Oriented Party (POP)

A *Product-Oriented Party* argues for what it stands for and believes in. It assumes that voters will realise that its ideas are the right ones and therefore vote for it. This type of party refuses to change its ideas or product even if it fails to gain electoral or membership support.

### *A model of the Product-Oriented Party*

A Product-Oriented Party goes through a five-stage marketing process, as shown in Figure 1.2.

*Stage 1: Product design*
The party designs its behaviour according to what it thinks is best.

*Stage 2: Communication*
This includes the so-called near or long-term campaign but also ongoing behaviour. Not just the leader, but all MPs and members, send a message to the electorate. The organisation is clear and effective; designed to advance the party's arguments to voters.

*Stage 3: Campaign*
The official election campaign period leading up to the election.

*Stage 4: Election*
The general election.

*Stage 5: Delivery*
The party should deliver its promised product in government.

**Figure 1.2** *The marketing process for a Product-Oriented Party*

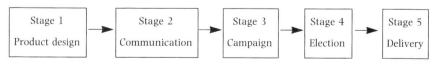

## The Sales-Oriented Party (SOP)

A *Sales-Orientated Party* focuses on selling its argument to voters. It retains its pre-determined product design, but recognises that the supporters it desires may not automatically want it. Using market intelligence to understand voters' response to its behaviour, the party employs the latest advertising and communication techniques to persuade voters that it is right. A Sales-Oriented Party does not change its behaviour to suit what people want, but tries to make people want what it offers.

*A model of the Sales-Oriented Party (see Figure 1.3)*

*Stage 1: Product design*
The first stage is to design its behaviour according to what the party thinks best.

*Stage 2: Market intelligence*
A Sales-Oriented Party then aims to discover voters' response to its product. It tries to find out which voters do not support the party, but might be persuaded. Communications can the be targeted on this section of the electorate. Market intelligence can be derived informally, through 'keeping an ear to the ground'; talking to party members; creating policy groups; and holding general meetings with the public. Formally, parties use quantitative research (electoral results, public opinion polls and privately commissioned studies) and qualitative research such as a focus group.

*Stage 3: Communication*
This includes the so-called near or long-term campaign but also ongoing behaviour. With all parties, it is not just the leader, but all MPs, candidates for office, and members send a message to the electorate. The party therefore attempts to ensure all communication helps it achieve electoral success: that the party is portrayed in a positive light. It attempts to influence others in the communication process, such as journalists and television news programmes. The party formulates an effective and clear communication plan which is well organised. It is designed not just to advance arguments but to persuade the voter that the party is right. It uses all available selling techniques such as direct mail and targeted communications to persuade voters to agree with the party.

*Stage 4: Campaign*
This is the official election campaign period leading up to the election. It utilises sales techniques in the same way as the communication stage.

*Stage 5: Election*
The general election.

*Stage 6: Delivery*
The party delivers product in government.

**Figure 1.3** *The marketing process for a Sales-Oriented Party*

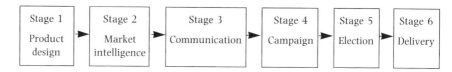

## The Market-Oriented Party (MOP)

A *Market-Oriented Party* designs its behaviour to provide voter satisfaction. It uses market intelligence to identify voter demands, then designs its product to suit them. It does not attempt to change what people think, but to deliver what they need and want.

A Market-Oriented Party needs to ensure it provides voter satisfaction to reach its goal. It will not simply offer voters what they want, or simply follow opinion polls, because it needs to ensure that it can deliver the product on offer. If it fails to deliver, voters will become dissatisfied and the party will risk losing electoral support in the long term. It also needs to ensure that it will be accepted within the party and so needs to adjust its product carefully to take account of this. A Market-Oriented Party therefore designs a product that will actually satisfy voters' demands: that meets their needs and wants, is supported and implemented by the internal organisation, and is deliverable in government.

## A model of Market-Oriented Party behaviour (see Figure 1.4)

Because parties are moving towards the Market-Oriented Party, this model will be discussed in more detail.

### Stage 1: Market intelligence

The first stage a Market-Oriented Party goes through is market intelligence: finding out the needs, wants, behaviour and demands of the voters whose support it seeks. Market intelligence can be derived from many

**Figure 1.4** *The marketing process for a Market-Oriented Party*

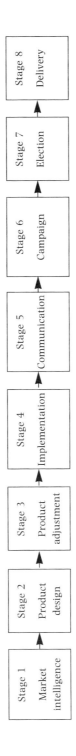

sources and in different ways and is concerned with party–voter communication in its broadest sense.

*Informal market intelligence*
Parties can get ideas about what voters want by 'keeping an ear to the
ground' or talking to party activists. Hall *et al.* (1996: 137) noted how
managers in profit-making organisations 'also place stress on having a feel
for the market'. They can call meetings and have discussions with
members or voters, especially as this not only lets the party understand
what the people want, but helps people feel that the party is interested in
them. The leadership can also set up policy groups within the party
consisting of politicians, professionals and members.

*Formal market intelligence*
As technology has advanced, parties have more tools at their disposal to
understand their market, even given the increase in its size and complex-
ity. Formal market intelligence can come from primary or secondary
sources and be created using quantitative or qualitative methodology.

Quantitative secondary sources include electoral results, and public
opinion polls conducted by specialist research firms such as Gallop and
MORI. The party can also create primary data sources through privately
commissioned studies (see Moon (1999) for further detail). Qualitative-
based intelligence can take the form of less structured, interactive
discussion that enables a detailed exploration of voters' demands. One
example of this is a focus group. It can be more effective in helping a party
identify voters' long-term (as opposed to short-lived) demands, or which
demands take precedence over others. For example, it may be the case that
quantitative surveys reveal that every voter wants lower tax, but they also
want good public services. Assuming that a medium level of tax needs to
be paid to ensure good public services, voters might rather pay slightly
more tax to have satisfactory public services, rather than pay the lowest
level of tax and not be satisfied. Qualitative methodology could help reveal
the optimum (and an achievable) combination of voters' demands and also
helps assess the likely impact of new policy ideas.

*Organisation of market intelligence: professionals versus members*
A party will probably use professionals in gathering market intelligence.
These include market research firms, polling organisations and advertising
agencies. Such people bring professional expertise. They are less likely to
have personal career ambitions within the party and will be more willing
to raise all possible issues which need to be addressed by the party. As
Moon (1999: 177) observed, 'the fact that they are outsiders means that
the pollsters are able to take a more dispassionate view'. However, the

'politics' of a political party mean that market intelligence needs to be carefully organised, much more so than with a business organisation. The leadership also needs to involve MPs and members. The results of professional research should be made fully available to them. This will increase the chances of them accepting any necessary change in behaviour. For example, in seeing the results of opinion polls themselves, they might accept that despite the arguable value of the party's current policies, voters will not support them, and thus help engender a market orientation rather than a product orientation. They can also help gather marketing intelligence from informal sources. It can also promote a feeling of involvement, value and worth amongst those within the party. Both professionals and party members need to be involved together in committees or policy groups. This will increase co-operation and understanding between them and help to reduce the chances of an 'outsider/insider' (professional/party member) distinction developing.

### Stage 2: Product design

The party will then design its 'product' according to the findings from its market intelligence to suit electoral demands. It creates a model product design or picture as to how the party would behave if it followed voters' demands. This means changing, where necessary, not just the policy of a party but aspects such as its leader (or leadership style), the behaviour of the party's MPs and/or candidates for office, organisational structures and membership rights.

Depending on the results of market intelligence and the party's existing behaviour, this may not involve much change. As Moynihan and Titley (1995: 197) argued, adopting a marketing orientation may require complete product-change or otherwise 'simply re-marketing them as being improved or different in some way, for example by re-launching the product with a new trademark or logo'. Similarly, market intelligence may confirm support for the party's behaviour. Nevertheless there will undoubtedly be occasions where the results from market intelligence show that the party needs to make dramatic changes in its behaviour to respond to voters' demands and become market-oriented. This can be problematic for a party, especially if it has previously been more product-oriented in attitude. The next two stages of the marketing process are therefore important in easing the implementation of a change in behaviour.

### Stage 3: Product adjustment

The product design then needs to be adjusted according to four factors:

1 *Achievability*: the party should not promise what it cannot deliver in government.
2 *Internal reaction*: the party should change the design to ensure that it will obtain the support of enough MPs and members to ensure its implementation.
3 *Competition*: the party should find out the opposition's weaknesses and highlight its own corresponding strengths.
4 *Existing/needed support*: the party should focus on winning the support of voters it does not have but needs if it is to win power.

*Achievablity*
A Market-Oriented Party would not 'promise the earth'. It must ensure that the promised product will be achievable in government, especially where policy proposals are concerned. Promises to reduce tax and then a failure to do so, for example, would only result in voter dissatisfaction.

*Internal reaction analysis*
Although a party needs to respond to voters' concerns, because it is different to a business, and serves not just voters at large but its members as well, it needs to adjust its product design carefully. As Harmel and Janda (1994: 261) noted, any decision to change a party's behaviour, including its organisation, issue positions or strategy, will 'face a wall of resistance common to large organisations'. It is important that a party considers all of its supporters on an internal as well as external level in order to ensure that it will be implemented through the party and not simply the top leadership. Members are also a source of informal feedback from different parts of the country. Additionally, they can help generate external support (Seyd and Whiteley (1992) and Whiteley *et al.* (1994)). Alienation of such members, particularly those most active and loyal, could similarly lose support for the party. The party leadership needs to understand the views of all within the organisation and alter the product accordingly to ensure that it will gain the necessary level of acceptance.

In particular, leaders who seek to change their party's behaviour are always constrained by a party's ideology and history (see Dunleavy with Ward (1991: 131–3) and Rose and McAllister (1990: 178)). Ideology is often a source of motivation for members and MPs. Changes in policy thus need to be placed within or with reference to the party's traditional ideological framework, wherever possible. This will be a sometimes delicate, yet essential, balancing act between the demands of external (voters) and internal (members) supporters. One way to ease the process might be to consult the membership and MPs on how the party might change.

*Competition analysis*
A party also needs to adjust its product design according to the competition, taking into account the strengths and weaknesses of the opposition parties. It should alter its design to ensure that it is not simply the same as those of other parties; and that it has strengths where the other parties are weak. The marketing framework that can be used for this analysis is SWOT analysis: Strengths, Weaknesses, Opportunities and Threats (see Box 1.1). The party should consider the strengths, weaknesses, opportunities and threats, on two levels: both itself and the opposition party.

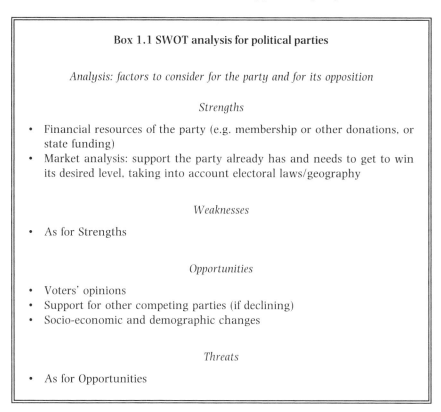

**Box 1.1 SWOT analysis for political parties**

*Analysis: factors to consider for the party and for its opposition*

*Strengths*

- Financial resources of the party (e.g. membership or other donations, or state funding)
- Market analysis: support the party already has and needs to get to win its desired level, taking into account electoral laws/geography

*Weaknesses*

- As for Strengths

*Opportunities*

- Voters' opinions
- Support for other competing parties (if declining)
- Socio-economic and demographic changes

*Threats*

- As for Opportunities

For example, after the 1997 election, a presentation by Andrew Lansley (1997) from the Conservative Party showed attempts to engage in SWOT analysis: see Box 1.2.

This is in line with basic rational-choice theory (see Downs (1957) and, amongst others, Dunleavy with Ward (1991: 113)) but unlike some of these accounts suggest, this does not mean that all parties will become the same. As Downs (1957: 97) himself noted, a party must ensure it stands out from its competition, for 'citizens will see little point in voting if all choices are identical'. In marketing terms this is called product differentiation and SWOT analysis can lead into this. Although it may be researching the same electorate as its major rival, it needs to create a product design that will be different in some way. Differences will inevitably occur as the party adjusts its behaviour to suit its internal support, because each major party has a different historical and ideological background. Additionally, the party may highlight or downplay a particular ideological difference with the competition, depending on whether it is a strength or weakness. A party needs to determine what it can offer which the other(s) cannot, and ensure that they stand out from their rivals, with different key attributes or issues. A party which simply copies another which seems to be electorally successful would not be using political marketing correctly.

---

**Box 1.2 SWOT analysis of the Conservative Party**
**following the 1997 election**

*Strengths*

- Conservative Party seen as the party of government
- Tradition of policy success
- 200 strong constituencies
- Conservative voters may have left the party, but can come back
- Conservative Thatcher's children – still materialistic and goal-oriented, have only lapsed; there are lots of lapsed Conservatives in the electorate

*Weaknesses*

- Age, gender and ethnicity lacking in profile
- Sleaze
- Divisions/factionalism
- Party perceived as out of touch

*Opportunities*

- The co-operation between Labour and the Liberal Democrats reduces the importance and support of the latter
- The Conservatives performance in local government could improve – and increase membership incentives
- There are some big hitters in the party, even if they're not all currently in parliament
- Opportunity for policy innovation while out of office

---

---

*Threats*

- Lib Democrat increase in strength
- Factionalism within party since 1992; if this continues in opposition, could lead to realignments
- How to sustain party organisation in really low Conservative-supporting areas
- Devolution (especially Scotland)
- Europe (not quite as big an issue; policy should be equivocal as public is like that); transaction with the public
- Generally, not radicalism for sake of being radical; follow what public want; don't be extreme
- Build policy on understanding of public opinion
- Possible loss of business support, with the Labour Party in favour now

*Source:* Lansley (1997).

---

*Support analysis*

A party must take into consideration its existing and required (but as yet, not attracted) support. If it already has long-term, loyal support from one section of society, it may reduce the aspects of the product design that suit its demand and alter its behaviour to suit another section of society which makes different demands but whose support the party does not yet have but needs to win power, as long as it can make these changes without alienating its existing support. This analysis would provide the basis for target marketing, both in the product adjustment stage and the later stages of communication and campaign.

After considering factors a–d, the party should have a new (adjusted) product design.

*Stage 4: Implementation*

For marketing to be effective, the findings from Stages 1–3 must be implemented. This is not easy to do within any organisation, especially a political party. There are significant organisational and communication factors the leadership needs to consider. A party leadership intent on making the organisation market oriented will inevitably encounter some hostility and resistance from some party members. It is highly likely that the basic idea of adopting a market orientation and thus following public opinion rather than ignoring or trying to change it will arouse some opposition. Furthermore, the use of marketing will probably result in a reallocation of power within the party (see Kotler and Andreasen (1991) and Anderson (1982: 86)). It is likely that conflicts will occur between different levels and groups within the party organisation, especially between those seeking power resources to influence leadership decisions. Those not within the marketing team 'are likely to view appeals to the marketing concept merely as a bargaining ploy' (Anderson (1982: 87)), possibly for more power within the party. Additionally, many party figures may be hostile to marketing because they have misconceptions or a lack of knowledge about it. A party needs to be aware of these potential problems and either take measures to avoid them or be ready to respond to them.

---

**Box 1.3 Guidelines for the implementation of marketing in a political party**

The party leadership must take the required steps to ensure that everyone else in the party (especially all other areas of power/leadership within the party – head of MPs, head of constituency chairmen, all constituency chairmen, head of research, head of communications/policy development etc.) understands what a market orientation is, accepts that it should be used by the party and implements it. They can do this in a variety of ways:

- Create a feeling that everybody in the party can contribute to making it market-oriented and successful.
- Acknowledge that the party may already be doing many things that would be classed as marketing activities.
- Encourage all members of the organisation to suggest ideas as to how the party might respond more effectively to voters.
- Create a system which enables all forms of market intelligence to be disseminated as widely as possible through the organisation.
- Present market intelligence reports from professionals, especially in the form of statistics, in a way that everyone in the party can understand.
- Appoint a marketing executive (or equivalent) to handle market intelligence from within the party and professional research firms.
- This executive should meet various groups within the party to learn what they think about the party and voters: first, explaining their job position, the nature of marketing and its uses, and then encouraging open discussion, inviting ideas for change within the party.
- The importance of views other than those of the majority of the electorate and the party's history should be acknowledged.
- Those within the party who support the idea of being market-oriented should be promoted to encourage market-oriented behaviour.
- Emphasise that becoming market-oriented is the means to achieve the party's goal; it is not the goal in itself.

---

Ensuring that marketing will be accepted in an organisation is therefore a political activity in itself. It is also extremely important because all within the party need to understand, accept and implement the concept if the party is to take on a marketing orientation. Box 1.3 contains a list of guidelines. These are adapted from the management literature studying business organisations, which includes Levitt (1960), Anderson (1982), Kotler (1979), O'Leary and Iredale (1976), Payne (1988), Kohli and Jaworski (1990) Hooley, Lynch and Shepherd (1990), Kotler and Andreasen (1991) and Lancaster and Massingham (1993: 14–15). Achieving a market orientation arguably takes some time, especially if it necessitates major changes in values and beliefs. It is also unlikely that the leadership will achieve 100 per cent party unity or complete acceptance of a market orientation, but it would aim for a majority of support for the new behaviour.

### Stage 5: Communication

Having implemented the new product design, the party must convey this to the electorate using the most appropriate and effective communication techniques. Communication is concerned with providing and influencing information given out through various media to the party's market about its product. It occurs continually, not just in a campaign. The party communicates with both internal and external supporters. It includes activities such as press releases or advertising, but also work done on behalf of the party to increase its support by activists from within the party membership. As Kotler and Andreasen (1991: 505) argue, everything 'about an organisation – its products, employees, facilities, and actions – communicates something'. Not just the leader, but all MPs and members send a message to the electorate. The party will also attempt to influence others in the communication process, such as journalists and opposition parties. It will seek to ensure that all the communication it has with all its publics will help it achieve electoral success. However, money spent on communications cannot make up for a poor product (see Shapiro (1973: 18)). But even a good product needs to be communicated to voters.

### Stage 6: Campaign

The election campaign is the final chance of the party to convey its behaviour in a positive way. The party will appoint a campaign manager who has clear control of the campaign and can communicate with others in the campaign organisation. The party will train and support all campaign workers, to ensure that they possess a clear knowledge of the product or party and can convey this in a intelligible and attractive manner to voters. It will also communicate regularly with candidates for office.

There are an array of marketing tools which politics can take from business, such as the use of slogans, catch phrases and advertisements: all of which will also be used in the communication stage. Nevertheless, as with general communication, a campaign is unlikely to make the difference between winning and losing the election. Chris Powell (Gould (1998b: 81)), one of Labour's professional advertising advisers, noted of the party's 1987 election campaign:

> In a way, we demonstrated the weakness of advertising ... It makes very little difference how well or how professionally you do the campaign if your leader and your policies are not likely to appeal to the broad mass of the population.

## Stage 7: Election

This is quite simply the general election, when, if the party's marketing strategy has been successful, the people 'buy the product' and thus vote for the party. A Market-Oriented Party will be better placed to attract support at all phases of the electoral cycle, although the focus remains on the general election because this is the deciding factor in whether the party gains control of government.

## Stage 8: Delivery

Delivery is crucial to the ultimate success of marketing and therefore political marketing. In their discussion of business organisations, Moynihan and Titley (1995: 259–60) note that production is not complete until the good or service reaches the consumer, who is likely to want to receive it as quickly as possible and warn (1995: 260) that an 'organisation that is unable to satisfy these desires will not achieve its aims of expanding market share ... There will be no repeat sales or customer loyalty from a dissatisfied customer'. In politics, if parties fail to deliver on policy promises, voter dissatisfaction is unlikely to decrease. In fact it may increase because voters were offered what they wanted but did not receive it.

A Market-Oriented Party will focus on the need to deliver in order to achieve voter satisfaction. The original design of the product will be mediated by the need to achieve internal party support and ensure that the product is achievable. Although many barriers exist to impede parties' ability to deliver (see Denver (1998: 46) and Rose (1997: 754–5)), these difficulties are those associated with governing rather than political marketing. Conservative Governments between 1979 and 1997 did not deliver on all their promises. Indeed, between 1992 and 1997 in particular they were perceived by voters to fail in many respects. The current

Labour Government frequently discusses its record on delivery since getting into government: indeed, the party initiated issuing an annual report on its delivery of its promises. Its web-site in the summer of 1999 took the reader straight to a page listing its successes: see Box 1.4. Delivery is the key to the ultimate success of political marketing, particularly in reducing voter dissatisfaction.

---

**Box 1.4 The Labour Party web-page, August 1999**

**Delivering on our pledges – the facts:**

**Since 1 May this government has been serving the people, spending more than the last government's plans in key areas, and keeping our election pledges**

- The Bill to cut class sizes for all 5, 6 and 7 year-olds is law: the first £22 million is going into cutting class sizes for 100,000 children.
- An extra £1.3 billion has gone to improving school buildings and equipment, plus an extra £1.25 billion to raise standards in schools.
- The NHS is getting £2 billion more than under the last government's plans.
- The windfall tax is already going into the biggest ever programme to get the young and long-term unemployed back to work.
- Corporation tax has been cut to the lowest level in Europe.
- Child care has been put within reach of all families, with £300 million over five years going to providing after-school places for nearly a million children.
- All handguns have been banned.
- The poorest 20 per cent of families will gain four times as much as the wealthiest 20 per cent from the announcements made in the Budget.
- We have won referendums for the Scottish Parliament and the Welsh Assembly.
- All pensioners are getting generous cash payments to cope with winter fuel bills on top of the cut on VAT.
- VAT on heating has been cut to its lowest level to help pensioners.
- The Crime & Disorder Bill is before the House to deliver 12 manifesto commitments, including our pledge to ensure swift justice for persistent offenders.
- All the above has been achieved without raising income tax, plus sound economic management and inflation under control.

*Source:* http://www.labour.org.uk/core.html (8 August 1999).

---

## Cyclical marketing

Once a party has gone through the whole process and become market-oriented, in order for it to maintain this position and electoral support it needs to engage in continual market intelligence to ensure that it does not go back to being a Sales or Product-Oriented Party. In the lead-up to the next election, it may adjust its behaviour if voter opinion changes, and essentially go through the whole process again, making it cyclical.

### The three party models compared

Although this book argues that the Market-Oriented Party model is becoming the dominant form of behaviour, all three party types are useful for understanding party politics. The difference between the three orientations is extremely important. Figure 1.5 outlines the difference between the three orientations and the broader scope of political marketing. It is important to note what is 'missing' from the process for the first two orientations: there are certain stages that only a Market-Oriented Party would go through. There are also important differences in the order. Like a Market-Oriented Party, a party with a sales orientation engages in market intelligence but only *after* designing its behaviour, in order to determine how to sell its product to voters: what popular characteristics to highlight, what to try to hide. With the Market-Oriented Party, identifying voters' needs and wants comes before a party determines how to behave. This results in potentially divergent products.

The sales orientation helps to explain why political marketing has hitherto been seen as nothing more than spin-doctors and sound-bites and why it can be criticised as not being new. Substantial political communication literature already exists to demonstrate that politicians use communication techniques. Early works such as Rose (1967) and Robertson (1976) have already suggested that this type of behaviour occurs. If parties adopt this approach, they do focus on using selling techniques and accusations that marketing is about presentation have some foundation. However a sales orientation adds two significant contributions to our understanding of this type of behaviour. Firstly, in terms of the concept, if political organisations adopt this focus they will be likely to produce the most effective presentation of the political product because all energy is put into communication. Secondly, in terms of tools, communication is designed in conjunction with results from market intelligence and can be used with marketing techniques, such as target marketing and direct mail.

This diverges slightly from Scammell (1999: 733) who, working without the differentiated three orientations, notes that the difference between Labour before and after the 1987 campaign might be the use of

**Figure 1.5** *The marketing process for Product-, Sales- and Market-Oriented Parties*

| Product-Oriented Party | Sales-Oriented Party | Market-Oriented Party |
|---|---|---|
| **Stage 1**<br>Product design | **Stage 1**<br>Product design | **Stage 1**<br>Market intelligence |
| | **Stage 2**<br>Market intelligence | **Stage 2**<br>Product design |
| | | **Stage 3**<br>Product adjustment |
| | | **Stage 4**<br>Implementation |
| **Stage 2**<br>Communication | **Stage 3**<br>Communication | **Stage 5**<br>Communication |
| **Stage 3**<br>Campaign | **Stage 4**<br>Campaign | **Stage 6**<br>Campaign |
| **Stage 4**<br>Election | **Stage 5**<br>Election | **Stage 7**<br>Election |
| **Stage 5**<br>Delivery | **Stage 6**<br>Delivery | **Stage 8**<br>Delivery |

marketing tools and the adopting of the marketing approach. Rather, the difference is better explained by differentiating between a sales orientation and a market orientation. Tools were used in both periods of behaviour, but post-1987 Labour moved towards a market orientation; the 1987 election represented more a triumph of a sales orientation with the focus on running the most effective campaign possible. Another important aspect of the Sales-Oriented Party concept is that such parties do engage in persuasion and try to make voters want what the party offers. This type of party is therefore most amenable to the normative criticism conventionally surrounding political marketing generally.

However the Market-Oriented Party is arguably even more contentious, although for different reasons. The idea that political parties should design their product to suit voters, rather than argue their case, works against traditional views of politics. Alternatively it could be argued that it shows parties are becoming more responsive to people, which is good for democracy. Either way, it has profound implications for the way parties work, for the political system and democracy as a whole.

### The potential and limits of this theoretical framework

Like any theoretical framework, it is subject to the usual qualifications. The three party concepts indicate what behaviour to look for and provide a greater understanding of reality: they do not attempt detailed predictions of behaviour at all times and under every circumstance. The orientation of an organisation is a question of degree and there would be overlap between each stage of the marketing process. The desired behaviour may not be easy to achieve internally but party (or any organisational) change is typically difficult to bring about. With regard to the Market-Oriented Party in particular, the idea that parties aim to provide voter satisfaction may be a hostage to fortune, but this is what the marketing literature argues about business organisations. It helps to convey the attention that the market-oriented approach gives to responding to voter demands in order to achieve the organisation's goal, rather than simply focusing on the goal itself. Measuring satisfaction is difficult, but we can (and parties do) use polls, surveys and focus groups which evaluate party behaviour. The ultimate judgement is obviously the general election, but just because a party wins does not mean it will provide satisfaction. Delivery is the other most notable contention. This is a key characteristic of marketing: making sure the consumer actually gets the good and its works. In politics, however, conventional wisdom and public opinion polls suggest that parties never keep their promises once in power. Studies of policy implementation might argue that there are too many barriers to delivery: governing is never easy. There are several responses to this criticism:

- If we really believe parties can never deliver, why do we have them? Why do we study them?
- If parties have not kept their promises in the past, this does not mean they never will in future, especially the greater the extent to which they become market-oriented and voters become aware of it.
- If there are problems in the delivery part of the system – legislation, policy implementation etc., MOPs may in time do more to address them, given that they are now so reliant on successful delivery to obtain electoral support.

*The three orientations and winning elections*

The three orientations are not simply useful for classifying different types of behaviour: they can be linked to organisational success. The discipline of marketing argues that, over time, the majority of businesses have first adopted a product orientation, then a sales orientation, and finally a market orientation. This is because the effectiveness of each orientation depends on the circumstances of the time. A business that has a product orientation will succeed in a market where demand exceeds supply, and the business has complete or virtual monopoly over the market. A sales orientation is most suitable in a market where competition is high and there is excess supply. Simply producing goods efficiently is not enough and necessitates effective selling techniques that will create the demand for an organisation's product. Cannon (1996: 10) notes how a sales orientation is often taken by a firm 'that seeks to buy its way out of trouble. A decaying product, being overtaken by technology or consumer tastes, will often be heavily promoted to extend its life'. A business needs to be market-oriented if its market has customers who are more affluent, with high disposable incomes and are thus more choosy about what they buy. It is also required where supply exceeds demand and there are high levels of competition, which can occur unexpectedly or as a result of rapid techno-logical change. Attracting custom is more difficult and only an organisation that is market-oriented, and understands its consumers and changes its product accordingly, will be successful.

A market orientation is currently dominant. There are, however, product- and sales-oriented firms that still survive because the market for their particular product has not developed as it has for others. Product-oriented businesses can be successful if, for example, they are a monopoly or their competition is also product-oriented. They may also be found to be sales- or product-oriented and failing. A business may go through several as it changes in response to changes in its environment (see Foxall (1989: 13), Houston (1986: 85) and Webster (1992: 15 and 31)). Like a business, a party may adopt any of these orientations, but it will reduce its chances of achieving electoral success if it does not move towards the orientation most suitable for the current nature of the market. A Product-Oriented Party would be most successful in market conditions similar to the type of society that emerged in Britain and Europe in the early twentieth century. The franchise was fully extended and the party organisation played a significant role in enabling parties to communicate, contact and mobilise their voters (Katz (1990: 143), Mair (1995: 41) and Rohrschneider (1993: 166)). Parties had strong links with the community through members and organisation, which helped them to generate and maintain both external and internal support

(Panebianco (1988: 264) and Ware (1996: 75 and 224)). As Mair (1995: 49–50) observed:

> In the past ... the dominant image of party was that of a more or less 'closed community.' Parties ... enjoyed very distinct identities. Each, to a greater or lesser extent, had its own 'natural' constituency, whether defined in terms of class, religion, occupation, or region, the core of which identified with and belonged to the particular party concerned and would rarely, if ever, consider voting for an alternative. Each party also controlled its own organisational resources, whether these be drawn mainly from ordinary supporters, from registered members, or from particular donors. Each more or less maintained its network of communications, in the form of its own internal press or a sympathetic but ostensibly autonomous 'public' newspaper. Each had its own distinctive programme and ideology which was geared to the needs of its own specific constituency.

These strong and stable bases of support meant that in marketing terms, parties could be product-oriented. This type of market can still exist in other countries with a different electoral history. Similarly, parties may still adopt this attitude even where the market nature is not suitable for a product orientation, but their electoral success would be limited.

A Sales-Oriented Party would be appropriate when parties' social basis of support begins to decline and so does support for their existing product. Parties respond by becoming sales-oriented and trying to persuade voters that the party they had once identified with was still the one they should vote for. Many parties act in this way, and indeed have done so to some extent since the emergence of mass politics. This type of behaviour has attracted attention more recently because parties have begun to use the most modern and technologically innovative selling techniques. They have also recruited professional experts, skilled in advertising and public relations, who have become known to the public. This has led to some criticism that there is too much focus on style over substance. Voters appear increasingly unwilling to accept this type of party, however, as they become more critical of parties and politics in general.

Indeed, given the changes to the electoral market in Britain that we have already discussed, a major party needs to adopt a market orientation in order to win a general election. As Philip Gould (1999), an adviser to the Labour Party, argued when questioned at the 1999 political marketing conference, 'the era of producer politics has gone'. As voters have become more educated, informed and critical of politics and parties, levels of party identification and membership have declined, the 'market' nature has become more heterogeneous. The demands made by voters have become less class-based and parties need to offer a product that will be supported by a diverse majority of the electorate. This has to be determined by a careful analysis of what it is that voters want; the party, and not what the voters want, has to change. Parties have to become Market-Oriented Parties.

It can be argued that political parties have gone through a similar developmental process to business: moving from product, to sales and then a market orientation as the market nature has changed. The overall trend may be in this direction, but an individual party may take on a market orientation, gain power and move back towards a product orientation. A party, once market-oriented, might, over time, prove less inclined to engage in thorough market intelligence. If a party wins power with a market-oriented product, over time it may remain convinced of its worth, and be unwilling to see it changed. While the electorate wants this product, this will be fine. If demands change and the party digs its heels in and refuses to respond, it will slip back into a sales or product orientation. Kotler and Levy (1969: 15) observed how 'parties become unresponsive after they enjoy power for a while and every so often experience a major upset'. Of course a party may fail to maintain a market orientation, yet retain power, if there is a lack of competition from other parties or a time lag from change in demands to rise in voter dissatisfaction/loss of electoral support. If such parties remain in power then voter dissatisfaction will most likely increase. Therefore, although parties in Britain may adopt different orientations at any time, a market orientation has the greater chance of helping them achieve their goal. The following chapters analysing party behaviour will show this. Clearly this argument cannot be 'proved' scientifically and because models are only ideal types a party may win an election without being 100 per cent market-oriented. Overall, however, the empirical evidence for the success of the market-oriented party model over any other types of behaviour is compelling.

## Summary

This chapter has shown how many social, technological and economic changes have eroded parties' traditional political environment. Voters do not simply support a party because of their background, parents or ideology. They are more critical, less easy to please and more demanding of their politicians. Parties need to respond to this new electoral market. They can do so using political marketing, most particularly being market-oriented. Political marketing is about more than how parties advertise themselves. It is concerned with how they understand voters, whether they decide to behave according to what they think, or respond to voters' demands. Parties can be product-oriented and simply argue their point of view. They can try to persuade voters to agree with them, employing all manner of sales techniques, and become a Sales-Oriented Party. Or, if they really want to be successful in today's electoral environment, they become a Market-Oriented Party. The theoretical framework set out above shows how. The rest of the book will examine when parties were product-, sales- or market-oriented and what consequence this had for their electoral support. This raises questions for how parties survive in today's electoral market and the nature of the political system as a whole.

## 2

# Thatcher the marketing pioneer

In 1979 Margaret Thatcher, the leader of the Conservative Party, won the general election and became Britain's first woman Prime Minister. This achievement followed careful use of political marketing. Thatcher recognised the need to apply marketing to not just the presentation but the nature of the party's product. Thatcher's marketing, at least in the early period of her time in office, went beyond that of mere advertising and followed the Market-Oriented Party model to win the 1979 general election. This chapter will explore how. It analyses the rest of Thatcher's premiership, examining the party's ability to deliver on promises in government. It discusses the extent to which the Tories remained responsive to voters between 1979 and 1987 and then how problems emerged for Thatcher in particular between 1987 and 1990. In this latter period, the leader's increasing strength and control over her party made it difficult for her to maintain a market orientation. She became increasingly out of touch and unwilling to respond to voters. Market-oriented political marketing can be extremely successful but problems quickly emerge if a party or leader begins to neglect it.

### The Conservatives in 1979

The Conservatives were successful ... because their product, the particular brand of conservatism offered by Mrs Thatcher, came closest to satisfying the needs of many voters. (Whyte (1988: 48–9))

Margaret Thatcher became leader of the Tories in 1975 and proceeded to lead her party to three successive election victories. Over time she gained a reputation for being a politician of conviction and even dogma. But her success in 1979 came after a period in which the Conservatives made substantial attempts to act in a way that responded to voter concerns. They utilised the techniques of marketing intelligence and communication, but more significantly, altered many aspects of their behaviour to attract more support from voters. In short, they were a Market-Oriented Party. To show this, analysis will explore the extent to which they went through all eight stages of the marketing process for a Market-Oriented Party.[1]

### Stage 1: Market intelligence

The Conservative Party engaged in substantial market intelligence using a variety of methods.

*Informally*
Thatcher encouraged general debate and discussion within the party that occurred in the following ways:

- The Party's Research Department produced ideas about what voters wanted.
- Thatcher listened carefully to the views of senior colleagues.
- Policy groups within the party, made up of both MPs and outside experts, discussed policy proposals.
- Sir Keith Joseph, who ran the Centre for Policy Studies, chaired an overall Advisory Committee on Policy, which consisted of MPs, peers and party in the country.

These all then fed into the policy design process, producing documents from which the final manifesto was drawn.

*Formally*
Both qualitative and quantitative research was conducted.

- The Opinion Research Centre (ORC) conducted quantitative polling for the party: surveys to identify particular policies as most likely to attract support, such as lower taxation and the sale of council houses.
- Saatchi and Saatchi, the party's advertising group, conducted focus groups to identify issues and in-depth interviews with people from four target groups.

Overall this gave the party several sources of understanding about what voters wanted and the opportunity to develop ideas about how to respond.

### Stage 2: Product design

The party was successful in producing a product design that matched the demands of voters discovered in Stage 1.

*Leadership*

Despite the contemporary view that Margaret Thatcher was highly princi-
pled and a politician of conviction, she pushed for policies that reflected the
views of the electorate. She had a strong style of speaking and labelled
herself a conviction politician, but this was nonetheless market-oriented.
Voters wanted a strong leader who would not go back on promises as
previous leaders had done, would have the determination to face the
nation's problems and end the politics of consensus which had previously
failed to deliver. The policies the party produced were moderate and
reflected public opinion, arguing against high levels of public spending and
tax, as well as the loss of individual freedom. Thatcher was pragmatic and
careful in her party management. Her Cabinet was appointed with the
desire to create ideological balance to reflect different views within the
party, and she retained most of the previous leader's former colleagues.
The Shadow Cabinet had the opportunity to discuss policy ideas fully. As
King (1981: 65) argued, 'she listened; she argued, but she also listened, at
least to those in her own party'.

*MPs*

Thatcher reflected the different views in the rest of the party and communication between the different parts of the organisation was high. The
policy groups created to inform the design of policies involved both MPs
and outside experts also facilitated good relationships between politicians
and professionals working for the party. Otherwise it was left to local party
associations to determine the nature of MPs and candidates for office.

*Staff*

The Conservative Party made effective use of staff. The party organisation
was run well. Lord Thorneycroft, Chair of the party, established a good
relationship with the leader and the constituencies that helped the party to
work most effectively. Departments at CCO (Conservative Central Office)
focused on improving voter support in different areas. For example, the
Department of Community Affairs worked to improve relations between
the party and various sub-groups of society such as youth, ethnic minori-
ties and trade unions. The party was also able to draw upon work done by
the Research Department. A Director of Publicity with professional experience was appointed: Gordon Reece, in February 1978. Reece not only had
expertise (he had experience as a television director and of the 1976 US
presidential election) but built up a good relationship with the party leader,
gaining her trust and confidence. Reece then appointed Saatchi and
Saatchi, the fourth largest advertising agency, in March 1978 to do the
party's advertising.

*Policy proposals*

The party's manifesto was market-oriented (see The Conservative Party (1979) for detail). The main proposals were:

- cutting public expenditure in almost every area;
- cutting the top rate of income tax to 60 per cent and reducing the bottom rate of tax;
- leaving pay deals to the private sector to decide;
- selling council houses to tenants;
- privatising nationally-owned industries;
- exercising stronger control of the money supply and inflation and reducing government borrowing;
- changing trade union law: limiting secondary picketing, providing compensation for workers who lose their jobs as a result of closed shops, granting a right of appeal against exclusion or expulsion from a union and financing postal ballots through the state;
- introducing stricter crime and immigration laws;
- improving Britain's defences: increasing spending in this area.

These proposals reflected public opinion to a significant extent. For example, the BES showed that a total of 77 per cent of respondents wanted either no more nationalisation or actual privatisation (see Table 2.1). The manifesto noted how the 'British people strongly oppose Labour's plans to nationalise yet more firms and industries' and stated that a Conservative Government would sell back the recently nationalised aerospace and ship-building industries (The Conservative Party (1979), Section 3: 'A More prosperous country').

**Table 2.1** *Voters' views on nationalisation, 1979*

*Question asked: There has been a lot of talk recently about nationalisation, that is, the Government owning and running industries like steel and electricity. Which of these statements comes closest to what you yourself feel should be done?*

|  | % |
| --- | --- |
| No more | 40 |
| De-nationalise some | 37 |
| Total | 77 |

*Source:* BES (1979).
*Note:* n = 1,893.

In terms of cutting public expenditure, a majority also thought that welfare payments had gone too far (see Table 2.2).

**Table 2.2** *Voters' views on welfare benefits, 1979*

*Question asked: Thinking about the welfare benefits that are available to people today, would you say that these have gone:*

|  | % |
| --- | --- |
| Too far | 48 |
| About right | 32 |
| Not far enough | 17 |
| Don't know | 3 |

*Source:* BES (1979).
*Notes:* n = 1,893. 'Too far' combines all respondents who said 'Much too far' and 'A little too far'. 'Not far enough' combines respondents who said 'Not quite far enough' and 'Not nearly far enough'.

The plan to introduce stricter legislation on crime reflected polls that indicated that law and order increasingly became a problem in voters' eyes. Butler and Kavanagh (1980: 37–8) report that by 1978 it was the fourth most important issue: first was unemployment; second strikes; third inflation. The party also adapted early drafts of the manifesto in light of most recent events, producing a tougher line on trade union power after the Winter of Discontent. The proposal to sell council houses was very popular, especially in the Midlands and in New Towns, thus increasing and widening the Tories' voter-support (see Table 2.4 below, Butler and Kavanagh's (1980: 190) comments from campaign canvassing and Crewe's (1981: 293) post-election survey). Surveys also found that the Conservatives' proposals were widely known and even a majority of Labour voters approved the majority of their policies (see Table 2.5 below). Polls also showed that voters expected the Conservatives to be more successful in achieving their objectives. As Clemens (1983: 19) argues: 'The Conservative manifesto was the most directly responsive to public demands. It presented clearly its policies on the issues that concerned the public.'

*Stage 3: Product adjustment*

*Achievability*
The Conservatives avoided detailed policy commitments. Between 1977 and 1979 the Shadow Treasury team met with the shadow ministers one by one to discuss how to reduce the expenditure of their proposals. The party also avoided making great promises. In the foreword to the manifesto Thatcher argued:

It contains no magic formula or lavish promises. It is not a recipe for an easy or a perfect life. But it sets out a broad framework for the recovery of our country, based not on dogma, but on reason, on common sense. (The Conservative Party (1979))

Indeed, the manifesto qualified its potential achievements, arguing that 'repeated disappointment of rising expectations has led to a marked loss of faith in politicians' promises. Too much has gone wrong in Britain for us to hope to put it all right in a year or two' (The Conservative Party (1979: Section 7, A new beginning)). Polls indicated that voters believed the Conservative proposals to be more achievable than Labour's (see Table 2.6 below).

*Internal reaction analysis*
The leadership took various steps to ensure that the product would achieve broad support within the party. The policy groups created to inform the design of policies involved both MPs and outside experts. The manifesto built on earlier policy documents which were taken through the party to gain support. *The Right Approach* (1976) gained Heath's approval, for example, and *The Right Approach to the Economy* (1977), which used the work of policy groups, included signatures of Joseph, Sir Geoffrey Howe and Jim Prior which gave it a broad party backing. The Shadow Cabinet had full opportunity to discuss these documents. Tim Bell (1982: 11), who was involved in the party's advertising, recalled how during the campaign the Research Director, Chris Patten, constantly 'checked back that we were continuing to sell policies which fairly represented the Party rather than just those we felt were most attractive'.

*Competition analysis*
The Conservative Party responded to the Opposition weaknesses. In its manifesto it pointed out how the Conservatives stood for reducing tax, government intervention and public expenditure but the Labour Party proposed to increase them all (see The Conservative Party (1979)). It also managed to turn what had been an Opposition strength into its own strength. The Winter of Discontent undermined Labour's traditionally positive relations with the trade unions. Thatcher then put forward stronger proposals for trade union reform in a party political broadcast in January 1979 and her poll ratings subsequently increased. The Conservatives re-defined the trade union issue from being about inflation and incomes policy to being about industrial relations and strikes, where Labour had been proved weak by events. They also avoided their own weaknesses: Clemens (1983: 20) observed that Thatcher's speeches tended to deal less often with jobs: 'the one issue on which the Conservatives were well behind in the polls.'

*Support analysis*

Saatchi and Saatchi conducted quantitative research which identified four target markets: first-time voters; women; skilled workers; and the party faithful. First-time voters were believed to be 'available' to the party because of increased electoral volatility and decreased party identification and research indicated that skilled workers would find tax cuts attractive. Policies and speeches were geared to suit these groups.

### Stage 4: Implementation

The 'product' design was relatively well implemented, aided by Thatcher's careful party management and involvement of different parts of the party within the product design stage. Any remaining major differences over policy were resolved far in advance of the election in the period leading up to the production of the documents *The Right Approach* (1976) and *The Right Approach to the Economy* (1977). The drafting of the manifesto was also begun early in preparation for an early election date in the autumn of 1978. The process was very clear and involved the Research Department, senior party figures and the Shadow Cabinet. The manifesto was then updated for the actual 1979 date, but without any trouble. Overall, despite some inevitable remaining disagreement in the party, it was broadly united behind the product. Additionally, the grass roots were at this time generally deferential to the leadership and accepting of the changes Thatcher made.

### Stage 5: Communication

The Conservatives began to engage in communication before the campaign even started. They began regular press advertising eighteen months before the election. Gordon Reece, Director of Publicity, conducted market intelligence and then advised Thatcher on her speaking style and physical appearance. Tim Bell, the Managing Director of Saatchi and Saatchi, developed a strategy early on. The agency created posters with slogans which included the infamous 'Labour isn't working' and 'Britain's better off with the Conservatives'. They also appealed to one of the party's target groups, the C2 social group of skilled workers, producing an advert in the popular press entitled: 'Why every Trade Unionist should Consider Voting Conservative.' This had very detailed positive argument and conveyed the feeling that the Labour Party was not necessarily the only party they could vote for.

*Stage 6: The election campaign*

The official campaign period was five weeks, but the Conservatives refused to start campaigning until Easter Monday, 16 April, giving them two and a half weeks of electioneering. The election campaign was built on careful market intelligence and used target marketing. It was well organised and the communication lines between party headquarters and the leader were clear. It was also very obvious what the role and power of everyone in the Conservative campaign group were. In complete contrast to Delaney in the Labour Party, Tim Bell from Saatchi and Saatchi was given free access to all research relevant to the agency's role and had clear contact to the highest levels of the party such as the chairman and the leader. It was also left alone to do its job. There was even good organisation and communication at the local level. The Organisation Department was in continual communication with the local agents, candidates and associations and offered constant support, information and advice. The party provided summaries of stated party policy, including analysis of Labour proposals and general advice to all candidates which assured some continuity between different levels of the party, and supported activists in their 'sales force' role. The UK was divided into twelve areas and effort targeted at the weakest.

The party held a press conference each day, designed to ensure visual effectiveness and offer a sound-bite for the television news. Common advertising techniques were used through bill board posters across fourteen hundred sites. Reece organised a seven-day-a-week operation throughout the campaign, producing various publications such as *Conservative News*, *Briefing Notes*, *Politics Today* and *Speaker's Notes* to keep the media supplied with information.

Margaret Thatcher did not figure heavily in the campaign because the Conservatives wanted to focus on the policy part of their product design, not just the leader. Her advisers (Thorneycroft, Whitelaw and Reece) stopped her engaging in a television debate with Callaghan, arguing that it would focus the campaign on the television interview rather than the issues at stake. For the appearances Thatcher did make, Reece persuaded her to appear on less traditional political programmes, such as the *Jimmy Young Show*, to attract support from target voters. Indeed, the campaign throughout was directed by an awareness that the party needed to win the support of its target market. The themes employed in the advertising: freedom under the law; incentives; Labour's failures; the threat of economic decline; and the general message of 'time for a change' were designed to suit the target voters. The advertising mediums were also chosen with the target markets in mind; newspaper adverts focused on the popular papers such as the *Mirror* and the *Sun*, women's magazines and also the cinema to attract support from first-time voters. The party placed major advertisements during the last five days of the campaign in the most popular papers. And as Livingston (1981: 141) noted, Thatcher's speeches were designed to appeal:

> Not only to convinced Conservatives but to wavering Labourites. Her audiences were full of cheering and cheerful supporters, but her words were often aimed over their heads to traditional Labour voters who might be persuaded to join the crusade.

Competition and SWOT analysis were used again in this stage. The campaign criticised Labour's weaknesses with regard to the Winter of Discontent, unemployment, standard of living and the economy.

Despite the role played by Saatchi and Saatchi, Tim Bell himself admitted that their 'contribution on its own did not win the campaign' (1982: 11/25). This highlights how marketing is not just about selling. Indeed Bell (quoted in Worcester and Harrop (1982: 32)) argued 'what we do is present the policies which we are given by the Party. We do not tell the Party what policies to adopt; we simply present the facts that we're given'. Even Delaney (1982: 30–1) conceded that Saatchi and Saatchi did not sell the Conservative Party as if it were soap-powder. They simply brought professionalism to the party's communications, influencing the presentation of its ideas rather than seeking to change them.

### Stage 7: Election – the party's success in attracting support

The consequences of this market-oriented behaviour on party support can be evaluated in three ways: the results of the general election, membership levels and voter evaluations of the party.

1 *The general election*: The Conservative Party won the election, with 44 per cent of the popular vote and 339 seats (compared to Labour's 269). It was the largest lead in votes over Labour since 1935 and the largest lead overall since 1945. Thatcher was even successful in capturing working-class voters to the Conservative Party.
2 *Membership*: Membership, however, followed a general pattern of decline, falling from 1,500,000 in 1974 to 1,350,000 in 1979, reflecting societal changes but also the fact that marketing was not applied to the membership part of the product.
3 *Voter evaluations of party behaviour*: The Conservative policies were preferred by the majority of voters, as measured by both opinion polls and the BES. The BES found that Conservative policy was preferred over Labour's on all six areas of trade unions, nationalisation, unemployment, taxes and services, the Common Market and welfare: see Table 2.3.

**Table 2.3** *Preferred party policy, 1979*

*Question asked: When it comes to the question of [policy area], do you prefer any of the parties? [If yes] Which party?*

|  | Party policy preferred<br>(% lead over the opposition) |
| --- | --- |
| Regulating the activities of trade unions | Conservative (26) |
| Nationalisation | Conservative (25) |
| Unemployment | Conservative (13) |
| Taxes and Government services | Conservative (8) |
| Britain's attitude to the Common Market's economic policies | Conservative (4) |
| Social services and benefits | Conservative (2) |

*Source:* BES (1979).
*Note:* n = 1,983.

Conservative support above Labour was also shown in MORI polls taken in May, and a more specific BBC/Gallup survey which asked about particular manifesto proposals also found that the Conservative proposals received more support: see Table 2.4. Furthermore, even Labour voters supported Conservative proposals: see Table 2.5

**Table 2.4** *Support for Conservative and Labour manifesto proposals, May 1979*

*Question asked: I am going to read out some of the proposals that the different parties have put forward in this election. In each case I would like you to say whether you think the proposal is a good idea or a bad idea.*

| Proposal | All voters (%) |
| --- | --- |
| *Conservative* | |
| Ban secondary picketing | 91 |
| Have a free vote in the House of Commons on the death penalty | 90 |
| Sell more council houses to tenants | 80 |
| Stop social security payments to the families of strikers | 81 |
| Cut top income tax rate for people with large incomes | 57 |
| Put up VAT in order to reduce income tax | 51 |
| *Average for Conservative* | 71.5 |
| *Labour* | |
| Take tougher stand against the Common Market's agricultural policy | 94 |
| Give Government subsidies where that is necessary to protect jobs | 79 |
| Introduce a wealth tax | 49 |
| Give trade unions seats on the boards of major companies | 45 |
| Reduce the powers of the House of Lords | 43 |
| *Average for Labour* | 62.0 |

*Source:* Crewe (1981: 294–5), from a BBC Gallup survey, 2–3 May 1979.
*Note:* n = not known.

**Table 2.5** *Labour voters' views on Tory aims, April 1979*

*Question asked: Should the next Government attempt to achieve these objectives?*

| Objective | Yes | No | Don't know |
|---|---|---|---|
| Reduce violent crime and vandalism | 95 | 3 | 2 |
| Reduce supplementary benefit for strikers | 63 | 30 | 7 |
| End secondary picketing by strikers | 78 | 14 | 3 |
| Reduce income tax, especially for the higher paid | 52 | 45 | 3 |
| Give council house tenants the right to buy their homes | 75 | 20 | 5 |
| Reduce the number of civil servants | 70 | 22 | 8 |
| Sell off parts of some state-owned companies | 40 | 49 | 11 |

*Source: Observer,* 22 April 1979.
*Note:* n = not known.

The popularity of the Conservative Party was also on issues that the voters held as most important, such as inflation, tax, law and order and strikes (as shown by the BES).

In terms of ability to deliver, the Conservative Party benefited from voters' relatively low evaluations for the Labour Government's handling of problems, especially strikes. 68 per cent of respondents to the BES said the country was in poor shape and 62 per cent believed their income had fallen behind. The Conservatives received hypothesised perceptions of how they might have handled various problems that were higher than Labour, particularly on crime. For example, 85 per cent of respondents felt the Tories would have handled law and order well compared with only 53 per cent for Labour. This was also an area high on voters' list of important issues. Conservative proposals were also viewed as more achievable: see Table 2.6.

**Table 2.6** *Credibility of Conservative and Labour proposals*

| | % saying the party would succeed in achieving these objectives minus % saying it would not |
|---|---|
| *Conservative* | |
| Give council house tenants the right to buy their homes | + 61 |
| Reduce income tax, especially for the higher paid | + 49 |
| Reduce supplementary benefit for strikers | + 42 |
| Reduce violent crime and vandalism | − 20 |
| | |
| *Labour* | |
| Reduce income tax, especially for the lower paid | + 30 |
| Bring inflation down to 5% a year within 3 years | − 41 |
| Prevent increases in Common Market farm prices | − 29 |
| Achieve a long-term understanding with trade unions on wages | − 3 |

*Source:* RSL survey, 17–18 April 1979, quoted in Crewe (1981: 286).
*Note:* n = 1,199.

*Stage 8: Delivery*

Clearly, the next stage that Thatcher had to lead her party through was delivery. In 1979, however, voters had to choose according to expected delivery. Whether the Tories were successful in delivery in government will be examined in the section on marketing in government on pp. 61–63.

## Market-oriented Margaret Thatcher

It is clear that political marketing is about more than just the use of snappy slogans or spin-doctors. It holds the potential to influence all aspects of a party's behaviour, as seen in this analysis of the Conservatives in the run-up to the 1979 election. Contrary to conventional wisdom, Thatcher did use political marketing. This has been advanced previously by Scammell (1994, 1995 and 1996) but the influence of political marketing was actually even more comprehensive. Not only was marketing used in the design of the leader's image, it influenced policy to a greater extent than just setting the parameters. Although Thatcher's own claims to be a politician of conviction contradict this, academic analysis needs to reach deeper than the assertions of particular politicians. CPM analysis which considers not just the leader and the use of polls but party behaviour as a whole has revealed subtle aspects of political marketing which are important to its success. Thatcher accepted the basic market-oriented concept: that parties change their behaviour to suit what voters want. She then led and supported the necessary activities to do this, identifying voters' needs and wants through various forms of market intelligence and ensuring leadership behaviour and the policies on offer were in line with public opinion. The Conservatives were consequently successful in ensuring high party unity and conveying 'what was on offer' to the electorate.

There were limits to this. Thatcher did not apply the market-oriented concept to all aspects of party behaviour, leaving those such as candidates for office and party membership alone. Nevertheless, the use of political marketing was sufficient to not just win the general election but to attract a wide range of electoral support, providing further evidence of how the market has indeed changed and is more open. The rest of the chapter will examine the successes and failures of Thatcher's Conservatives in government: where the fulfilment of promises rather than just their reflection of voters' demands becomes important. After a successful change in party behaviour and good result in the general election, the remaining question for the leader was how to maintain such success.

**Marketing in government: The Conservatives, 1979–87**

After winning the 1979 election, Margaret Thatcher went on to win a further two elections, staying as party leader and Prime Minister for eleven years until 1990. This section will analyse the party's success in delivering on promises as well as its ability to remain responsive to voters while still in government between 1979 and 1987.

*The Conservatives from 1979 to 1983*

Between 1979 and 1983 the Conservative Party maintained its market orientation. It achieved some success in delivering on its 1979 promises and continued to conduct market intelligence and change its behaviour accordingly. Its actions were somewhat constrained by being in government, but this did not prevent it from paying attention to the views of the electorate.

The first stage to consider is Stage 8 – delivery on promises made in 1979. This book is concerned with voter perception of party behaviour: it does not claim to make an academic assessment of policy effectiveness. It therefore makes general assessments based on this and the party's election pledges.

*Previous marketing – Stage 8: Delivery*

*Problems*

There are various areas in which the Conservative Government can be criticised for failing to meet election pledges:

- Public expenditure as a share of GNP increased: 41 per cent (1979) to 44 per cent (1983).
- VAT was doubled in the June 1979 budget from 8 per cent to 15 per cent.
- Unemployment grew to three million by January 1982. At 12.7 per cent it was the highest it had been for fifty years.
- Government continued to provide large subsidies to industries such as British Leyland and British Steel.
- There was a second hike in oil prices after the fall of the Shah of Iran and susbsequent international economic problems.
- Riots broke out, for example in Brixton, Bristol and Toxteth.

Unsurprisingly, during the first two years of being in government the party's standing in opinion polls fell considerably.

*Successes*
On the other hand, there were some successes:

- Unions: the Party delivered almost by default. A steel strike in early 1980 lost the industry customers and profit and eventually led to big redundancies which helped to deter other strikes and encouraged lower pay claims. The Employment Acts of 1980 and 1982 reduced union power.
- Privatisation: by 1983, plans had been put in place for this, such as the sale of shares in British Petroleum and British Airways. Postal and telephone services were separated in preparation for selling off British Telecom at a later date.
- Income tax was cut: in the 1979 Budget the top rate was reduced from 83 to 60 per cent and the standard rate from 33 to 30 per cent.
- The inflation rate declined significantly, down to 5 per cent in early 1983, which was the lowest level it had been for 10 years.
- Tighter financial controls were introduced into the public sector.
- Rhodesia: here an agreement was reached under the Government's direction, settling a long-standing unresolved issue.
- Europe: in 1980 Thatcher was also successful in securing an £1,800 million rebate on the British contribution to Europe.
- The Falklands War: British troops were successful in recapturing the Falkland Islands after the Argentines seized them. Susbsequently Thatcher's standing as leader improved and criticism from within her party lessened.
- Council houses: The promise to sell council houses was also fulfilled through the 1980 Housing Act. This not only increased and extended the sale of houses, it provided local authority mortgages to help people buy. It proved popular with voters: see Table 2.7.

**Table 2.7** *Voters' views on the sale of council houses, 1983*

*Question asked: I want to ask about some changes that have been happening in Britain over the years. For each one I read out can you say whether you think it has gone too far, not gone far enough, or is it about right: the sale of council houses*

|  | % |
| --- | --- |
| Gone too far | 13 |
| About right | 66 |
| Not gone far enough | 21 |

*Source:* BES (1983).
*Note:* n = 3,760.

*Success in negating blame*

Unemployment remained a problem but not for the party's electoral support. Voters did not hold the Tories responsible. They were more inclined to blame factors outside the party's control, such as the international recession. Table 2.8 reports results from the BES which support this argument by showing voters' ambiguity towards whether the Government was to blame for unemployment.

**Table 2.8** *Voters' views on whether unemployment is Government's fault, 1983*

*Question asked: Please say whether you agree or disagree that the high level of unemployment in Britain is mainly the British Government's fault.*

|  | % |
| --- | --- |
| Agree | 41 |
| Not sure | 9 |
| Disagree | 50 |

*Source:* BES (1983).
*Note:* n = 3,955.

An alternative argument is that the Government did not have enough time to deliver. Thatcher had argued before 1979 that she would need two terms of office to achieve her goals and surveys indicated that voters accepted that it would take time before the Conservative policies would yield results.

Overall, therefore, the Conservatives were broadly successful in delivery: at least in the voters' eyes. Failures were negated by the lack of time and other successes. The Tories' position was also helped by, as will be discussed in a subsequent chapter, the alternative choice (Labour) being product-oriented. The other aspect to consider is how the Conservatives went through the marketing process again in time for the next general election.

*Stage 1: Market intelligence*

The Conservative Party continued to conduct varied market intelligence and used it extremely effectively.

*Informally*

• About seventy Conservatives (including MPs, peers, MEPs and local government activists) were invited to take part in policy committees, charged with finding policies for the future. They produced reports that then fed into the manifesto process.

- The party drew on pressure groups and think tanks, such as the Centre for Policy Studies, the Institute of Economic Affairs and the Adam Smith Institute.

*Formally*

- Harris (formerly the Opinion Research Centre) conducted quantitative research for the party. It conducted an attitude poll to identify the most important issues to voters and surveys.
- Marplan were commissioned to do some polling early in their period of office.
- The party followed the Gallup omnibus survey.
- It also analysed reactions to the SDP through by-election results and nation-wide surveys.
- Qualitative research was also conducted, using focus groups, which discovered how voters did not blame the Government for unemployment.

The results of this were all made readily available to the Number 10 policy unit for the drafting of the manifesto.

*Stage 2: Product design*

*Leadership*

Margaret Thatcher continued a strong and determined leadership style once in office. Her popularity was poor in the first few years of office but turned more positive towards the end of the Government (see Tables 2.14 and 2.15). Nevertheless, her relationship with her party was somewhat problematic in government. Her argumentative style, particularly in view of her being a woman, was not always well received. She attempted to appease different points of view by giving office to most of Heath's Shadow Cabinet as well as her closest supporters. The problem with this was that strong critics of the party's new behaviour remained in Cabinet. During the first two years of government, Thatcher battled against them; ministers were divided, there were many leaks and she met numerous defeats. Over time, Thatcher demoted her critics in re-shuffles and promoted those who were behind the promised policies. Overall she remained resolute and determined. Given that voters wanted strong leadership, and new policies, that her leadership style helped to deliver these was in itself market-oriented.

*MPs*
The local party associations continued to control the selection of candidates.

*Membership*
The Conservative grass roots remained generally deferential to and supportive of Margaret Thatcher.

*Staff*
The party's use of staff was mixed. Thatcher herself drew on a number of advisers with relevant experience, such as Alan Walters, an economist and Sir Anthony Parsons, previously an Ambassador to the United Nations. Ferdinand Mount organised the Policy Unit: Mount had been political editor of the *Spectator*. However some of them lacked substantial political experience which compounded Thatcher's problem of being a relative outsider in the Conservative Party.

The party's chairmanship experienced some difficulties. Lord Thorneycroft remained as Chair of the Party after the election and worked to cut the party's £2.2 million deficit in 1980–81. Although successful in this he proved to be a strong critic of the Government's economic policy and Thatcher replaced him with Cecil Parkinson in September 1981. Parkinson's chairmanship was particularly effective in improving the party's communications. He created a Department of Marketing that held overall responsibility for communications strategy. The Head, Chris Lawson, had significant experience: he had been involved in election campaigns in the USA and was the managing director of a large US company. A series of direct mail-outs was initiated in December 1982, to focus on key voters in critical constituencies and to ask for donations: a technique copied from the US Republican Party. The Department of Press and Public Relations was left to deal with the mass media.

The Research Department, however, suffered from a loss of morale and standing during 1979–83. The first Director of the Research Department cut expenditure, the second was too close to the Party Chairman to pull back its independence. Staff left. Control of survey research was given to the new Marketing Department. The involvement and influence of the Research Department on policy also declined. Thatcher called more on the Centre for Policy Studies and civil service ministers.

Other posts in the party suffered from turnover and confusion. For example, when Gordon Reece left his position as Director of Publicity, he was replaced firstly by Sir Harry Byne, then David Boddy, until in March 1983 Anthony Shrimsley (who had editorial experience) was appointed Head of the Press and Publicity Department. Nonetheless, the Department continued to dispense useful advice to different parts of the party.

*Policy proposals*

The manifesto (see The Conservative Party (1983)) took into account the party's position in government and related the party's promises for the future to its actions over the last four to five years. The party thus persisted with many of its previous promises and themes, focusing on three areas: defence, employment and the economy. It promised to continue to pursue firm control of public expenditure, the money supply and public sector pay, aiming to further reduce inflation and tax rates. This responded to public opinion: Table 2.9 shows how voters thought high income tax made people work less hard and people relied too much on state provision.

**Table 2.9** *Voters' views, 1983*

*Question asked: Please say whether you agree or disagree with each of these statements, or say if you are not sure either way.*

| | Agree (%) | Not sure (%) | Disagree (%) |
|---|---|---|---|
| High income tax makes people less willing to work hard | 70 | 8 | 22 |
| Too many people these days like to rely on Government handouts | 68 | 9 | 23 |

*Source:* BES (1983).
*Note:* n = 3,955.

The Conservative manifesto also proposed more changes in legislation for trade unions and the privatisation of state industries such as British Telecom, British Airways, British Steel and British Leyland.

Results from the BES show that these proposals reflected voters' views. Table 2.10 indicates that 74 per cent of respondents believed that trade unions still had too much power.

**Table 2.10** *Voters' views on trade unions, 1983*

*Question asked: Thinking now of trade unions in this country – do you think they have . . .*

| | % saying trade unions have . . . |
|---|---|
| Too much power | 74 |
| Not too much power | 26 |

*Source:* BES (1983).
*Note:* n = 3,755.

Table 2.11 suggests that a majority of voters were against nationalisation.

**Table 2.11** *Voters' views on nationalisation, 1983*

*Question asked: Should there be more or less nationalisation or de-nationalisation?*

|  | % |
| --- | --- |
| Nationalise (a lot or a few) more industries | 18 |
| Nationalise no more | 39 |
| De-nationalise | 43 |

*Source:* BES (1983).
*Note:* n = 3,491.

Following results from its marketing intelligence, the party continued with its policies on unemployment because although it was a problem for the country, voters did not blame the party for it: there was no need for the party to change its existing 'product' or policy. The party also knew that voters still wanted the public services maintained. The manifesto might have been more radical were it not for the results of marketing intelligence. Overall, the Conservatives were the most popular party in various respects (see Tables 2.12 and 2.13).

### Stage 3: Product adjustment

*Achievability*
The Conservative Party's manifesto did not contain many spending promises. Each one was examined by the Financial Secretary to the Treasury, Leon Brittan, who made sure that the costs outlined in the manifesto were in line with previous government budgets and white papers. One participant in the manifesto-drafting process commented how 'unlike previous governments we did not want to make lavish promises, raise expectations and then disappoint them' (quoted by Butler and Kavanagh (1984: 41)). The party also tried to make voters have realistic expectations of what government could do. The party focused on the causes of unemployment and other economic problems and argued that its policy solutions would deliver the best results in the long term.

*Internal reaction analysis*
Thatcher's resolute determination to do as she had planned inevitably led to criticism. She responded to those who opposed her by demoting them in Cabinet re-shuffles which caused significant problems in the long term. At

this time, however, it can be viewed as reasonable given that they criticised behaviour which the party had promised to deliver and for which the public had voted. Thatcher was also hindered by her staff's lack of political experience, as well as her own outsider status and gender. She was, however, successful in attracting more secure support on the back benches. The manifesto was drawn up after policy groups within the party and discussions between the Prime Minister and Cabinet Ministers.

*Competition analysis*
This was used in the campaign itself. For example, emphasis was placed on Thatcher's strong leadership style that also exploited Labour's weak leadership. Market intelligence revealed that in relation to the Labour Party the Conservatives were generally weaker on issues such as pensions and the NHS. Thatcher therefore reiterated the party's commitment to public services. Research also showed that the contents of the Labour Party's manifesto would prove unpopular with voters and the Conservatives thus focused on Labour's manifesto wherever possible.

*Support analysis*
Unlike in 1979 the party did not make any special attempt to seek support outside that it already had: only the leader's tour and advertising in the campaign were designed to secure this.

### Stage 4: Implementation

In the early part of 1979–83, Cabinet unity was poor because Thatcher met significant opposition from ministers sceptical of the policies. Over time, she promoted those who supported the new product design and became more involved in departmental matters and with the civil service to ease implementation. By the time of the election, her critics had generally been defeated or taken away from key positions, so the overall consequence was one of a unified and coherent message in the campaign. More significantly, voters viewed the party as unified (see Tables 2.16 and 2.17).

### Stage 5: Communication

The Tories neglected this stage, except for the usual communication a government makes with the public.

### Stage 6: The election campaign

The campaign itself was generally well prepared and organised. Preparation began at least a year before the election. Communication within the campaign organisation was well co-ordinated and integrated, with close links between different sections of the party organisation. Market intelligence was conducted throughout the campaign. Cecil Parkinson stayed at the centre during the election to provide rebuttal to any criticisms that arose. The party had access to mini-polls each day, a weekly survey and general polling conducted by Harris. A few potential problems occurred but did not materialise into big issues.

The party's advertising was run by Saatchi and Saatchi again. A committee consisting of three MPs, four people from Saatchi and Saatchi (as well as Tim Bell and Michael Dobbs) and Chris Lawson and Keith Britto met from January 1983 onwards to oversee it. BJM Research Associates conducted qualitative research for Saatchi and Saatchi which informed the design of advertising. The agency argued that the party must encourage realistic expectations from voters, focus on Conservative strengths and the weaknesses of the opposition. One negative development was that Saatchi and Saatchi had much less access to senior party figures than before.

The Prime Minister's trips were designed to gain maximum coverage on the national television news, creating attractive photo opportunities. Cabinet ministers were also sent on trips, designed to reach all parts of the country and gain local media attention. At the local level, campaign effort was targeted on 103 seats defined as critical marginals. They received greater help from agents and professionals and the Conservatives were successful in winning 98 of them. Overall the product was communicated very coherently.

*Stage 7: Election – the party's success in attracting support*

*The general election*
The 1983 general election gave the Conservatives an increased majority from 43 to 144. They gained 397 seats compared with Labour's 209. The Conservative majority was the largest in terms of seats since 1945 and largest in terms of votes since 1935.

*Membership*
This continued to follow a general pattern of decline, falling from 1,350,000 in 1979 to 1,200,000 in 1983.

*Voter evaluations of party behaviour*
The Conservatives came out as the party with the best policies in a BBC Election Day Survey, the BES and MORI opinion polls taken just before the election. Table 2.12 reports the MORI results.

**Table 2.12** *Best party policy on key issues, 1983*

*Question asked: I am going to read out a list of problems facing Britain today. I would like you to tell me whether you think the Conservative Party, the Labour Party or the Liberal Democrats has the best policies on each problem.*

| | Labour or Conservative better policy (% lead over the other) |
|---|---|
| Defence generally | Conservative (34) |
| Common Market | Conservative (27) |
| Taxation | Conservative (19) |
| Nuclear arms | Conservative (19) |
| Law and order | Conservative (31) |
| Education | Conservative (8) |
| Industrial relations/strikes | Conservative (4) |
| Unemployment | Labour (4) |
| Housing | Labour (6) |
| National Health Service | Labour (7) |
| Pensions | Labour (8) |

*Source:* MORI polls.
*Notes:* n = c. 1,000 or 2,000, surveys based on GB residents aged 18 +. Poll taken 1–3 June, except for pensions which was any time in June.

BES data also showed that those issues on which the Conservatives led were also seen by voters as the most important. For example, crime, which is a traditional Conservative strength, was chosen by respondents in the BES as the most desirable option: see Table 2.13.

**Table 2.13** *Voters' most desirable option, 1983*

*Question asked: If you had to choose from among the items on this card, which are the two that seem most desirable to you?*

| | Order of that chosen by most respondents (1 = the highest) |
|---|---|
| Maintaining order in the nation | 1 |
| Fighting rising prices | 2 |
| Giving people more say in important political decisions | 3 |
| Protecting freedom of speech | 4 |

*Source:* BES (1983).
*Note:* n = 3,955.

The Conservatives also had the most popular leadership. It came out top when the BBC Election Day Survey asked respondents which party had the best team of leaders. The BES results also indicated that 91 per cent of respondents viewed Thatcher as an effective Prime Minister, whereas in sharp contrast 70 per cent said that the Labour leader, Michael Foot, would have been ineffective (see Table 2.14).

**Table 2.14** *Effectiveness of party leader as Prime Minister, 1983*

*Question asked: On the whole, how effective or ineffective do you think Mrs Thatcher [Mr Foot] is [could have been] as Prime Minister?*

|  | Effective (%) | Ineffective (%) |
|---|---|---|
| 1 Thatcher | 91 | 9 |
| 2 Foot | 30 | 70 |

*Source:* BES (1983).
*Notes:* n = 3,955. 'Effective' combines those saying 'Very effective' and 'Fairly effective'; 'Ineffective' combines those saying 'Fairly effective' and 'Very ineffective'.

Table 2.15 also shows that Thatcher led Foot on voters' perceptions of their ability to get things done, improve the nation's standing abroad, get the most out of a team and unite the nation.

**Table 2.15** *Most able Prime Minister, 1983*

*Question asked: At the time of the general election, which one do you think would have been the Prime Minister most able to …*

|  | Thatcher or Foot lead (% over the other) |
|---|---|
| Get things done | Thatcher (60) |
| Improve Britain's standing abroad | Thatcher (51) |
| Get the most out of a team | Thatcher (45) |
| Unite the nation | Thatcher (40) |
| Have concern for all groups in society | Thatcher (3) |
| Be most in touch with ordinary people's problems | Foot (6) |

*Source:* BES (1983).
*Note:* n = 3,955.

Thatcher also received more positive evaluations than Foot on qualities such as toughness, determination, decisiveness and the ability to stick to principles.

The Conservative Party as a whole was viewed by 70 per cent of respondents in the BES as being united, compared with 92 per cent who thought Labour was divided (see Table 2.16).

**Table 2.16** *Party unity, 1983*

*Question asked: Would you describe the Conservative/
Labour Party nowadays as united or divided?*

|  | United (%) | Divided (%) |
|---|---|---|
| Conservative | 70 | 24 |
| Labour | 8 | 92 |

*Source:* BES (1983).
*Note:* n = 3,955.

Table 2.17 shows that Conservative policies were also seen by voters as being clearer.

**Table 2.17** *Implementation of product design, 1983*

*Question asked: On the whole, do you think the
Conservative/Labour Party has clear or vague policies?*

|  | Clear (%) | Vague (%) |
|---|---|---|
| Conservative | 82 | 18 |
| Labour | 38 | 62 |

*Source:* BES (1983).
*Note:* n = 3,955.

The Tories had greater general credibility in governing. The BBC Election Day Survey found that 75 per cent of respondents had confidence in Conservative politicians to deal wisely with Britain's problems, whereas only 25 per cent had this confidence in Labour. Voter assessment of the Government's handling of particular problems was positive: Table 2.18 shows that the large majority of voters felt that it had handled the inflation and strikes well, although 72 per cent viewed its handling of unemployment negatively. As already discussed, this did not translate into lost votes because the electorate could negate the blame onto external factors and the Tory Party was, in comparison with other parties, seen as the best party to deal with it in future.

Conservative success was therefore substantial but not complete. The BES reveals that whereas a majority of respondents felt that the Government had been successful in keeping taxes down, they were less positive about improvements in their standard of living: see Table 2.19.

**Table 2.18** *Voters' evaluation of the Conservative Government's handling of problems, 1983*

*Question asked: On the whole, do you think the Conservative Government over the last four years has handled [. . .], very well, fairly well, not very well, or not at all well?*

|  | Well (%) | Not well (%) |
|---|---|---|
| The Falklands Dispute | 77 | 23 |
| The problem of inflation | 80 | 20 |
| The problem of strikes | 73 | 27 |
| The problem of unemployment | 28 | 72 |

*Source:* BES (1983).
*Notes:* n = 3,955. 'Well' combines those who said 'Very well' and 'Fairly well'; 'Not well' combines those saying 'Not very well' and 'Not at all well'.

**Table 2.19** *Voters' evaluation of the Conservative success in government, 1983*

*Question asked: On the whole, do you think the Conservative Government over the last four years was successful or unsuccessful in . . .*

|  | Successful (%) | Unsuccessful (%) |
|---|---|---|
| 1  Keeping taxes down | 66 | 34 |
| 2  Improving your standard of living | 45 | 55 |

*Source:* BES (1983).
*Notes:* n = 3,955. 'Successful' combines those who said 'Very successful' and 'Fairly successful'; 'Unsuccessful' combines those who said 'Fairly unsuccessful' and 'Very unsuccessful'.

Overall though, the party received positive evaluations: certainly more positive assessment than the Labour Party. The BES showed that far more voters believed that the Conservatives were most able to keep prices down, prevent strikes and reduce unemployment: see Table 2.20.

**Table 2.20** *Parties' possible performance in government, 1983*

*Question asked: Which party do you think would be the most likely to [. . .] over the next four–five years?*

|  | Conservative | Labour |
|---|---|---|
| Keep prices down | 43 | 25 |
| Prevent strikes | 48 | 25 |
| Reduce unemployment | 46 | 27 |
| Improve the standard of living | 18 | 49 |
| Look after the health and social services | 20 | 54 |

*Source:* BES (1983).
*Note:* n = 3,955.

Furthermore, these areas were also those that voters held as their priorities and most important in their decision about who to vote for.

Overall, the Conservatives managed to maintain a market orientation between 1979 and 1983. Their policies were broadly in line with market opinion, were seen as credible and the party held general governing competence. The party also offered strong leadership and organisational coherence. In terms of electoral success, it was clearly aided by an unpopular Opposition: rather than providing clear competition, Labour moved away towards a product orientation, as will be discussed in a subsequent chapter. Nonetheless the basic assumption of CPM theory is that the party which is the most market-oriented wins and the 1983 result supports this.

## The Conservatives from 1983 to 1987

The Conservative Party entered the 1987 election very much a party of government: it had been in office for two terms and, perhaps understandably, it neglected certain activities necessary to maintain a market orientation in the long term. The leader became more dominant within the party which unfortunately reduced the level of critical analysis of future policy promises. Communication between different sections of the party organisation also declined. Nonetheless, the party responded to the results from market intelligence that suggested that voters thought the Government had run out of steam and overall the behaviour of the Conservatives remained closest to public opinion of any major party.

### *Previous marketing – Stage 8: Delivery*

*Problems*

- Embarrassments: Cecil Parkinson, the former Party Chairman, resigned from the Cabinet in October 1983 when it was revealed that he had had an affair with his secretary. The 'Westland affair', where members of the Government disagreed about how to respond to a company floundering, was fully covered by the media and increased voters' perception of Thatcher as being too bossy and damaged the standing of the party as a whole.
- Scotland: The party had poor results in the 1985 local elections after a re-valuation of rates. This stimulated the introduction of a new tax, the community charge or poll tax.
- Unemployment rose again during 1983–87 from 3.1 to 3.3 million. Indeed, voters felt that unemployment and crime had increased and the standard of health and education had fallen (see Table 2.29).

74

*Successes*

- Unemployment: voters did not punish the Conservatives for the increase in unemployment.
- Rise in living standards for some: for those in work, their disposable income increased between 1983 and 1987.
- Inflation rate: was 3.5 per cent, well below that held in the majority of other major democracies.
- Interest rates: were reduced to 9 per cent in 1987 and the public perception of the economy was generally positive.

The Conservative Government succeeded in delivering a number of other 1983 pledges:

- It privatised a third of public enterprises, such as Jaguar Cars, British Telecom, British Aerospace, British Gas and British Airways.
- The number of private shareholders increased and the policy proved popular: very large profits were made by initial investors.
- Prices and incomes policies were abandoned.
- Tax: High marginal tax rates were reduced from 80 to 60 per cent and the basic level from 33 to 26 per cent. Indirect taxes had increased, but these were less noticeable. Indeed the BES found that the most voters felt that taxes had stayed the same or fallen (see Table 2.29 below).
- Trade unions: in 1984 the Government passed a Trade Union Act, which required postal ballots at least every five years for all union offices. Its reaction to the miners' strike of 1984–85 proved popular. The strike lost public support. It was not condoned by the Labour Party and a miners' union in the East Midlands broke away to form the UDM and the NUM was defeated in Spring 1985. The Government's policy thus appeared successful, especially because overall relatively few days were lost in disputes during 1983–87.

The delivery record was generally mixed, therefore, but with a number of notable successes that proved popular with voters. During 1983–87, the party's adherence to the Market-Oriented Party model nevertheless declined although overall it remained more market-oriented than Labour.

*Stage 1: Market intelligence*

The party had access to plentiful but sometimes contradictory market intelligence during 1983–87.

*Informal*

- Small policy groups were created to advise on the manifesto. Members consisted of MPs, academics and businessmen. These reported to the Strategy Group led by Margaret Thatcher.

*Formal*

- Harris conducted tracking polls every fortnight in the run-up to the election.
- The party bought the results of regular Gallup surveys which provided a large, nation wide sample which could then be broken down by region or attitude.
- The party also analysed published or public polls.

But the leadership received advice from a number of different sources:

- Saatchi and Saatchi, the official agency, gathered market intelligence using BJM Research Associates, which revealed some problems for the party. Voters thought the party had nothing new to offer, it might be 'time for a change', Thatcher was perceived as being too fixed on doing what she wanted without being clear about what that was and Conservative action on health and education was not satisfactory. Thatcher's response was to commission alternative research.
- Young and Rubicam conducted a series of long interviews to discover what voters wanted, why and what benefits they expected to get. The reports were more positive about Thatcher and called for stronger leadership.
- Thatcher also received advice from Tim Bell who had previously worked for Saatchi but now had his own firm.

This multitude of information was difficult for the party to absorb and input into its product design. Overall the party's use of market intelligence was not as effective as in previous years.

### Stage 2: Product design

*Leadership*
Thatcher continued to attracted admiration, if not popularity, from voters for being a strong leader but characteristics which were once perceived as strengths were now weaknesses. As Sharkey (1989: 64) explains, 'her determination was perceived as stubbornness, her single-mindedness as inflexibility, and her strong will as an inability to listen'. Within her party, Thatcher became dominant, using Cabinet re-shuffles to increase her power without taking account of how this aroused discontent within the organisation. Furthermore, by surrounding herself with only those who supported her, Thatcher also cut herself from alternative points of view, eroding an important source of feedback on how the public was respond-

ing to the Government's behaviour. This had the positive effect of eliminating those who disagreed with her from positions of power but the negative consequence of failing to resolve the disagreement itself.

*MPs*

Cabinet became dominated by Thatcherite supporters. Evans (1997: 24) observed how only 'those she believed to be true believers of her version of politics' were promoted. For example, Francis Pym was sacked as Foreign Secretary and replaced by Sir Geoffrey Howe; Nigel Lawson was promoted to Chancellor of the Exchequer.

*Staff*

The Conservatives experienced some difficulties in their handling of staff during this period. The party's chairmanship was subject to change and problems. John Selwyn Gummer took the position, but lacked the political weight and managerial skills to match the requirements of the job. Norman Tebbit, who had greater standing, agreed to take over in September 1985 but his relationship with Thatcher suffered from poor communication and increasingly public divisions. The party's number of agents fell so that only all the most critical seats had full-time agents; nearly half of constituency associations did not. Communication efforts also suffered from a lack of permanent, experienced staff. For example, they did not appoint a specific Director of Communications because Thatcher and Tebbit could not agree on who should be appointed. The Department of Marketing was disbanded, although its director, Chris Lawson, was appointed in March 1986 to head a Special Services Unit responsible for computers, direct mail and private polling. The party's use of advertising professionals was also confused. Saatchi and Saatchi were maintained as the main agency but only after debate and other sources of advice were sought.

*Activities*

The party made effective use of its pre-election annual party conference in October 1986. It was designed to respond to voters' desire for a new direction. The fundamental idea behind the design of the conference was to focus on the future. Saatchi and Saatchi, the party's advertising agency, created the theme *The Next Moves Forward*. Tebbit (1989: 46) noted how this theme:

> played to our strength by emphasising government and party unity, purposefulness and competence. It also projected the Government's plans and actions through and beyond the forthcoming general election.

*Policy proposals*

The Conservative Party succeeded in changing its behaviour in response to market intelligence while still in government. In late 1986, spending on health and education was increased, plans for re-shaping SERPS (State Earnings-Related Pension Scheme) were scaled down and it was suggested that higher education would be expanded. The party outlined the achievements of its past behaviour by producing a document entitled *The First Eight Years*. The party then outlined promises for a third term of office in its manifesto.

The manifesto was entitled *The Next Moves Forward*, using the theme set at the pre-election conference (see The Conservative Party (1987)). It was longer than that for the two preceding elections: nearly eighty pages. It pledged to continue what had been successful, such as sound economic management and encouraging home ownership, but also included more radical policy initiatives in response to market intelligence. New policies were proposed in areas voters were most concerned about (see Tables 2.21 and 2.22), such as the National Health Service (NHS), education, law and order and housing. For example, the manifesto proposed that:

• local authorities would lose their automatic right to completely control education, housing and local planning: for example schools would be able to opt out of LEA control;
• domestic rates would be abolished and a new community charge (or poll tax) put in its place;
• university education would be expanded and a review of the student grant system completed, which would consider the possibility of introducing top-up loans;
• there would be further privatisation, such as the privatisation of the water authorities and electricity boards;
• share ownership would be extended;
• there would be further reform of trade unions, in particular to protect individuals within unions and to ensure that ballots on strikes were secret and fair;
• there would be further cuts in income tax, in particular a reduction in the basic rate to 25p in the pound.

It reflected voters' views in many respects. Table 2.21, for example, shows that 50 per cent of respondents to the BES felt that government should introduce stricter laws to regulate the activities of trade unions. Table 2.22 also indicates some support for further privatisation.

**Table 2.21** *Voters' views on what government should do, 1987*

*Question asked: Please say whether you think the Government should or should not ...*

|  | Should (%) | Shouldn't (%) |
|---|---|---|
| Get rid of private education in Britain | 17 | 59 |
| Put more money into the NHS | 90 | 5 |
| Spend more on education | 86 | 7 |
| Reduce Government spending generally | 43 | 39 |
| Introduce stricter laws to regulate the activities of trade unions | 50 | 33 |

*Source:* BES (1987).

*Notes:* n = 3,826. 'Should' combines those saying 'Definitely should' and 'Probably should'; 'Shouldn't' combines those saying 'Definitely shouldn't' and 'Probably shouldn't'.

**Table 2.22** *Voters' views on nationalisation, 1987*

*Question asked: Do you think there should be more nationalisation or privatisation?*

|  | % |
|---|---|
| More nationalisation | 17 |
| More privatisation | 32 |
| Leave as it is | 51 |

*Source:* BES (1987).

*Note:* n = 3,826.

Table 2.23 also shows support for further reform of trade unions because voters believed them to be responsible for unemployment. It also suggests support for further income tax cuts in so much as a majority thought that high income tax made people less willing to work and that too many people relied on government.

**Table 2.23** *Voters' views, 1987*

*Question asked: Please say whether you agree or disagree with each of these statements:*

|  | Agree (%) | Disagree (%) |
|---|---|---|
| Much of our unemployment has been caused by trade unions | 80 | 11 |
| Too many people these days like to rely on Government handouts | 61 | 27 |
| High income tax makes people less willing to work | 65 | 22 |

*Source:* BES (1987).

*Notes:* n = 3,826. 'Agree' combines those saying 'Strongly agree' and 'Agree'; 'Disagree' combines those saying 'Strongly disagree' and 'Disagree'.

*Stage 3: Product adjustment*

*Achievability*
Unlike past elections, there was little indication of a Conservative attempt to scale down promises, even if the product appeared more achievable than Labour's.

*Internal reaction analysis*
Attempts were made to involve the party in preparation for the next election. A Strategy Group was formed whose members included Thatcher and a number of senior party figures. The leadership also sought opinions on policy from small groups created a year before the election and draft proposals from ministers before drafting the manifesto. On the other hand, the actual influence of these policy groups was limited. Certain aspects of the manifesto were also criticised from within the party, especially the more radical aspects, such as proposals on managing schools and council homes. Although this did not prevent the party from winning the election, it meant that new policies were not fully discussed: policies that when implemented after the election would create voter dissatisfaction.

*Competition analysis*
The Conservatives fully exploited Labour's weaknesses, particularly extremism; defence; and handling of the economy. They also anticipated the possible charge from Labour of 'time-for-a-change'. The Tory Party also tried to differentiate its product. It put particular emphasis on its tax and defence policies because this is where it differed most from Labour.

*Support analysis*
The party carried out significant support analysis. Over a year before the election, the Chairman, Norman Tebbit, conducted a broad audit of the constituencies, taking into account previous election results, social change and strengths or weaknesses of the local party (organisation, candidate or members). From this he drew up a list of which were most crucial to the outcome and more campaign support was sent to those which the party needed to win in order to maintain its majority. The effort made to target voters whose support the party needed but did not already have was nevertheless limited however because as Tebbit (1989: 48) argued, the manifesto and general appeal of the party was 'to the nation as a whole'.

*Stage 4: Implementation*

The Conservative 'product' was effectively well implemented. The Party Leader enjoyed relatively unchallenged power within her party. The attitude of the leader herself, however, was not conducive to a market orientation. As already noted, Thatcher's response to negative results from market intelligence was to commission another study. In the short term, the Conservative Party maintained behaviour that was more in line with public opinion than the Opposition but in the long term Thatcher's leadership style gradually eroded a market orientation and caused problems not just for her but for the party.

## Stage 5: Communication

Communication efforts began twenty months before the election. The Chairman began an ongoing process of creating a document entitled 'The War Book' that laid out a detailed plan. The communications effort was highly disciplined.

## Stage 6: The election campaign

The campaign was short and well planned but lacked a clear chain of command. The leadership was provided with an advertising plan from Saatchi and Saatchi, Michael Dobbs composed a 100-page report on strategy and various meetings were held. Each campaign day was organised around a press conference. Meetings occurred throughout the day, ensuring that all feedback from polls, the media and the regions was discussed. Thatcher visited places that displayed economic progress, to indicate the success of Conservative policies. Saatchi and Saatchi created the slogan 'Britain's Great Again. Don't Let Labour Wreck It'. The party took out substantial press advertising in the last week of the campaign but overall advertising was criticised for being weak, especially in comparison with a much more professional effort from the Labour Party.

Norman Tebbit (1989) argues that the party tried to focus on its strengths and downplay its weaknesses. These were 'mirror images' of the Labour Party. It also dealt with the more problematic issues such as unemployment early on, highlighting the more positive issues such as defence and economy later on in the campaign. The Conservatives attempted to reduce Labour strengths, the more 'caring issues', claiming that Labour's proposals would cost £35 billion. They also criticised Labour's 'looney left' and the defence policy. One advertisement featured a soldier with his hands up, and the slogan 'Labour's Policy on Arms'.

Although the campaign went generally as planned, it suffered from not having a Director of Communications in sole control of all communication activities. The lack of harmonious relations between the Party Leader and other important players in the campaign: the official advertisers; CCO; and the Party Chairman; made this situation worse. One consequence of this may have been the peculiar episode that took place between 3 and 4 June: the so-called 'Wobbly Thursday'. During this time Thatcher tried to over-turn the entire campaign strategy. The issue was resolved but is indicative of the personal tensions, rivalries and poor communication between those involved in the campaign. Tebbit (1989: 48) noted that one lesson from the campaign might be: 'too many cooks can always spoil the broth – espe-cially if some of them are intent on trying their own recipes without telling the chef.'

Nonetheless, despite these problems, the party's actual product remained more in line with public opinion than the opposition. Butler and Kavanagh (1988: 254) cite someone 'close to Mrs Thatcher' who said he had thought the party had no strategy, but:

> In fact we probably did have one, but only realised it at the end. We stood for something which the voters wanted, whereas the opposition stood for something they did not want. That is why we won.

### Stage 7: Election – the party's success in attracting support

*The general election*
The Conservatives won the election on 11 June 1987 with 42.3 per cent of the total popular vote. Conservatives won 376 seats with a 102 majority. Support was regionally biased, however: the party attracted much more support in the South of England than Scotland and Wales. Additionally, as Tebbit (1989: 48) conceded, the cuts in public services alienated many within the middle class who worked in the public sector.

*Membership*
Membership declined from 1,200,000 in 1983 to 1,000,000 in 1987.

*Voter evaluations of party behaviour*
The Conservatives generally proposed popular policies. Table 2.24 shows that MORI polls also indicated that the Tories had more popular policies than Labour in the majority of areas.

Conservative policies also reflected voter priorities as measured by the BES but also a MORI panel survey. For example, MORI asked respondents which two or three issues would be most important to them in deciding which party to vote for: 27 per cent said defence and 18 per cent law and order. The Conservative Party had the most popular leader: see Table 2.25.

**Table 2.24** *Best party policy on key issues, 1987*

*Question asked: I am going to read out a list of problems facing Britain today. I would like you to tell me whether you think the Conservative Party, the Labour Party or the Liberal Democrats has the best policies on each problem.*

|  | Labour or Conservative better policy (% lead over the other) |
|---|---|
| Defence generally | Conservative (26) |
| Law and order | Conservative (18) |
| Disarmament | Conservative (15) |
| Taxation | Conservative (11) |
| Trade unions | Conservative (3) |
| The natural environment/conservation | equal |
| Education/schools | Labour (3) |
| Unemployment | Labour (5) |
| Housing | Labour (6) |
| National Health Service | Labour (13) |

*Source:* MORI polls.
*Notes:* n = c. 1,000 or 2,000, surveys based on GB residents aged 18 +. Poll taken 3–4 June, except for taxation which was taken 3–4 November 1986.

**Table 2.25** *Best Prime Minister, July 1987*

*Question asked: Who would make the best Prime Minister?*

|  | % |
|---|---|
| Thatcher | 42 |
| Kinnock | 31 |
| Owen | 17 |
| Steel | 10 |

*Source:* Gallup Political Index Report No. 323
(July 1987), quoted by Heath *et al.* (1994: 130).
*Note:* n = 4,886.

Furthermore, in terms of more detailed perception of leader characteristics, although Kinnock was seen as being more likeable and caring, Margaret Thatcher was seen as a stronger leader and better at getting things done (see Table 2.26).

This trend was also shown in the MORI panel survey which indicated that Thatcher was seen as more capable than Kinnock; 45 per cent to 27 per cent said Thatcher would make the most capable Prime Minister.

One of the biggest differences between the parties was voters' perceptions of party unity. 76 per cent of BES respondents thought the Conservatives were united, but the same figure thought Labour was divided (see Table 2.27).

**Table 2.26** *Voters' perceptions of the party leaders, 1987*

*Question asked: Would you describe Mrs Thatcher/Mr Kinnock as . . .*

|  | Thatcher (%) | Kinnock (%) |
|---|---|---|
| Good at getting things done | 90 | 45 |
| Bad at getting things done | 6 | 34 |
| | | |
| Capable of being a strong leader | 96 | 51 |
| Not capable of being a strong leader | 2 | 42 |
| | | |
| Looks after one class | 59 | 48 |
| Looks after all classes | 36 | 42 |
| | | |
| Extreme | 68 | 35 |
| Moderate | 24 | 56 |
| | | |
| Likeable as a person | 41 | 63 |
| Not likeable as a person | 50 | 30 |
| | | |
| Caring | 50 | 78 |
| Uncaring | 42 | 13 |

*Source:* BES (1987).
*Note:* n = 3,826.

**Table 2.27** *Party unity, 1987*

*Question asked: Would you describe the Conservative/Labour Party nowadays as united or divided?*

|  | United (%) | Divided (%) |
|---|---|---|
| Conservative | 76 | 24 |
| Labour | 24 | 76 |

*Source:* BES (1987).
*Note:* n = 3,826.

The Conservatives were not perceived to be successful in delivering a better life, in so much as voters' perceptions of life under the Government as measured by the BES indicated that since the last election, unemployment and crime had increased and the standard of health and education had fallen (see Table 2.28).

Nonetheless, voters' evaluation of the Government's response to these problems was not all negative: over 70 per cent thought they handled the issues of crime, defence, education and taxes well: see Table 2.29.

**Table 2.28** *Voters' perceptions of life under the Conservative Government,*
*1987*

*Question asked: Since the last general election in June 1983, would you say that [...]*
*has increased or fallen?*

|  | Increased (%) | Stayed the same (%) | Fallen (%) |
|---|---|---|---|
| Prices | 92 | 5 | 3 |
| Unemployment | 74 | 9 | 17 |
| Taxes | 36 | 20 | 44 |
| The standard of the health and social services | 10 | 24 | 66 |
| Crime | 91 | 5 | 4 |
| The quality of education | 8 | 22 | 70 |
| Britain's safety from the threat of war | 30 | 53 | 17 |

*Source:* BES (1987).
*Note:* n = c. 3,826. 'Increased' combines 'Increased a lot' and 'Increased a little';
'Fallen' combines 'Fallen a little' and 'Fallen a lot'.

**Table 2.29** *Voters' evaluation of the Conservative Government's handling of*
*issues, 1987*

*Question asked: Between 1983 and 1987, how well or how badly do you think the*
*Conservative Government handled the following issues?*

|  | Well (%) | Not well (%) |
|---|---|---|
| Crime | 75 | 25 |
| Defence | 74 | 26 |
| Education | 73 | 27 |
| Taxes | 69 | 31 |
| Prices | 66 | 34 |
| Health and social services | 29 | 71 |
| Unemployment | 29 | 71 |

*Source:* BES (1987).
*Notes:* n = 3,826. 'Well' combines those who said 'Very well' and 'Fairly well';
'Not well' combines those saying 'Not very well' and 'Not at all well'.

Thus it would seem that although there were still problems to be dealt
with, voters felt that the Tories were the best party to deal with them. The
Conservatives were also seen as more capable generally of strong government and getting things done. Table 2.30 below indicates that nearly all
voters perceived the Conservatives capable of strong government whereas
only 36 per cent of respondents to the BES thought this of Labour.

**Table 2.30** *Party's capability of strong government, 1987*

*Question asked: On the whole, would you describe the Conservative/ Labour Party as capable or not capable of strong government?*

|  | *Capable (%)* | *Not capable (%)* |
| --- | --- | --- |
| Conservative | 95 | 5 |
| Labour | 36 | 64 |

*Source:* BES (1987).
*Note:* n = 3,826.

This was also reflected in evaluations of the leaders as shown above in Table 2.26. From this, the Conservatives gained general governing capability and ability to deliver.

Between 1983 and 1987, the Conservative Party was broadly market-oriented, and certainly more so than Labour. It did not, however, use the full potential of marketing in this period. Organisationally, potential problems were created by its use of market intelligence, the power structures within the campaign organisation and the leader's attitude to the opinions of senior MPs. Although this did not prevent the party winning in the 1987 election, it did prevent the discussion of new policies created in response to voters' demand for something new. These were not necessarily what voters desired therefore and it was not clear that once they were implemented they would provide voter satisfaction. This laid the ground for problems after the election.

### 1987–90 and the fall of Margaret Thatcher

Superficially then, the 1987–92 period began positively for the Conservatives. Margaret Thatcher had achieved a third election victory and with it apparent domination of the Conservative Party. Thatcher's very success nonetheless laid the foundations for failure: her strength enabled her to exhibit an attitude more in line with a product orientation. This, combined with the implementation of untested new policies, created many problems for the leader and illustrates the difficulty of marketing in government.

*Previous marketing – Stage 8: Delivery*

Even only a few years into the term of office, there were a number of significant problems with delivery that reflected badly on Thatcher in particular.

*The poll tax*

The Conservatives encountered significant problems with their implementation of the community charge or poll tax. The existing tax system for local government had come under significant criticism as it was regarded as increasingly inequitable. The poll tax was levied on each individual rather than the property and it was argued that it would be fairer because it would make citizens more aware of the cost and standard of local services and thus increase the accountability of local government. The new system was introduced into Scotland in 1989 and then England and Wales in Spring 1990, under the 1988 Local Government Finance Act constituencies. The Bill was not passed easily and the public response was highly negative. An extra-parliamentary lobby group emerged and demonstrations took place across the country. The tax also suffered from high levels of non-payment.

Margaret Thatcher failed to respond to this discontent. She completely refused to do a U-turn on the tax. The 1992 BES showed that the vast majority of voters thought that tax was a bad idea: see Table 2.31.

**Table 2.31** *Voters' views about the poll tax, 1992*

*Question asked: Thinking about the poll tax, which of these statements comes closest to your view of the poll tax: it was ...*

|  | % |
| --- | --- |
| A good idea | 35 |
| A bad idea | 65 |

*Source:* BES (1992).
*Note:* n = 2,797.

*The economy*

This worsened during 1987–92. Inflation began to rise until it reached 11 per cent at the end of 1990. Interest rates and mortgages also rose; this affected the housing market badly. This in combination with the poll tax hit various sections of society badly, including core Conservative constituencies. Norton (1992: 46) explains how:

> New homeowners were threatened by repossession. Small businesses increasingly found it difficult to survive. The Party's natural constituency – those whom Margaret Thatcher liked to call 'our people' – were feeling the pinch.

The response of Thatcher's Government was ineffective, hindered by disputes between her and the Chancellor of the Exchequer.

*Europe*

Margaret Thatcher's stance on Europe became increasingly problematic and unpopular. She gave several highly negative speeches about the European Community, most particularly one in the House of Commons on 30 October 1990 in which she said:

> I do not want the Commission to increase its powers at the expense of the House. ... Mr Delors said ... that he wanted the European Parliament to be the democratic body of the Community, he wanted the Commission to be the Executive and he wanted the Council of Ministers to be the Senate. No. No. No.

Thatcher's approach to the issue appeared to be fostering a difficult relationship between Britain and Europe, a development criticised by Conservatives as much as the Opposition and the public. It also became one of the catalysts for the resignation of a senior party figure.

*Privatisation*

This was a problematic success. The Conservatives fulfilled their promise of further privatisation. Rover and British Steel were sold off in 1988. Water was privatised in 1989 and electricity in 1990. They attracted applications for shares, increasing government revenue, but engendered more criticism than previous privatisations, because they are natural utilities that people cannot do without. Attempts were also made to introduce an internal market into the National Health Service. NHS hospitals could become trusts and doctors could apply for the right to allocate their own budgets which was heavily criticised by Labour. Polls indicated that the public was at the very least unsure about this change.

In addition to problems in the delivery stage, the activities a Market-Oriented Party needs to engage in for the next election were not fulfilled successfully.

### Stage 1: Market intelligence

Market intelligence was significantly neglected under Thatcher's leadership. The party's Research Department was undermined as an independent source of ideas and Thatcher herself was cut off from feedback from senior colleagues because she demoted those who disagreed with her. Policy groups were only set up just before she left office.

### Stage 2: Product design

*Staff*

Thatcher experienced significant problems in her use of staff. Firstly, she made increasing use of outside, independent advisers that proved to be to the detriment of her relationship with her most senior ministers. For example, her continued reliance on an economic adviser, Sir Alan Walters, prompted the resignation of her Chancellor, Nigel Lawson. Secondly, as in 1983–87, Thatcher had difficulty in appointing a Chair of CCO. The position was offered to Lord Young, but he declined because he wished to remain Secretary of State at the Department of Trade and Industry. It was then given to Peter Brooke, a junior minister at the Treasury. Brooke was a good manager: he was successful in re-organising CCO into three sections (community, research and organisation), tightening budget control and assigning a new Director of Communications. Brooke, however, lacked political standing in the party and poor results in the June 1989 European elections prompted Thatcher to appoint a new Chair. Kenneth Baker took the position.

Baker was a senior minister and skilled in public relations. He proved to be a useful communicator between the party and the media and built up a good relationship with Thatcher and No. 10. Under his chairmanship, the Conservative Research Department lost further importance and influence, however. Emma Nicholson (1996: 101) argues that under Thatcher, and particularly after the 1987 election, the Research Department moved from being 'a forum for thinking from first principles into a compliant generator of propaganda – another mechanism of central control'. The head of the department, Robin Harris, left at the end of 1989 to move to the No. 10 Policy Unit. The party did, however, have a number of staff to draw on in terms of its communications but, as argued throughout this book, communications cannot make up for a poor product.

The party's finances were also a continual problem. Lord McAlpine, Treasurer, left in June 1990. Lord Beaverbrook and Sir Hector Lang took responsibility for trying to increase funds. The situation was made worse by the European elections, the modernisation of CCO and the installation of a new computer system. Donations from firms also declined during this period.

*MPs*
The Conservative Parliamentary Party suffered from high-profile ministerial resignations and criticisms of the leadership. Edwina Currie, Junior Minister for Agriculture, had to resign because of remarks she made about salmonella poisoning in eggs. Nicholas Ridley left the Cabinet in July 1990 over comments in an interview which were intensely anti-German. MPs became increasingly critical of the leadership while Thatcher was Prime Minister, especially over the unpopular poll tax.

*Policy*
While Margaret Thatcher was leader, little attention was paid to new policy design.

*Leadership*
The unprecedented third victory in the 1987 election gave Margaret Thatcher apparent invincibility. Her power within the party seemed firm and secure; she possessed clear dominance of her Cabinet. Nonetheless Thatcher's leadership of the Conservative Party encountered many difficulties after the 1987 election. In some ways these problems were laid before the 1987 term began: for example the vast majority of respondents in the 1987 BES viewed her as extreme (see Table 2.32).

**Table 2.32** *Voters' perceptions of the party leaders, 1987*

*Question asked: Would you describe Mrs Thatcher/Mr Kinnock as . . .*

|  | Thatcher (%) | Kinnock (%) |
| --- | --- | --- |
| Extreme | 68 | 35 |
| Moderate | 24 | 56 |

*Source:* BES (1987).
*Note:* n = 3,826.

In many ways what were once strengths in Thatcher's leadership style became weaknesses. Thatcher's determination to pursue a chosen path through to the end may have worked when that path was broadly market oriented, but it was not so effective with policies that proved unpopular. The most notable example was the poll tax, for she refused to alter the policy despite substantial protest from the public. Her attitude towards its unpopularity was dismissive, if not downright arrogant. She failed to respond to voter dissatisfaction, or even to try to *appear* to respond; furthermore she seemed to think she should not be expected to respond. It was as if she believed that voters had no right to criticise something she thought to be right: it was almost the complete opposite of a market orientation.

The other issue that caused problems was Europe. Thatcher's approach to the European Community became increasingly negative and isolationist and also differed significantly to that of her Chancellor and Foreign Secretary. Nigel Lawson and Sir Geoffrey Howe were in support of further moves towards a European Single Market and entry into the Exchange-Rate Mechanism (ERM). Lawson and Howe used threats of resignation to persuade her to lay down terms under which Britain would join the ERM at the European Summit in Madrid, June 1989.

Intra-party relations were extremely problematic. The longer Thatcher held office, the less attention she paid to party management and her relationship with the parliamentary party in particular seriously declined. A significant number of senior party figures such as Norman Tebbit resigned after 1987. In her memoirs, Thatcher (1993: 587) recalls the loss this meant: 'I did bitterly resent his decision. I had too few like-minded supporters in the Government, and of these none had Norman's strength and acumen.' Two other long-serving ministers, Norman Fowler and Peter Walker, resigned in early 1990. The most public and notable resignations were those of Nigel Lawson and Sir Geoffrey Howe. Lawson resigned in October 1989. He felt undermined by Thatcher's reliance on the adviser Sir Alan Walters.

This was followed by the resignation of Sir Geoffrey Howe in November 1990. He was then Leader of the House, having been removed from the Foreign Office by Thatcher in July 1989. Howe was a very senior party figure and had been a loyal supporter of Thatcher, but she had demoted him after he, together with Lawson, pressured her into agreement over Europe. Apart from this demotion, the major source of his discontent was Thatcher's negative attitude towards Europe, the catalyst for his resignation being her speech in the House of Commons on 30 October 1990. The next day the Prime Minister criticised his preparation of the parliamentary legislative programme at a Cabinet meeting; that evening, he informed her of his resignation. Thatcher attempted to make light of his resignation, claiming it was simply a matter of style. Howe, however, gave a damning resignation speech televised live in the House of Common on 13 November, in which he criticised Thatcher's approach to Europe:

> People throughout Europe see our Prime Minister finger-wagging, hear her passionate 'No. No. No.' much more than the content of carefully worded texts. The task has become futile ... of trying to pretend there was a common policy when every step forward risked being subverted by some casual comment or impulsive answer. ... That is why I have resigned.

The resignation had substantial political impact. These resignations also robbed Thatcher of skill and experience and increased her reputation as 'a prime minister who traded on the strength of conviction leadership yet who could not tolerate equally strong opinions in others' (Evans 1997: 110).

Thatcher's leadership style therefore became more a problem than a reason for success. In some respects this was due to the difficult path she had to tread to get to be Prime Minister in the first place. King (1981: 65) noted how Margaret Thatcher:

was a tough politician and proud of it. She wanted to reach the top in a man's world, and ... sought to do so by cultivating masculine virtues and what she saw as masculine ways of thought. She sometimes chided her male colleagues for their sentimentality and for their failure to think through problems in a sufficiently rigorous, tough-minded fashion.

In her first term of office, Thatcher had faced much opposition from her Cabinet. From then on, as she became more successful, she naturally promoted those who supported her and demoted dissenters. The negative consequence of this was that she lost a vital source of market intelligence and feedback: she was stronger superficially, but in the long term her position became weaker. Added to this was the general human tendency to obtain a feeling of invincibility and superiority once at the top of any profession. This was reinforced by winning three consecutive general elections and being the nation's first woman Prime Minister. These conditions worked against maintaining a market orientation.

### Thatcher's downfall

In many ways Thatcher's leadership style set the foundations for her downfall. Additionally, she made no attempt to respond to signs of discontent: rather, as Norton (1992: 41) observed, she 'made it clear that she did not intend to change'. The first formal challenge to her leadership occurred in December 1989, by Sir Anthony Meyer MP. Thatcher won the election easily but a significant proportion of the parliamentary Conservative Party withheld its support and a number of 'yes' voters made it clear that they remained critical of her leadership. She failed to respond to this and immediately following Howe's resignation Michael Heseltine launched a serious challenge to her leadership.

This challenge was launched after a period of growing disquiet in the parliamentary party. During this time voters appeared increasingly dissatisfied with the party as a whole. Conservative electoral prospects looked poor. The party was doing badly in opinion polls and it lost seats in by-elections, such as the safe seat of Eastbourne on 18 October. The poll tax was extremely unpopular and strongly linked to Thatcher: it seemed that the tax would only go if she did. MPs began to think that the answer to these problems might be a change in leader.

Thatcher's campaign for the election was badly organised and ineffective. She stuck to her normal daily routine, not bothering to try to rally support. Although she won a majority in the first ballot, she was 4 votes short of the 15 per cent lead required to win. Punnett (1992: 69) contends that the leadership contest:

was greatly influenced by the MPs' perceptions of the potential leaders' impact on the Party's electoral prospects. Although surveys of constituency opinion suggested that Mrs Thatcher retained the support of the majority of the Party members and activists, the MPs looked over the heads of the activists to consider the inclinations of Conservative voters and potential voters.

In this respect, then, it could be said that the MPs were acting in line with public opinion and moving the party closer to a market orientation.

Minutes after the result, Thatcher declared that she would fight on. However, she had not consulted her Cabinet, 'was attacked for acting arrogantly' and lost support in the days that followed. Upon returning to London, she met Cabinet members individually and realised that she might not survive a second ballot. Thatcher announced her intention to withdraw from the contest at a Cabinet meeting at 9 a.m. on 22 November 1990. Margaret Thatcher had led the Conservative Party to three election victories but, in the end, became an electoral liability. Although many factors contributed to her downfall at that particular time, the party stood a better chance of winning the next election if it elected a new leader. In this respect, the party as a whole succeeded in maintaining a market orientation even when the leader herself did not.

## Conclusions

The Conservative Party won three elections under the leadership of Margaret Thatcher, and did so using political marketing, by being a Market-Oriented Party. It adhered to the concept of identify voters' demands and then attempting to devise behaviour to suit them. It engaged in market intelligence, changed its policies and geared its leader's style towards the results, and achieved electoral dividends as a result. In government, despite some problems, it generally achieved satisfactory success in delivery. Over time, however, the market orientation of the party declined. It became harder for the party, and in particular its leader, to remain in touch with the public. Although in 1983 and 1987 it was aided by a product- or sales-oriented opposition, voter dissatisfaction with Thatcher's own product orientation became increasingly apparent in the 1987–92 period.

In many ways, the way in which Margaret Thatcher changed the behaviour of the Tory Party to respond to public opinion and achieve electoral success makes her the political marketing pioneer of Britain. At the start of her leadership, she utilised the basic concept of marketing, conducting market intelligence and responding to it. Towards the end, however, she neglected the more subtle organisational aspects of political marketing and took on a product orientation with regard to the party and indeed the country. Even in 1979 she indicated a stubborn frame of mind. During the campaign she declared:

I am what I am. Yes, I do believe certain things very strongly. Yes, I do believe in trying to persuade people that the things I believe in are the things they should follow ... I am far too old to change now.

Although such comments were to an extent rhetorical, because Thatcher's beliefs and policies were in line with public opinion, a product-oriented attitude will not secure success in the long term. As a successful party leader it can become extremely difficult to remain in touch with voters: this is why it is important that market intelligence is conducted continually and organisational and party aspects of the model are not neglected. A leader cannot maintain a market orientation by themselves.

The 1979–90 period is an example of how successful political marketing can be, but also an example of the problems that can emerge if a party or leader begins to neglect it. Product-oriented political marketing is not accepted in today's market. The next chapter will also show this by examining more obvious cases of Product-Oriented Parties.

### Note

1 All empirical analysis in Chapters 2–5 draws on a wide range of sources. Unless otherwise stated directly within the text because of particular originality or primary nature, this chapter as a whole draws on the secondary empirical descriptive accounts of the time period listed below. Details of other works consulted and directly cited are in the full bibliography at the end of the book.

*For the 1979 election*

Behrens (1980), Bell (1982), Blake (1985), Butler and Kavanagh (1980), Clemens (1983), Delaney (1982), King (1981), Leonard (1981), Livingston (1981), Rathbone (1982), Rosenbaum (1997), Scammell (1995), Whyte (1988).

*1979–83*

Butler and Kavanagh (1984), Blake (1985), Evans (1997), Pearce and Stewart (1992), Kavanagh (1987), Burch (1986), Rosenbaum (1997), Scammell (1995), Parkinson (1986), Tebbit (1989), Peele (1990), Sharkey (1989), Scammell (1994).

*1983–87–90*

Butler and Kavanagh (1988), Evans (1997), Scammell (1995), Evans (1997), Rosenbaum (1997), Sharkey (1989), Tebbit (1989), Peele (1990), Sharkey (1989), Scammell (1994), Scammell (1996), The Conservative Party (1987), Kleinman (1987), Heath *et al.* (1994), Norton (1992), Pearce and Stewart (1992), Nicholson (1996), Punnett (1992), Thatcher (1993), King (1981).

# 3

# The death of political conviction: how voters rejected Product-Oriented Parties

Organisations can grow set in their ways and unresponsive to new opportunities or problems ... Political parties become unresponsive after they enjoy power for a while and every so often experience a major upset. (Kotler and Levy (1969: 14–15))

The problem of the Labour Party in the Seventies and Eighties is not complex – it's simple. Society changed and the Party didn't. So you've got a whole new generation of people with different aspirations and ambitions, a different type of world, and we were still singing the same old songs that people had sung in the 40s and 50s. (Tony Blair (BBC 1995))

The Conservatives face the threat of becoming the victims of their own success. The longer the Party remains in office, the greater the risk that its leaders become so enamoured of the authority of office that they forget it depends upon a frequent renewal of their mandate through success in competing with opponents increasingly keen to win office. (Rose and McAllister (1990: 179))

The Labour Party under Mr. Foot ... adopted a typical product oriented approach to the market. Indeed, some members of the Party persist in their error, when they claim that they lost the election because their policies were badly presented and misunderstood – a reaction which caused Mr Healey to quote Oscar Wilde – 'The play had been a great success; it was the audience which was at fault.' (Whyte (1988: 48–9))

Whether in government or opposition, for a variety of reasons, a party may choose not to be market-oriented and be more product-oriented in the approach it takes to its behaviour. This chapter explores three examples of POPs (Product-Oriented Parties): Labour in 1979, the Conservatives in 1997 and Labour in 1983. In each case, these parties neglected to apply marketing to many aspects of their behaviour, taking a more traditional approach, seeming not to appreciate the need to respond to voters' demands. The first two had the added problem of difficulties in delivery. Labour in 1983 was not impeded by the constraints of being in office but actually took the strongest product-oriented attitude. Indeed, it is the classic example of a Product-Oriented Party. The left wing became dominant both organisationally and ideologically and was not concerned with designing its product to respond to voters. They simply wanted to make their argument. The party's manifesto was far removed from the concerns of the majority of ordinary voters. These POPs did not win the election, however. Voters will not support parties that simply appeal for support on the basis that they are right or are arguing for a normatively valuable ideology. The politics of conviction no longer seems a viable approach for a major political party in Britain.[1]

## Labour in 1979

The Labour Party's attempts to win the 1979 election were largely devoid of an awareness to respond to voters' demands. The party did not use market intelligence to inform its behaviour. Its structure, culture and ideology worked against a market orientation. Its communication and campaign effort was hindered by organisational disunity.

### Stage 1: Market intelligence

The party did not go through this stage of the marketing process effectively. There was significant opposition within the Labour Party marketing intelligence. Polling was cut back after the 1974 election. There was only a focused survey on Scottish and women voters and marginal seats in England. Furthermore, results did not influence the product design. Results were not disseminated: for example, the party's advertising group was forbidden access to the results! The Party Leader, James Callaghan, made no attempts to seek market intelligence or ideas from his Cabinet: he formed the party's strategy himself.

### Stage 2: Product design

Indeed, Labour in 1983 began with product design, as the marketing process for a Product-Oriented Party would suggest.

#### Leadership
Jim Callaghan attracted higher levels of popularity than the Opposition leader, Margaret Thatcher, but appeared to be product-oriented, acting as if he knew best, in a number of respects. One example is that he appeared to be out of touch during and after the 1978–79 'Winter of Discontent'. On his return from a foreign trip in January 1979, his response to the

strikes was inappropriate: unappreciative of voters' concerns about the issue. Another is that he neglected to consult senior colleagues, even over issues such as the crisis with the trade unions and when to call the election.

*MPs*
The Parliamentary Labour Party suffered from substantial ideological divisions over policy. The Cabinet was dominated by the right wing of the Labour Party, but the Conference and the National Executive Committee (NEC) remained left-wing. Organisational and constitutional power lay with the latter. Decision-making therefore produced unstable compromises or open conflict, especially when it came to policy.

*Staff*
Callaghan appointed a number of staff to help with communication, but he kept overall control. Although many of them had some kind of professional expertise, those such as Tim Delaney who led an 'Advertising Team' were not well integrated into the party organisation.

*Policy proposals*
The manifesto was entitled *The Labour Way is the Better Way* and launched on 6 April 1979 (see The Labour Party (1979)). It included several proposals for expanding the role of the state in the economy and the redistribution of wealth. The key proposals were:

- to cut the inflation rate to 5 per cent by 1982, by strengthening the Price Commission's power to reduce prices, reform the Common Market's Agricultural Policy and 'work with' the Trade Union Congress using collective bargaining;
- reduce unemployment by expanding training, increasing the powers of the National Enterprise Board, creation of jobs through public ownership and government investment;
- increase pensions and child benefit;
- impose a wealth tax for those who have more than £150,000 in personal wealth;
- invest in new housing and oppose council house sales in areas of serious housing need.

These policies did not reflect voters' opinions. All surveys of public opinion picked up negative reactions to Labour proposals (see Tables 3.1 and 3.2 and Crewe (1981: 293–4) for details of a post-election survey). Additionally, although most Tory voters completely opposed Labour's proposals, a significant majority of Labour voters supported those of the Conservatives.

*Stage 3: Product adjustment*

The Labour Party did not use this stage well, which is further indication of its remoteness from the Market-Oriented Party model.

*Achievability*
The party did not seriously try to ensure that its product was achievable.

*Internal reaction analysis*
Callaghan failed to seek Cabinet advice on strategy and he dominated the final drafting of the manifesto. The manifesto-drafting process was long and problematic because of divisions in the party, but the result was an incoherent manifesto which still could not satisfy internal party views.

*Competition analysis*
Labour did not engage in anything like competition analysis. For example, one of the party's traditional strengths was relations with the trade unions. The Winter of Discontent eroded this because the Government was not perceived to respond effectively to the strikes. Although it criticised the Opposition in the campaign it did not try to adjust its own behaviour accordingly.

*Support analysis*
The Labour Party's target marketing was inherently flawed. The party focused on those traditional Labour voters, whose support could most likely be guaranteed anyway, rather than those it needed to win power but did not have.

*Stage 4: Implementation*

Labour's organisational structure made implementation difficult. The manifesto-drafting process was long-winded and problematic, involving the annual conference, several policy groups and ministerial–NEC working groups. Two separate groups, Callaghan's staff and the NEC, each drew up a draft manifesto. The final document was only produced through time pressure, Callaghan's force of argument that Clause 5 of the constitution entitled him to have the final say, and his threat of resignation if certain proposals, such as abolishing the House of Lords, went through. The party had clearly not taken on a market orientation: there was huge inconsistency between different parts of the party, with some clearly out of line with market views.

## Stage 5: Communication

Planning for the party's publicity was also embroiled in power-battles and confusion. Callaghan kept control and organisation of communications. Although from February 1978 he held meetings at No. 10 for some staff and MPs, they were kept secret. Another illustration of Labour's resistance to respond to voters' views is its attitude towards advertising. Tim Delaney (1982: 29) recalls how the party's negative attitude towards advertising also made communication difficult:

> Although the people with whom we dealt in Number 10 were sympathetic to a professional attitude, the same cannot unfortunately be said of Transport House. Even though Transport House likes to have advertising people around and uses them freely, there is and always has been a deep suspicion of professional advertising people there.

This indicates how the party was not only not market-oriented, but it did not fit the model of a Sales-Oriented Party either. Attention was focused instead on the campaign, with Edward Booth-Clibbon, Organiser of Publicity, arguing for a longer campaign than normal to allow enough time to 'win the argument' and persuade people of Labour's view. This is a product-oriented attitude to winning the election.

## Stage 6: The election campaign

The campaign was nonetheless badly run, with power and authority (both formal and unofficial) located in different power centres: No. 10, Transport House and the advertising team. Power struggles and confusion occurred throughout the poorly organised campaign. Callaghan retained overall control over the campaign and dominated all discussions about it. It also focused on him, yet he was reluctant to engage in professional communication and campaigning techniques. Transport House, the party's headquarters was a major source of problems. It had its own publicity group and co-operation between this and Booth-Clibbon's Group (encompassing Delaney's advertising team) was not good. Transport House launched a poster campaign in January 1979, at the same time as the lorry drivers' strike, with slogans which included 'Keep Britain Labour and it will keep on getting better'. It was rejected as the group to produce the party's election broadcasts but this left the other group little time to prepare because it was only told a few days after the election had been called. Bob Worcester (quoted in Gould (1998b: 45–6)) noted how:

> In the 1979 election, you had the White Room group who were doing some advertising PR, research people, and you had the Transport House group, of which I was a part, and literally on the day before the election, this group working with the Campaign Strategy Committee, dealing with them every

day, you had those guys being faced with an alternative final-day advertising strategy and a set of ads. And in a room over at the St Ermin's Hotel I witnessed an industrial relations guy called Michael Callaghan being shown two alternative advertising executions and someone saying 'Michael, which one do you think your dad would prefer?' That was forty-eight hours before the General Election.

Internal disputes prevented a clear message being presented to the electorate. Additionally, the number of full-time agents acting for the Labour Party had fallen to its lowest level since 1918: in 1951 there had been 296, but by 1979 this had been reduced to 70 and even these were not focused in marginal areas. Furthermore, in terms of issues, Clemens (1983: 21) noted how early press releases focused on the Party's proposals such as an increase in pensions, income tax cuts for the low-paid, which 'although attractive to individual sub-groups in the electorate, were not issues of concern to the electorate at large'. The campaign seemed to ignore the issues that were important to voters.

Overall, Labour's internal structure, policies and attitude to politics were devoid of a market orientation: the focus was more within the party than towards the voters.

### Stage 7: Election – the party's success in attracting support

All indications – votes, membership and public opinion assessments – suggest that voters did not evaluate the party's behaviour very positively.

*The general election*
Labour lost the election: it went down to 37.8 per cent of the vote and only 269 seats. The swing was 5.2 per cent away from Labour: the biggest since the war.

*Membership*
Labour's overall membership suffered from a sharp decline: from 659,737 in 1974 to 284,000 in 1979.

*Voter evaluations of party behaviour*
Labour's policies were clearly not popular: Conservative policies were preferred by the majority of voters, as measured by both opinion polls and the BES survey: see Table 3.1 (and Tables 2.3 and 2.4 in Chapter 2 for further detail).

More significantly, even Labour voters supported Conservative proposals (see Table 2.5 in Chapter 2). And Labour was unpopular on those issues which voters held as most important. Their stand on nationalisation and trade unions went against the grain of voter opinion. For example,

Table 3.2 shows that Labour was perceived by 66 per cent of respondents to the BES as being too willing to listen to the trade unions.

**Table 3.1** *Best party policy on key issues, 1979*

*Question asked: I am going to read out a list of problems facing Britain today. I would like you to tell me whether you think the Conservative Party, the Labour Party or the Liberal Democrats has the best policies on each problem.*

|  | Labour or Conservative better policy (% lead over the other) |
| --- | --- |
| Law and order | Conservative (39) |
| Taxation | Conservative (26) |
| Schools and education | Conservative (16) |
| Common Market | Conservative (10) |
| Housing | Conservative (9) |
| Unemployment | Conservative (6) |
| Industrial relations/strikes | Labour (2) |
| National Health Service | Labour (1) |

*Source:* MORI polls.

*Notes:* n = c. 1,000 or 2,000, surveys based on GB residents aged 18 +. Poll taken 4–6 May, except for education, health, housing, strikes which were taken April 1978.

**Table 3.2** *Voters' perceptions of party attitude towards trade unions, 1979*

*Question asked: Do you think that the Labour Party is too willing to listen to the trade unions or not willing enough? Or that things are about right?*

|  | Too willing to listen (%) | About right (%) | Not willing enough (%) |
| --- | --- | --- | --- |
| Labour | 66 | 28 | 6 |

*Source:* BES (1979).
*Note:* n = 1,893.

Labour encountered various problems in government and this was reflected by voters' low perceptions of living standards: see Tables 3.3–3.5.

Labour's policy proposals for 1979 and beyond were considered to be far less credible than the Conservative policies: see Table 3.6.

**Table 3.3** *Voters' perception of living standards: I, 1979*

*Question asked: All in all, would you say that the country is in very good shape, fairly good shape, poor shape, or that something is very wrong?*

|  | % |
|---|---|
| Good shape | 32 |
| Poor shape | 68 |

*Source:* BES (1979).
*Notes:* n = 1,893. 'Too far' combines all respondents who said 'Much too far', and 'A little too far'. 'Good shape' combines respondents who said 'In very good shape' and 'Fairly good shape'; 'Poor shape' combines those who said 'In poor shape' and 'Something very wrong'.

**Table 3.4** *Voters' perception of living standards: II, 1979*

*Question asked: Looking back over the last year or so, do you think your income has fallen behind prices, kept up with prices, or has gone up by more than prices?*

|  | % |
|---|---|
| Income fallen behind | 62 |
| Kept up with prices | 32 |
| Income up by more | 6 |

*Source:* BES (1979).
*Note:* n = 1,893.

**Table 3.5** *Voters' perception of living standards: III, 1979*

*Question asked: Looking back over the last year or so, would you say that the state of Britain's economy has stayed about the same, got better, or got worse?*

|  | % |
|---|---|
| Got better | 22 |
| Stayed about the same | 30 |
| Got worse | 48 |

*Source:* BES (1979).
*Note:* n = 1,893.

**Table 3.6** *Credibility of Conservative and Labour proposals, 1979*

| | % saying the party would succeed in achieving these objectives minus % saying it would not |
|---|---|
| *Conservative* | |
| Give council house tenants the right to buy their homes | + 61 |
| Reduce income tax, especially for the higher paid | + 49 |
| Reduce supplementary benefit for strikers | + 42 |
| Reduce violent crime and vandalism | − 20 |
| *Labour* | |
| Reduce income tax, especially for the lower paid | + 30 |
| Bring inflation down to 5% a year within 3 years | − 41 |
| Prevent increases in Common Market farm prices | − 29 |
| Achieve a long-term understanding with trade unions on wages | − 3 |

*Source:* RSL survey, 17–18 April 1979, quoted in Crewe (1981: 286).
*Note:* n = 1,199.

Labour clearly neglected many aspects of political marketing. It failed to utilise marketing intelligence, suffered from a lack of governing competence, perceptions of low living standards and an unpopular product. It is one example of why, although Product-Oriented Parties can still be found in Britain, they are not the ones winning the election.

### The Conservatives in 1997

The tale of the Tories in 1997 is a cogent reminder that in the current electoral market parties cannot rest on past achievements but must continue to be responsive to changes in society if they wish to remain in power. The election saw the Conservative Party left with only 165 MPs and no seats at all in Scotland and Wales. But the party had become increasingly product-oriented between 1992 and 1997: its behaviour indicated an increasing ignorance of the need to attend to the demands of the electoral market. There were a number of crises, high levels of public disunity and voters appeared increasingly dissatisfied. In many ways the Conservative Party's behaviour was similar to Labour in 1979, but its problems were compounded by having held office for eighteen years. On one hand, voters perceived them as to blame for any problems, on the other the years in power encouraged the party's politicians to feel above criticism and more complacent.

*Previous marketing – Stage 8: Delivery*

There were a number of problems or failures in the post-election delivery stage.

*Taxes*

In the 1992 election the Conservatives claimed that the Labour Party would increase direct taxes, whereas they were a party which would reduce the tax burden on voters. They then significantly increased indirect taxes, for example raising taxes on alcohol and tobacco at a rate above inflation, reducing tax allowances for married couples and extending VAT to domestic fuel and power. The Government reduced the basic rate of income tax in 1995 and 1996 (one penny less in each) but this did not serve as fulfilment of campaign promises as far as the electorate was concerned. Indirect taxes always hit the lower-paid more so the average voter was being hit harder by these increases despite the reduction in income tax. The Conservatives therefore lost their position as the best party on tax.

*Privatisation*

Public opinion turned increasingly negative towards privatisation between 1992 and 1997. Although the party had technically delivered its promised product, voters did not like its end consequences. The product did not deliver the expected result. Water companies such as Yorkshire failed to deliver the water when the weather turned hot, despite an increase in charges to customers, large salaries for the management and healthy profits for shareholders. Although technically these were not the fault of the Conservative Party because the utilities were now in the hands of private companies, the party was blamed because it put them there. Furthermore, the Conservative Party did not respond effectively to the problem. Although Major set up a Cabinet committee to examine the situation, it failed to reach any conclusion and the Government refused to change its policy of opposition to regulation. Public dissatisfaction was not diminished. The Conservative response was product-oriented: it refused to change its policy of privatisation and even engaged in further privatisation, such as the selling of British Rail, despite evident opposition in public opinion polls.

*Health and BSE*

The BSE crisis began in March 1996. Despite having made protestations to the contrary in the mid–1980s, the Government admitted that there might be a link between the BSE or so-called 'Mad-Cow' disease and the human disease Creutzfeld-Jakob. Following this an EC ban was imposed on the export of British beef and domestic sales of the meat suffered a huge drop.

*Management of the economy and the ER*
Britain joined the Exchange-Rate Mechanism (ERM) under Thatcher's leadership in October 1990, when John Major was Chancellor. This restricted Britain's ability to change interest-rates and a crisis emerged during the deep recession in summer 1992. Furthermore, the Government's response was easily criticised. At first, it declared that nothing would change, then on 16 September (now called 'Black Wednesday') when the rate of sterling suddenly fell despite intervention by the Bank of England, sterling was taken out of the ERM. This was a complete reversal of the Government's stated economic policy. The episode damaged the party's traditional reputation for economic competence.

*Other problems*
The crisis also encouraged factionalism in the party, increasing Tory doubts about the future of European Integration and related matters such as the Maastricht Treaty. The press became more critical of the Government. There were also other 'problem-areas', such as the Child Support Agency that was badly managed and created significant voter dissatisfaction.

*Successes*

The Conservative Government did, however, implement several popular policies:

- immigration was restricted;
- penal policy was tightened;
- police powers were increased;
- Major's handling of Northern Ireland was praised for giving peace a chance;
- unemployment and inflation were relatively low;
- overall the economy was sound.

*Lack of electoral dividends*
Despite some success, especially on economic indicators, as Denver (1998: 41) noted, 'even when their policies appeared to work – as in the case of the economy – they cut no ice among a sceptical and disillusioned electorate'. Although the economy was doing well according to aggregate measures, at the individual level not all voters were feeling the benefits of this. The BBC-commissioned NOP 1997 exit poll found that a majority of voters did not feel they were better off after the 1992–97 Conservative Government. People were hit by indirect taxes and also felt that the standards of services they now needed to use, such as health and education,

were declining sharply (see Table 3.14). The benefit from any improvement in the economy as a whole was offset by the poor service offered by these public institutions. What's more, this decline was believed to be the result of Tory actions (see Table 3.15). Crewe *et al.* (1998: xxii) pointed to this in their post-election analysis:

> Because the economy had ceased to be a problem, voters' concerns turned to other problems, notably spending on health, education and pensions, on which voters were massively dissatisfied with the Government.

Another explanation is that the party suffered from a credibility problem, arguably due to its failure to deliver on other areas of its promised product design. The ERM crisis made it appear incompetent so that voters did not believe the things they did like them saying. An April 1992 Gallup Poll indicated that only 16 per cent thought the Conservatives had told the truth about tax during the election, and 76 per cent thought they had been misled by the party. Table 3.16 indicates that a majority of voters perceived the Conservatives to have failed to deliver on their promises. The Conservative Party therefore had to make some serious changes if it were to ensure that its product became more market-oriented.

### Stage 1: Market intelligence

The Conservatives did not follow the model of a Market-Oriented Party, however. They neglected the first stage in the process: market intelligence. They failed to conduct effective post-electoral analysis. They did not really understand why they won in 1992. The party's success against the odds also made the Conservatives feel almost unbeatable and contributed to a sense of complacency. It may partly explain why the party paid less attention to market intelligence. The Research Department concentrated more on communications than policy development. It was only when Dr Brian Mawhinney became Party Chairman in the summer of 1996 that research began but, even then, survey and focus group work by ICM (run by Nick Sparrow) was closely guarded even from John Major. The Conservatives were more like a Product-Oriented Party.

### Stage 2: Product design

Similarly, there is no sense of the Conservative product being designed with voter demands in mind. It was derived, not designed, from existing behaviour, without thought, and had several unpopular aspects.

#### Leadership
John Major lost popularity, especially against the Labour leader, Tony Blair

(see Table 3.11). Although he began the 1992–97 period with a strong standing in his party, problems arose as the party's public standing declined. The Prime Minister's actions were constrained by a narrow parliamentary majority. The constant divisions made him appear weak. MPs failed to follow the party line over European issues, undermining Blair's leadership.

### MPs

The Parliamentary Party was increasingly damaged by scandal. Firstly, members of the Government were involved in sex scandals. This came after John Major had advocated a 'Back to Basics' move which had been interpreted as a reassertion of traditional moral values. The party therefore seemed hypocritical. Secondly, several MPs were involved in financial scandals. In every case the MPs were seen to be using the power of their elected office to make extra money. This made the Conservatives seem a selfish and corrupt party, full of politicians intent on getting what they wanted for themselves rather than the people. The leadership attempted to protect the MPs involved in such scandals, but this increased the image that the party was intent to go against the grain of public opinion. Major initiated a new Standing Committee on Standards in Public Life, under the direction of Lord Nolan, the report from which recommended various changes, yet many Conservative MPs resisted some of its proposals. A Labour amendment to carry its proposals even further and make the disclosure of MPs' outside earnings mandatory was then opposed by John Major, but supported by the House. The appearance of Tories being sleazy remained.

### Membership

The Conservative membership halved. It also aged, as the party failed to attract younger members. The 1992 study of the Conservative membership by Whiteley *et al* (1994) suggested that members were also less active. It suffered from poor morale. The leadership did nothing to resolve this.

### Staff

The Conservative Party's use of staff between 1992 and 1997 was problematic. The Tories were hindered by financial difficulties. Dr Brian Mawhinney, the Party Chairman, had much work to do to ensure that the organisation was ready for another election. Turnover of staff in key positions was relatively high: for example there were five different Directors of Communications. The Research Department also suffered from staff leaving: Andrew Lansley left to stand as an MP and although Danny Finkelstein became Head of Research he focused more on communications than policy development.

*Policy proposals*

Conservative policy in government was weak in areas of most importance. During the 1992–97 period health and education moved up the agenda to become the nation's most serious problems: see Table 3.7. But voters did not believe the Conservatives would deliver what they wanted in these areas.

**Table 3.7** *Voters' perception of the nation's most urgent problems, May 1992–April 1997 (%)*

| Year | Health | Education | Law and order | Unemployment | Cost of living |
|------|--------|-----------|---------------|--------------|----------------|
| 1992 | 18 | 11 | 5 | 66 | 25 |
| 1993 | 22 | 8 | 13 | 72 | 19 |
| 1994 | 26 | 11 | 18 | 65 | 16 |
| 1995 | 33 | 15 | 15 | 55 | 14 |
| 1996 | 32 | 22 | 16 | 48 | 10 |
| 1997 | 41 | 29 | 14 | 36 | 4 |

*Source:* King (1998b: 194) from *Gallup Political and Economic Index.*
*Note:* Figures show the annual percentage average of respondents identifying what they believe to be the two most urgent problems facing the country. n = not known.

Tax was also a problem for the Tories. Voters' willingness to pay higher rates of tax is always difficult to assess, but King (1998b: 196–7) argued that between 1979 and 1997 their willingness increased: 'by 1997 service-extenders had come to outnumber tax-cutters by more than 10 to 1': see Table 3.8. The 'market' changed its demands on this area, yet the Conservatives continued to offer the same product. A Market-Oriented Party would have adapted to this, but the Tories' product-oriented attitude did not allow them to respond. They simply argued the case for existing policy.

**Table 3.8** *Public views on tax and public spending, 1979–97 (%)*

| | 1979 | 1983 | 1987 | 1992 | 1997 |
|---|------|------|------|------|------|
| Taxes should be cut, even if it means some reduction in government services | 34 | 22 | 12 | 10 | 7 |
| Things should be left as they are | 25 | 22 | 21 | 20 | 18 |
| Government services should be extended, even if it means some increases in taxes | 34 | 49 | 61 | 66 | 72 |
| Don't know | 7 | 6 | 5 | 4 | 3 |

*Source:* King (1998b: 200) from *Gallup Political and Economic Index,* Report No. 441, May 1997: 30.
*Note:* n = not known.

Despite all the problems over Europe, the party's official policy of 'Wait and see' on the proposed exchange-rate mechanism was actually market-oriented. The BBC/NOP exit poll on 1 May 1997 lends further weight to this presumption about the voters: see Table 3.9.

**Table 3.9** *Voters' desired Government policy on EMU (%), 1997*

*Question asked: There are proposals for the pound to be replaced by a new single European Currency throughout Europe – the Euro. What do you think the Government's policy should be?*

|  | % |
| --- | --- |
| To say now that Britain will never join the single currency | 36 |
| To say now that Britain will join the single currency | 17 |
| To wait and see what happens | 47 |

*Source:* Kellner (1997: 620) – BBC/NOP exit poll, 1 May 1997.
*Note:* n = not known.

The problem instead was that voters were not convinced that the party really did offer what it promised. The behaviour of the party did not follow the official party line: whereas Major would say 'Wait and see' other senior party figures would declare something different. Voters could not trust the party to deliver what the leader promised.

As for future promises, unsurprisingly for a Product-Oriented Party, the final Tory manifesto, entitled *You can only be sure with Conservatives*, seemed devoid of any awareness of voters' opinions on their record in government. It was very detailed and heavily loaded with tables, graphs and statistics, as if to show how well the party had done in government. It was sales-, if not product-oriented. It simply stated that the party's product was the best, not why voters should want it and without reference to what voters wanted. For example, the foreword by John Major reads as a list of credits he claims the party had achieved, rather than showing that the party understood and would give the voters what they wanted. See below (quoted from The Conservative Party (1997a)):

> The Conservative administrations elected since 1979 are among the most successful in British peacetime history. A country once the sick man of Europe has become its most successful economy. A country once brought to its knees by over-mighty trade unions now has industrial peace. Abroad, the cold war has been won; at home, the rule of law has been restored. The enterprising virtues of the British people have been liberated from the dead hand of the state. There can be no doubt that we have created a better Britain.

The problem was that voters did doubt it, or at least they wanted more: they believed the Labour campaign theme, 'Britain deserves Better'.

*Stage 3: Product adjustment*

The party did not produce a clear strategy. It is almost as if it forgot it had a forthcoming election to contest.

*Achievability*
The party neglected the need to make its promises seem achievable. Its manifesto contained a large number of pledges: twenty-five in total, outlined in detail.

*Internal reaction analysis*
The lack of party unity indicates how the leadership failed to gain support for the product design. During 1992–97 a number of MPs even defected from the party. The leadership made some attempts to 'listen' to the rest of the party, announcing in January 1996 that it would give out a consultation paper on European Integration. In 1996 the party also ran a consultation exercise with the membership over Europe, called 'Our Nation's Future: Listening to the Conservative Party'. It then covered up the findings.

*Competition analysis*
Due to problems in delivery, previous Conservative strengths became weaknesses. For example, the party became weak on tax. It also failed to deal effectively with the competition. It did not know how to deal with Tony Blair and 'New Labour'. Willetts (1998: 115) contends that the criticism that Labour was simply copying the Conservatives was ineffective:

> If there were a competition to judge the least scary thing which any political party can say about its opponents it would be that they have stolen our clothes. It does not send a shiver down the spine of the electorate – indeed, it reinforced exactly the message which Tony Blair was trying to transmit: that now it was safe to vote Labour.

*Support analysis*
The party did not show any awareness of the state of its support within the electoral market.

*Stage 4: Implementation*

The Conservative Party has traditionally possessed an internal culture of electoral pragmatism that has proved amenable to the marketing concept, but this failed to prevail. The lack of unity over issues connected with Europe prevented at least one aspect of the product design being implemented. That these divisions occurred repeatedly and publicly also meant that voters' perception of the rest of the product, such as the leadership, was poor. Dissent was also well organised with a number of different Euro-sceptic and pro-Europe groups. Divisions also permeated the Cabinet. They also continued right up to the election. Appeals from the leadership for discipline were ineffective. Furthermore, voters noted these divisions: the BBC's exit poll on May 1 1997 also indicated that over 80 per cent of voters saw the Tories as divided (see Table 3.12).

## Stage 5: Communication

The party had difficulty communicating its product: it had not really designed one. Tim Bell was brought in to help, but a number of plans for strategy were made. There was a No. 12 Committee, run by the Chief Whip, to communicate Government action. In February 1995 this became the 'EDCP' and focused on the media. Michael Heseltine took over a chair in July 1995, and regular meetings took place with the Chief Whip and Party Chairman involved. The group was largely ineffectual because of party disunity. Plans to begin advertising in 1996 were hindered by events such as the BSE story. In the end, more harm than good had been done in the communications stage and the only opportunity left to do anything about it was the campaign.

## Stage 6: The election campaign

Political marketing is not just about election campaigns. Furthermore, political campaigning and salesmanship cannot make up for a poor product. The campaign was officially launched on 17 March, six weeks before the election. The behaviour of the Conservative Party in regard to setting a long campaign was arguably similar to the Labour Party in 1979: it hoped that the longer-than-average time-scale might provide the chance to catch up with the opposition. This type of behaviour is suitable for a Sales- or Product-Oriented Party but it could not win the election.

Furthermore the campaign was not run that effectively. It was led by Major, but various people, all with different opinions, were involved. At a lower level, the party organisation was in a poor state following decline in membership and poor morale due to a series of local election and by-election defeats. The party failed to adopt a clear strategy, fluctuating between pushing its own record in government (which was unpopular) and negative campaigning towards Labour (which voters liked). There was also a debate about how to deal with Labour: the Conservatives were torn between attacking it because of its past or its present character.

When they did discuss their own policy, this only served to reinforce divisions, because senior party figures focused on different areas at the same time. The official 'Wait and see' line on a single currency was defied by many Conservative candidates on their own addresses to constituents, and the *Daily Mail* newspaper published a national list of these Euro-sceptics on 14 April. Major's response was to drop a planned party election broadcast and make a direct appeal to the voters to trust him and ask his fellow MPs not to tie his hands over Europe. This made him look weak and highlighted how deeply divided the party was but it did not stop the debate. The next day an advertisement was launched featuring Blair sat as a puppet on the German Chancellor's lap. This was then criticised by senior Conservatives such as Kenneth Clarke. It was also out of line with public opinion because Europe was not a particularly important issue to voters.

The Conservatives failed to push their strengths and instead the campaign seemed to serve only to highlight their weaknesses. It was dogged by further sleaze stories surrounding Conservative MPs that resulted in the retirement of two back benchers and put pressure on standing MPs Neil Hamilton and Piers Merchant. The party tried to raise the tax issue, with Major claiming that the average family was better off now than in 1992, but tax was an area where they were now weak. Conservative claims were also discredited by a report from the Institute for Fiscal Studies that argued that the average family was in fact 2.6 per cent worse off because of tax and benefit changes. The Tories tried attacking Labour on the trade unions but this no longer held.

Their advertising was not very successful: but this was not surprising given the weakness of the product being sold. The old Saatchi and Saatchi had split into two groups so the party had to choose one, and chose M&C Saatchi to do its advertising, but only a year before the election. They used slogans – 'New Labour, New Danger' and 'Britain is Booming – Don't Let Labour Blow It' – but they did not increase Tory support. The negative advertising on the theme 'New Labour, New Danger', which consisted of a poster series with red devil's eyes, only produced criticism of and within the Conservatives.

Regardless of this, as Steve Hilton (1998: 48–9), who worked on the party's advertising campaign in 1992 and 1997, argued, they could not do anything with the advertising when voters' perceptions of the product, based on reality, were so negative. And this was not simply due to events immediately prior to the election such as BSE and sleaze. Willetts (1998: 112) recalls that when canvassing during the campaign 'it was striking how often one did not even need a political discussion with the voter on the door-step. They just had to define who they were – "I am a single parent", "I am a teacher", "I work in the NHS" – for it to appear obvious to them that they could not possibly vote Conservative'.

Overall, the campaign made very little difference to the party's electoral position. The Conservative Party not only lacked a market orientation, it lacked the *desire* to be market-oriented. It showed no attempts to try to give the voters what they wanted. It simply continued with what it deemed to be right: it was product-oriented. The party appeared insensitive and unresponsive to the needs of voters, particularly when it was criticised for failing to deliver on promises made in 1992. When the Government increased VAT, for example, Major said there would be 'no pain without gain', not understanding the effect on people's daily lives. Sanders (1998: 217) observed how the party's behaviour made it seem unresponsive and uncaring about ordinary people:

> More and more they enveloped harsh realities in clouds of official statistics. Asked about the length of hospital waiting lists, they recited meaningless statistics about the total number of people being treated by the NHS. Asked about falling educational standards, they cited statistics, which might or might not mean anything, about the numbers of pupils passing A-levels.

The party seemed to ignore all indications of voter dissatisfaction. The Conservatives neglected market intelligence, continuing to push their existing design, despite failure to deliver on promises made in 1992. Even where they did get product design right, the value of this was reduced because voters lacked faith in their ability to deliver on promises. Table 3.18 below indicates that a majority of voters did not think the Conservatives would keep their promises if they won office. They displayed public disunity and plans for the communication and campaign stages were haphazard, ever-changing and hindered by high turnover of staff.

### Stage 7: Election – the party's success in attracting support

The lack of a market orientation was reflected in the 1997 election results, but also membership decline and fall in public opinion ratings.

#### The general election

The Conservative Party did not just lose, but suffered heavy losses. It lost over 50 per cent of seats, including those of 7 current Cabinet members, with a vote-share of only 30.7 per cent (their lowest since 1883), 165 seats (their lowest since 1906). They failed to win any seats in Scotland and Wales. This was the first time in Scotland that this had ever happened and the first time in Wales since 1906. William Hague, who later became leader of the Tories, conceded (in the *Spectator*, 10 May 1997) that 'the Conservative Party was not merely defeated. It was humiliated'. The Tories even lost seats that were normally considered unwinnable by any other party.

*Membership*

The Conservative Party suffered from a loss in numbers but also an ageing and less active membership. The party's own study after the 1997 election admitted that it had 'failed to involve sufficiently those members we have recruited, to provide attractive new avenues for participation and as a result there has been a continuation of the decline in membership' (The Conservative Party (1997b)). This reflects how the Conservatives neglected to apply marketing to inform the design of their membership nature, structure or recruitment throughout the 1979–97 period.

*Voter evaluations of party behaviour*

Voters chose which party they expected to make things better in Britain and most voters believed that Conservative policies would make things worse (see Table 3.10).

**Table 3.10** *Voters' evaluation of expected party performance, 1997*

*Question asked: If Labour/the Conservatives wins the election, do you think that, overall, Labour/Conservative policies will make things in Britain a lot better, a little better, no different, a little worse or a lot worse?*

|  | Labour policies (%) | Conservative policies (%) |
|---|---|---|
| Better | 57 | 31 |
| No difference | 11 | 19 |
| Worse | 33 | 49 |

*Source:* Kellner (1997: 622), quoted from a BBC/NOP exit poll, 1 May 1997.
*Notes:* n = not known. 'Better' combines those saying 'A lot better' and 'A little better'; 'Worse' combines those saying 'A lot worse' and 'A little worse'.

The Conservatives were far behind Labour on the party with the best policies (see Chapter 5 for further detail). The Party Leader was also unpopular. Major received much lower evaluations by the public as measured by overall poll ratings (see Table 3.11) and more specific questions (see Chapter 5 for further detail); 47 per cent thought he was out of touch with ordinary people, compared with only 9 per cent thinking the same of Blair.

**Table 3.11** *Leader approval ratings, 1994–96*

|  | Blair (%) | Major (%) | Ashdown (%) |
|---|---|---|---|
| Aug–Dec 1994 | 41 | 16 | 14 |
| 1995 | 42 | 17 | 13 |
| 1996 | 39 | 19 | 14 |

*Source:* Denver (1998: 40) from *Gallup 9000*.

The exit poll on May 1 1997 showed that 84 per cent of voters thought the Conservatives were divided (see Table 3.12).

**Table 3.12** *Voters' perception of party unity, 1997*

*Question asked: Regardless of how you voted today, do you think that the Conservative/Labour Party is united or divided?*

|  | Conservative Party (%) | Labour Party (%) |
|---|---|---|
| United | 16 | 66 |
| Divided | 84 | 34 |

*Source:* Kellner (1997: 622) from a BBC/NOP exit poll, 1 May 1997.

The 1997 BES found that a majority of respondents felt that the party was good for only one class, one which broke its promises and was not capable of strong government: see Table 3.13. This also eroded the Conservatives' general governing ability.

**Table 3.13** *Voters' perceptions of the parties, 1997*

*Question asked: On the whole, would you describe the Conservative/Labour Party nowadays as . . .*

|  | Conservative (%) |
|---|---|
| Good for one class | 76 |
| Good for all classes | 34 |
| A party that keeps its promises | 16 |
| A party that breaks its promises | 84 |
| Capable of being a strong Government | 27 |
| Not capable of being a strong Government | 73 |

*Source:* BES (1997).
*Note:* n = 3,615.

As explored above, the Tories failed to deliver on their promises in many areas. The BES found that a majority of respondents felt that taxes and crime had increased whilst the quality and standard of education and the NHS had fallen: see Table 3.14. Furthermore, most felt these problems were mainly due to the policies of the Conservative Government (see Table 3.15).

**Table 3.14** *Voters' perceptions of life under the Conservative Government, 1997*

*Question asked: Looking back to the general election in 1992, would you say that since then [. . .] has increased or fallen?*

|  | Increased (%) | Stayed the same (%) | Fallen (%) |
|---|---|---|---|
| Taxes | 68 | 13 | 11 |
| Crime | 79 | 10 | 8 |
| Unemployment | 44 | 12 | 42 |
| The quality of education | 13 | 18 | 59 |
| The standard of the health and social services | 11 | 12 | 74 |

*Source:* BES (1997).
*Notes:* n = 3,615. 'Increased' combines 'Increased a lot' and 'Increased a little'; 'Fallen' combines 'Fallen a little' and 'Fallen a lot'.

**Table 3.15** *Change the result of government policies, 1997*

*Question asked: Do you think this is . . .*

|  | % saying mainly the result of the Conservative Government's policies |
|---|---|
| The standard of the health and social services | 83 |
| Taxes | 82 |
| The quality of education | 69 |
| Unemployment | 64 |
| Crime | 50 |

*Source:* BES (1997).
*Note:* n = 3,615.

This was also reflected by polls on their overall record of delivery: see Table 3.16.

**Table 3.16** *Voters' perception of the Conservatives' delivery in office, 1997*

*Question asked: On the whole, do you think that the Conservatives have or have not kept their election promises?*

|  | % |
|---|---|
| Have | 15 |
| Have not | 69 |
| Don't know | 14 |

*Source:* King (1998b: 191), from *Gallup Political and Economic Index* Report no. 428, April 1996: 5.
*Note:* n = not known.

It was also viewed as dishonest: see Table 3.17.

**Table 3.17** *Voters' perception of the Conservative Government's honesty, 1997*

*Question asked: Do you think the Conservative Government over the past few years has been basically an honest or basically a dishonest government?*

|  | % |
|---|---|
| Voters who thought the Government was basically honest | 29 |
| Voters who thought the Government was basically dishonest | 67 |

*Source:* King (1998b: 191), from *Gallup Political and Economic Index* Report no. 440 April, 1997: 9.
*Note:* n = not known.

The party, unsurprisingly, lost its 'delivery competence': see Table 3.18.

**Table 3.18** *Voters' belief in the Conservative Party's likelihood of delivery, post-1997*

*Question asked: If the Conservatives win the next election, how likely do you think they will be to keep the promises they make then?*

|  | % |
|---|---|
| Very/fairly likely | 28 |
| Not very/not at all likely | 65 |
| Don't know | 7 |

*Source:* King (1998b: 191), from *Gallup Political and Economic Index* Report no. 428, April 1996: 5.
*Note:* n = not known.

The Conservatives lost the general governing competence that they had enjoyed for most of the 1979–97 period. It was the ability to deliver generally, not just on the economy, which voters questioned. The economy may affect all other areas of delivery, which is why it is seen as an important variable in election results. Once the overall performance is broadly satisfactory, voters expect delivery in other areas: although the Tories had delivered a healthy economy this was not enough. The Conservatives also lost further credibility by holding official party policies such as that on Europe which were not implemented throughout the party. This inevitably led voters to question whether they could trust the Conservative Party to deliver any of the promises they made, even if they did like them.

Overall therefore, the 1992–97 Conservative Government provides another example of the importance of being market-oriented. Without this, voter dissatisfaction will rise. The party remained in power while losing its market orientation. Its leader became unpopular, it failed to deliver on past promises and displayed continual disunity. As Denver (1998: 16) observed, 'John Major and the Conservatives plumbed depths of unpopularity never before experienced by a modern government'. When such a party continues in government, it is entirely consistent that voter dissatisfaction will increase. Voters are much more likely to be critical of a party's failure to maintain a market orientation if that party is in government and thus greater influence over the system and their lives.

The Conservative losses also highlight the importance of the product adjustment/achievability and delivery aspect of marketing. This stage of the marketing process can be criticised for being naive on the grounds that delivery is impossible or simply related to economic performance. Delivery may be difficult, but is essential to the success of political marketing. Furthermore, why do parties exist if they cannot make a difference? In 1992 the Conservatives promised to deliver what they then proved unable to and they lost support as a consequence. On the BBC's election night coverage, when it became clear that the Tories had lost, Edwina Currie MP was asked 'Why do you think John Major lost, Mrs Currie?' She replied:

> Well, we all lost and this is part of the tragedy: we've lost most of the Cabinet, it sounds like, and most of the seats in Scotland. I think in the end we lost because we did not satisfy the British public about our probity, about our wisdom and our common sense.

When asked 'Do you blame the Euro-sceptics in particular?' she replied:

> It's more than that. It's not just the Europeans. We came in last time on the belief and the promise that we could keep taxes down, and that proved impossible. Perhaps we should have realised it, but in the end we put taxes up – the biggest peace-time hike in taxes we've ever seen, and the electorate didn't like it.

The 1997 case highlights that, as explored in Chapter 1, voters are increasingly critical and less willing to offer their support to political parties which encounter difficulties in delivering their promises. Analysis of electoral behaviour should include analysis of parties' delivery as well as general governing competence. Although this challenges some models of voting behaviour, it is becoming increasingly apparent that the outcome of an election depends not simply on party identification levels in the electorate, or the performance of the economy. It is also not just policies, but a wide array of aspects within party behaviour. Harrop (1997: 318) suggested that the 1997 election in particular:

should initiate a post-mortem among political scientists. And the most likely outcome of such deliberations ... will be a simpler, more convincing and more political account of electoral change. Instead of attempting to reduce electoral change to sociological, economic or even policy variables, we should recognise the primacy of general political factors, specifically ratings of the unity and overall governing competence of the parties. Such variables simply overwhelmed whatever benefit the Conservatives expected from an improving economy. Political professionals have always realised that perceived governing capacity is the crucial battleground; it is time political science caught up.

The 1997 election showed that the economy does not necessarily matter above all else. Everybody knows, or rather thought they knew, that voters reward governments when times are good and punish governments when times are bad. By all the usual indicators, times were exceptionally good in May 1997, with 3 per cent annual growth, historically low inflation, steadily falling unemployment. Yet the Government presiding over the best economic news and healthiest economy for two generations suffered a resounding defeat. Moreover, it was hit hardest where the economy was steaming ahead fastest – in London and the South East.

The case of the Tories in 1997 also shows how important it is that a party once successful in an election engages in cyclical marketing, or it can become unresponsive in power and voter satisfaction will decline. Kotler and Levy (1969: 15) noted that:

> All organisations are formed to serve the interest of particular groups: hospitals serve the sick, schools serve the students, governments serve the citizens, and labour unions serve the members. In the course of evolving, many organisations lose sight of their original mandate, grow hard, and become self-serving. The bureaucratic mentality begins to dominate the original service mentality. Hospitals may become perfunctory in their handling of patients, schools treat their students as nuisances, city bureaucrats behave like petty tyrants toward the citizens, and labour unions try to run instead of serve their members. All of these actions tend to build frustration in the consuming groups. As a result some withdraw meekly from these organisations, accept frustration as part of their condition, and find the satisfactions elsewhere ... But new possibilities have arisen, and now the same consumers refuse to withdraw so readily. Organised dissent and protest are seen to be an answer, and many organisations thinking of themselves as responsible have been stunned into recognising that they have lost touch with their constituencies. They have grown unresponsive.
>
> Where does marketing fit into this picture? Marketing is that function of the organisation that can keep touch with the organisation's consumers, read their needs, develop 'products' that meet these needs, and build a program of communications to express the organisation's purposes.

Additionally, all aspects of the model and the product are important. For example, between 1979 and 1997, the Conservatives neglected to apply marketing to the membership aspect of their product and lost not only a source of loyal support and a chance to satisfy members demands in particular, but a source of marketing intelligence. It made it easier for the party to lose touch. Members play many roles in helping to ensure the party continues to be responsive to voter demands.

The failure of Labour in 1979 and the Tories in 1997 reflects the parties' resistance against following a market orientation. The greatest example of this is nevertheless the Labour Party in 1983 that substantially rejected the idea of responding to what voters thought. Indeed, its behaviour is the closest example of a Product-Oriented Party.

## Labour in 1983

In 1983 Labour offered a programme far removed from the concerns of the majority of voters. Since 1979 the party had suffered from internal divisions and a debate between left and right which intensified into a bitter power-struggle with little consideration for the views of the electorate. The left wing of the party took over both organisationally and ideologically. It was not concerned with designing its product to respond to voters. It simply wanted to make its argument.

### Stage 1: Market intelligence

Labour commissioned significant formal market intelligence. MORI conducted qualitative and quantitative research and reported the findings to the party's committees during March and April 1983. This uncovered many weaknesses in the party's behaviour: see the summary below (quoted in Butler and Kavanagh (1984: 141)):

LABOUR
 – PARTY IMAGE POOR, DIVIDED, OUT OF TOUCH, DISORGANISED, LEFT-
   WING, INCONSISTENT, OLD FASHIONED, T.U. LINKED, BUT ... CARING
   FOR THE WORKING CLASSES (?), WELFARE
 – LEADERSHIP SHABBY, NOT OUTSTANDING, NOT PROJECTED, UNIN-
   SPIRING, INCONSISTENT, OLD, SINCERE BUT WEAK
 – POLICIES – LOW AWARENESS, LOW CONFIDENCE, NO BETTER THAN
   ALTERNATIVE, FOR WELFARE, LOOKING AFTER POOR/UNEMPLOYED

Polls were also conducted for the campaign during May and June 1983 and the results were reported to Walworth Road and then the Campaign Committee each morning. But the party paid little attention to the results: marketing intelligence did not influence the product design. MORI's polling was too close to the election to have significant influence on the party's behaviour. Additionally, the Labour Party's culture is traditionally against such research, a bias reinforced by the dominance of the left wing.

### Stage 2: Product design

For most of the 1979–83 period, there was no coherent 'product' as such because the party was too focused on internal battles. When one did emerge, nearer to the election, it was driven by the dominant left wing of the party and did not reflect public opinion.

### Leadership

Michael Foot, who became leader of the Labour Party in October 1980, was liked by voters but not viewed as a potential Prime Minister (see Tables 3.23 and 3.24). He was nearly 70 years old and, as Shaw (1994: 27) observed, 'regarded with incredulity by most of the electorate'. Roy Hattersley describes the election of Foot as 'a conscious decision by the parliamentary party to abdicate. Not to worry about the next election, not to worry about its popularity in the country' (BBC (1995)). Although one of the reasons his party elected him was to preserve party unity, ironically he also failed to do this. He appointed a balanced Shadow Cabinet, but failed to command strong support from it: his left-wing sympathies alienated right-wing party MPs. He could not prevent Tony Benn's long, drawn-out challenge to Healey for the deputy leadership in 1981. As Denis Healey recalls, this contest 'was profoundly repulsive to the average elector' (BBC (1995)).

### MPs

The behaviour and composition of the Parliamentary Labour Party were not designed to suit voters' demands. They reflected the divisions and debates within the party. It suffered from poor morale. Its composition kept changing because of retirements, defections and the de-selection of the more right-wing MPs. The left became more dominant. MPs who had been prominent members of previous Governments (David Owen, William Rodgers, Roy Jenkins and Shirley Williams: the so-called 'Gang of Four') left Labour in January 1981 to form a new party: the SDP. Thirteen Labour MPs joined it.

### Membership

The National Executive Committee (NEC) within the party had always been left wing but became increasingly so and more assertive over the party as a whole. After the loss of the 1979 election, activists, together with the NEC, severely and publicly criticised the previous Labour Government.

They argued that problems had occurred because the Government had not done what the whole party wanted them to. This provoked a campaign to change the party's organisational structure to prevent this happening in future: the Campaign for Labour Party Democracy (CLPD), led by Tony Benn. Benn argued that the Parliamentary Party must be made more accountable to the party conference and activists to ensure that socialism was actually implemented when the party was in government.

These changes gave activists more influence over policy-making and promises for the 1983 election reflected their views over voters. The activists were generally more ideological and left-wing and pushed for policies out of line with public opinion. Another problem was the Militant Tendency within the party. This was a Trotskyite organisation, formed in 1950, which worked through the Labour Party to secure revolutionary socialism. It permeated the youth of the party and some constituency parties. In 1981 the NEC began to try to remove it and instructed constituency parties to expel Militant supporters, but they did not all do so. The Militant presence lost the party support amongst the wider electorate. The party's internal composition also complicated the process of policy-making. It was influenced by both the Shadow Cabinet and the NEC. Arguably this prevented the party from being an effective Product-Oriented Party, let alone a Market-Oriented Party.

*Staff*
Labour lacked independent, professional expertise and the party's staff was not effective. Michael Foot relied on left-wingers for advice. The party's headquarters moved from Transport House in Smith Square, Westminster, to Walworth Road, South of the Thames: a move which was both costly and problematic because it reduced the contact with the Parliamentary Party. There were many staff changes at headquarters. Staff numbers overall were low and a wage-freeze had been imposed because of financial difficulties within the party. A new National Agent, David Hughes, was appointed but the number and experience of agents below him had been in decline since 1979. There was also much turnover in other posts. A new General Secretary, Jim Mortimer, was appointed just a year before the election. The Broadcasting Officer, Doreen Stainforth, retired in February 1983 and was not replaced. Peter Clark retired as Director of Publicity in 1979. Max Madden, a former Labour MP, took over but left to seek another seat in July 1982. A debate took place within the NEC as to who should succeed him, and eventually Nick Grant, who had experience in public relations, was appointed but only a few months before the election in January 1983. Consequently, the Party's General Secretary, National Agent and Director of Publicity were new in their position and did not have experience of running a general election from (a new) party headquarters.

*Constitution*

Three major changes to the party's constitutional and organisational arrangements facilitated protracted debate and the rise of the left. At the 1979 Brighton Conference, the NEC was granted control of the election manifesto; mandatory re-selection of MPs during the lifetime of a Parliament was introduced and the rule which had prevented policy and constitutional change being discussed less than every three years at a conference was abolished. In January 1981, the Wembley Conference established a new electoral system for the leader. This gave 40 per cent of votes to trade unions, 30 per cent to local constituency parties and 30 per cent to MPs.

*Activities*

The party's annual conference provided a most visible spectacle of its divisions. Conference was controlled by the left wing and became a deliberative policy-making body. Policy-decisions taken at the party's annual conference moved the party further and further away from voters' opinions. For example, in 1981 the party voted to leave the EEC and to abandon Polaris. In 1982, it voted for removing American military bases on British soil. It also voted to abolish the House of Lords. The televising of these conferences also meant that radical decisions over policy were clearly visible to the public way in advance of the election.

*Policy proposals*

The party's policies reflected its dominant left wing. The final manifesto built on a campaign document called *Labour's Plan: the New Hope for Britain* written in March 1983 which was agreed upon by the NEC and Shadow Cabinet, although it was pushed through very quickly and as Hattersley (BBC (1995)) recalls, 'virtually without discussion'. The process was therefore far from open: Labour was evidently unclear about its product design. The actual manifesto, launched on 16 May 1982, was called *The New Hope for Britain* (see The Labour Party (1983)). Gerauld Kaufman described it as the longest suicide note in history. He contended (BBC (1995)) that:

> It was a stupid document. It contained a number of extremist things. It contained also utter nonsenses. During the course of compilation of that document, we only narrowly staved off a proposal that we should have a Socialist policy for puppy farms. I kid you not.

The document was lengthy and highly detailed, with long lists of everything a Labour Government would do. Even the contents page had an unusually long list of some seventy items.

Labour proposed:

- substantial nationalisation;
- greater union influence in economic policy-making;
- a non-nuclear defence policy under which it would cancel Trident and refuse to have Cruise missiles stationed in the United Kingdom;
- the two sides of industry and government would decide the nation's economic priorities, including pay;
- any assets privatised by the Conservatives would be re-nationalised;
- there would be public investment in industry;
- unemployment would be reduced to under a million in five years;
- to remove Britain from the EEC;
- to make local authorities buy back any council houses already sold;
- to freeze rents for one year;
- to increase spending on housing by 50 per cent.

Many of the party's policies were disliked by voters, such as the policy to remove Britain from the EEC or Common Market, buy back council houses and re-nationalise industries, as shown by Tables 3.19–3.21.

**Table 3.19** *Voters' views on the Common Market, 1983*

*Question asked: Which of these three statements comes closest to your own views on the Common Market?*

|  | % |
| --- | --- |
| Britain should leave the Common Market | 16 |
| Britain should stay if it achieves better terms | 56 |
| Britain should stay anyway | 28 |

*Source:* BES (1983).
*Note:* n = 3,955.

**Table 3.20** *Voters' views on nationalisation, 1983*

*Question asked: Should there be more or less nationalisation or de-nationalisation?*

|  | % |
| --- | --- |
| Nationalise (a lot and a few) more industries | 18 |
| Nationalise no more | 39 |
| De-nationalise | 43 |

*Source:* BES (1983).
*Note:* n = 3,955.

**Table 3.21** *Voters' views on the sale of council houses, 1983*

*Question asked: I want to ask about some changes that have been happening in Britain over the years. For each one I read out can you say whether you think it has gone too far, not gone far enough, or is it about right: the sale of council houses*

|  | % |
|---|---|
| Gone too far | 13 |
| About right | 66 |
| Not gone far enough | 21 |

*Source:* BES (1983).
*Note:* n = 3,955.

As Fielding (1995: 65–7) commented, in 1979 the electorate voted against state collectivism, but in 1983 Labour offered more. Butler and Kavanagh (1984: 46) noted that people 'were voting Labour in spite of its policies, which increasingly reflected the views of its activists, not the voters'. Tony Blair (BBC (1995)) claimed that at the time he had:

> no doubt at all that the Party's position was going to lose us the election ... and that was precisely because we'd allowed a small group of people to determine the agenda of the Party who hadn't the faintest notion what was going on in the world out there ... and had constructed a whole set of policies that were absolutely nothing to do with the needs of real people.

### Stage 3: Product adjustment

*Achievability*
Voters also saw Labour policies as unrealistic. The manifesto was crammed with lists of promises, such as that to reduce unemployment to under a million in five years' time. Shirley Williams, the former Labour MP, declared at the time that the manifesto was 'an abuse of the common-sense of the British voter ... It promises billions to everyone ... it has no idea how to pay for those promises' (quoted in Butler and Kavanagh (1984: 91)). The party as a whole also lacked credibility with the public.

*Internal reaction analysis*
The party did take account of its members' views, but at the neglect of voters as a whole. Or, perhaps more accurately, the party took account of a certain section of its members. The policies in the manifesto that were against the views of the electorate were also against the views of the parliamentary party and leadership. The manifesto reflected the differences within the party.

*Competition analysis*

The Party's qualitative market intelligence highlighted how the Conservatives had many strengths, even in traditional Labour territory, whereas Labour was weak in many areas: it was seen as too left-wing, disunited, lacking leadership and dominated by the unions. But the party did not try to adjust its behaviour in response.

*Support analysis*

Labour also neglected to engage in support analysis and target marketing.

## Stage 4: Implementation

The debate within the party meant that even the product-oriented views of the left were not fully implemented. The most obvious indication that there was disagreement was the break-off by some of the party to form the SDP. They left after the Wembley Conference established the new electoral system for the leader, and the new party was formed on 26 March. Additionally, of those that remained, many did not accept the radical policies. There were divisions in particular on defence, Europe and pensions which became especially obvious during the election campaign. The most notable issue was defence. Gerauld Kaufman recalls (BBC (1995)) how

> One of the problems is that policy wasn't clear, policy was often damaging but not clear. There was one day when three different interpretations of Labour's defence policy were given on the very same day by Michael Foot, Denis Healey and by John Silken. It was utterly unco-ordinated. It was a shambles.

These divisions were also picked up by voters. The BES found that only 38 per cent of respondents felt that Labour had clear policies: see Table 3.22.

**Table 3.22** *Implementation of product design, 1983*

*Question asked: On the whole, do you think the Conservative/ Labour Party has clear or vague policies?*

|  | Clear | Vague |
|---|---|---|
| Conservative | 82 | 18 |
| Labour | 38 | 62 |

*Source:* BES (1983).
*Note:* n = 3,955.

### Stage 5: Communication

Labour did not develop a long-term communications strategy.

### Stage 6: The election campaign

> It was a hopeless campaign. The Labour Party was losing votes day by day: support was just sliding away from us. (Jack Cunningham, BBC (1995))

> The general perception from the outside was that the campaign was very badly run and inept. But I have to say that from inside it was even worse. (Jim Parish, Publications Officer in 1982, BBC (1995))

The election was really over before the campaign begun. Nonetheless, the campaign did not help matters: it was badly planned or not really planned at all. Jim Mortimer took over as General Secretary only twelve months before election day. The Campaign Committee did not meet until November 1982 – eight months before the election. Grant became Director of Publicity in January of the election year and claims that no real preparation had taken place by this time (see Grant (1986: 82–6)). Planning from thereon was also slow and cumbersome. Discussion between the leader and senior party members and staff only took place for one hour each month. Labour's approach was more in line with a product orientation. Grant (1986: 83) reveals how preparation was done 'as if all Labour had to do was attack the Government's disastrous economic policy and voters would throw off their doubts about Labour and return us to power'.

Organisational discipline was also lacking during the campaign. The Campaign Committee met every morning, but each time different people attended: it could include heads of department, spokesmen for that day, NEC members and others, as well as the Campaign Committee. Press Conferences, run at Transport House, started late and ended early. They rigidly adhered to one theme and were not effective in conveying the party's message. Indeed, the message itself was contradictory and disputes about policy came into the open. On 31 May Michael Foot pledged that there would be no increase in National Insurance charges, but the manifesto committed the party to raising £1 million by abolishing the £220-a-week ceiling on earnings-related contributions. Divisions also emerged between Healey and Foot on defence.

Labour appointed a professional advertising agency in 1983 at the last minute: Wright and Partners: a small, largely unknown company. The firm had to work under great time-constraints and pressure and rely on research and slogans created previously for the local elections. Wright (1986: 81) recalls that relations between the party and the agency were confused. Labour's natural distrust of advertising made the situation worse. Additionally, the instructions given to Wright and Partners indicates a more product-oriented attitude. They were told to put the Labour Party's case, i.e. the Keynesian logic for their economic policy, and to argue that government needed to invest to stimulate growth. The party simply thought 'this is what we stand for', ignored the views of the voters in the design of its product and attempted to convey its argument without any consideration for voters' views in the campaign. Indeed, Peter Mandelson (quoted in Gould (1998b: 47)) observed that: 'The idea of image-making comes hard to the Labour Party, because they're more interested in their product, they're more interested in getting over the nitty-gritty of their social welfare policy or their investment policy, or their exchange control policy.' The Party Leader was also reluctant to change his behaviour to suit television reporting. He was successful in attracting large crowds wherever he went, but would often focus on past rather than present and future battles, adding to the party's image of being out of touch.

Faults in the campaign organisation were not the major cause of electoral defeat however. At a meeting of the NEC on 12 September 1983, Denis Healey (quoted in Butler and Kavanagh (1984: 279)) declared:

> The election was lost not in the three weeks of the campaign but in the three years which preceded it ... In that period the Party itself acquired a highly unfavourable public image, based on disunity, extremism, crankiness and general unfitness to govern. The Party also managed to express many of its policies in terms remote from the lives and hopes of millions of voters and rendered itself politically vulnerable to attack on many issues.

The problem with the campaign was that what the party was selling – its product – was not wanted by a majority of voters in Britain.

### Stage 7: Election – the party's success in attracting support

Labour's product orientation did not attract support, even from the membership.

#### The general election
Labour suffered a substantial defeat in 1983. It went down to only 209 seats and 27.6 per cent of the total popular vote. The party had only 3 out of 179 seats in the south and east of London and came second in only 24 of them. It gained 25 out of 84 possible seats in the Greater London area. The party lost 119 deposits. It also lost working-class support, especially amongst skilled (C2) workers. Even amongst unskilled workers it only achieved a majority of those who were trade unionists. It was not just a party of the working class, but a sub-set within that.

*Membership*
Despite the changes within the party organisation to try to make it democratic and presumably more appealing, the size of the membership as a whole actually fell during this period. It reached its lowest level throughout the entire 1979–99 period in 1982, when it declined to 273, 803.

*Voter evaluations of party behaviour*
Labour's policies were not market-oriented. In the 1983 BES the Conservatives took the lead as the preferred party on the majority of issues, especially those considered important to voters (see Chapter 2 for details). Labour's party leader, Michael Foot, also suffered from a lack of popularity: 70 per cent of respondents to the BES thought he would be an ineffective Prime Minister (see Table 3.23).

**Table 3.23** *Effectiveness of party leader as Prime Minister, 1983*

*Question asked: On the whole, how effective or ineffective do you think Mrs Thatcher [Mr Foot] is [could have been] as Prime Minister?*

|  | *Effective (%)* | *Ineffective (%)* |
| --- | --- | --- |
| Thatcher | 91 | 9 |
| Foot | 30 | 70 |

*Source:* BES (1983).
*Notes:* n = 3,955. 'Effective' combines those saying 'Very effective' and 'Fairly effective'; 'Ineffective' combines those saying 'Fairly ineffective' and 'Very ineffective'.

Table 3.24 indicates that although Foot was perceived by more voters to be caring and likeable, far more voters thought that Thatcher was determined, tough and decisive. Additionally a fewer number of voters thought Foot was likely to get things done (see Chapter 2 for further details).

Labour suffered from high party disunity: 92 per cent of BES respondents thought it was divided (see Table 3.25) and 62 per cent thought Labour's policies were vague (see Table 3.22 above).

**Table 3.24** *Most able Prime Minister, 1983*

*Question asked: Which of these qualities on this card would you say Thatcher and Foot have?*

| | *Thatcher or Foot receiving higher number of voters saying they have that quality (% lead over the other)* |
|---|---|
| Tough | Thatcher (72) |
| Determined | Thatcher (64) |
| Decisive | Thatcher (53) |
| Sticks to principles | Thatcher (47) |
| Shrewd | Thatcher (34) |
| Caring | Foot (32) |
| Likeable person | Foot (23) |

*Source:* BES (1983).
*Note:* n = 3,955.

**Table 3.25** *Party unity, 1983*

*Question asked: Would you describe the Conservative/Labour Party nowadays as united or divided?:*

| | United (%) | Divided (%) |
|---|---|---|
| Labour | 8 | 92 |

*Source:* BES (1983).
*Note:* n = 3,955.

Labour also faced the barrier of relatively positive perceptions amongst voters about Conservative record of delivery and credibility in governing. The BES showed that far more voters believed that the Conservatives were more able to keep prices down, prevent strikes and reduce unemployment than Labour: see Table 3.26. This was an even greater obstacle to success given that these issues were those that voters held as their priorities and most important in their decision as to who to vote for.

**Table 3.26** *Possible party performance in government, 1983*

*Question asked: Which party do you think would be the most likely to [. . .] over the next four–five years?*

| | Conservative (%) | Labour (%) |
|---|---|---|
| Keep prices down | 43 | 25 |
| Prevent strikes | 48 | 25 |
| Reduce unemployment | 46 | 27 |
| Improve the standard of living | 18 | 49 |
| Look after the health and social services | 20 | 54 |

*Source:* BES (1983).
*Note:* n = 3,955.

Furthermore, Labour lacked general governing competence: a BBC Election Day Survey found that 75 per cent of respondents had confidence in Conservative politicians to deal wisely with Britain's problems, whereas only 25 per cent had this confidence in Labour.

## Conclusion

In 1983 Labour was a Product-Oriented Party, holding the view that politics is (and should be) about standing up for what you believe in. Philip Gould (1998b: 4) recalls having dinner with Michael Foot and his wife after the election: 'They could not understand why the Labour Party had lost the election that June. Labour had offered education, choices and opportunities, but the people had turned on them. They read the *Sun* and abandoned the Labour Party.'

Their view was that if people had not bought the product, it was because the people were wrong. Indeed, Foot's reaction during the campaign to the request to say less about the unpopular defence policy indicates a product orientation. Bob Worcester (BBC 1995), Labour's pollster at the time, recalls that:

> His colleagues were saying Michael will you please shut up about it. And he said at one point ... 'I am not going to be leader forever of a party. This is an opportunity that I have to get my message across and I am not going to lose that opportunity to communicate to the British electorate what I think so strongly about this policy.' Now you have to admire that kind of attitude, but as somebody said in the American context, 'this is a person who'd rather be right than President.' Well Michael clearly would rather be articulate on unilateral disarmament than be Prime Minister.

Similarly, the comments by Labour's General Secretary, Jim Mortimer, at the conference after the election, indicate a product orientation:

> It is not the Party's policy, but public opinion which needs to be changed. No socialist worthy of the traditions of the Labour movement should refuse, on occasions, to go against a strong current of public opinion if in doing so he believes that such a course is necessary for the purpose of social progress.

One question arising from this is why Labour was product-oriented. Gould (1998b: 23) suggests that Labour's resistance to modernisation was due to reasons deep in the party's history and also to do with its funding. He writes (1998b: 24) that 'Labour was ... too close to trade unionism; too obsessive about public ownership; too tied to myth; too rooted in the past'. Another explanation might be that Labour adopted a product orientation because it was out of touch and therefore did not realise that it would not be successful. It wanted its product to win the election, to win its own argument, but because they did not comprehend the nature (as well as the demands) of the market, it did not know this would not work. Major parties can no longer succeed in Britain if they adopt a product orientation. Tim Bell, a chief adviser to the Conservatives, said of Labour in 1983 'I think they were still deeply embedded in a concept of politics that had long gone by' (BBC (1995)). Indeed Philip Gould (1999) said at a conference on political marketing that 'the era of producer politics has gone'. The nature of the British electoral market, party competition and majoritarian democracy is such that a major political party which wants to win office, needs to be market-oriented in order to succeed. The normative implications of this are profound: conviction politics would seem dead on the ground in Britain. Or at least conviction politics where the beliefs held are not those of the majority of the population. As will be discussed later, there may yet be room for ideology and beliefs within a market-oriented framework. But a party that does not listen to the people and does not attempt to meet their demands in any way at all will not succeed electorally. This is a lesson the Labour Party in particular found hard to learn. After losing in 1983 it took the party a further three elections before it changed enough to win again.

## Note

1  Unless otherwise stated directly within the text because of particular originality or primary nature, this chapter draws on the secondary empirical descriptive accounts of the time period listed below. Details of other works consulted and directly cited are in the full bibliography at the end of the book.

### Labour, 1979

Butler and Kavanagh (1980), Byrd (1986), Crewe (1981), Delaney (1982), Gould (1998b), Leonard (1981), Livingston (1988), Rosenbaum (1997).

### The Conservatives in 1997

Ball (1998), Butler and Kavanagh (1997), Crewe *et al.* (1998), Denver (1998), Fielding (1997a), Finkelstein (1998), Gavin and Sanders (1997), Harrop (1997), Hilton (1998), Jones (1997, Kellner (1997), King (1998a), King (1999), Lansley (1997, Norris (1997b), Norris (1998a), Norton (1998), Powell (1998), Rose (1997), Sanders (1998), Whiteley (1997), Whiteley *et al.* (1994), Willetts (1998).

*Labour in 1983*

BBC (1995), Butler and Kavanagh (1984), Byrd (1986), Croft (1992), Fielding (1995), Gould (1998b), Grant (1986), Kavanagh (1982), Kavanagh (1992), McLean (1987), O'Shaughnessy (1990), Pearce and Stewart (1992), Punnett (1992), Rosenbaum (1997), Shaw (1994), Whiteley (1983), Whyte (1988), Wright (1986), Wring (1997b).

# 4

# The limits of sales-oriented marketing: why Labour did not win in 1987 and 1992

Between 1983 and 1992 Labour made significant attempts to change their behaviour to become more electable. Under a new leader, Neil Kinnock, the party used marketing to inform the way it presented itself. In 1987 it ran an extremely professional campaign, and is a perfect example of a Sales-Oriented Party. It broadly retained its pre-determined product design, but recognised that those whose support it needed to win the election would not necessarily vote for such a product. It therefore tried to persuade them that the party was right and focused effort on selling, but tried to sell a product that voters did not want. Labour did not win the next election because despite changing some of its behaviour to reflect electoral preferences, in 1992 it remained less popular on key parts of the product such as the leader, certain policies and overall party unity than the opposition.[1]

## A triumph of presentation over the product: Labour 1983–87

> Labour's emphasis on social issues, despite doubts about its approach to defence and the economy, resembled an airline with a safety problem marketing itself on the quality of its in-flight meals. The advertising was good but the strategy was doomed. (Harrop (1987: 281))

'We won the campaign, yes, but it could not win the election for us' (Hewitt and Mandelson (1989: 54)). Labour's attempts to win the 1987 election were based mainly on changes in how the party sold itself. As the Sales-Oriented Party model suggests, the focus was on the communication of the product, rather than product design.

### Stage 1: Market intelligence

The party's attitude towards market intelligence was very positive and it conducted various forms of formal research:

- The agency MORI, under Bob Worcester, was appointed immediately after the 1983 election. MORI conducted survey research, fast polling, and a panel study.
- Results went to those involved in strategy and campaign planning.
- Results showed the party's weaknesses, e.g. extremism and division; and that voters wanted a party that could improve their standard of living and would actually deliver on their promises.
- 200 qualitative focus groups were also conducted, mainly on lapsed Labour voters.
- Philip Gould (1998b: 49–50) also conducted focus group research which showed the 'gap between what Labour had become and what the British electorate wanted'.
- MORI conducted surveys of target groups and marginal seats for the actual campaign.
- The party established a system of overnight feedback which fed market intelligence results to the campaign control group each morning.

Nevertheless, being a Sales-Oriented Party rather than a Market-Oriented Party, results from market intelligence influenced only the presentation rather than the design of behaviour.

### Stage 2: Product design

*Leadership*
Neil Kinnock was elected party leader in 1983. Kinnock was not popular with voters: they did not think he possessed the necessary leadership characteristics (see Tables 4.1 and 4.2). His background was traditional Labour: he was from a mining community in South Wales and a typical left-winger who began to move towards the soft left after 1979. Kinnock was in a Catch-22 situation whereby he needed to appease the left in the party but also change Labour's reputation in the electorate. He faced many internal battles to change the party. The leader had to let some goals go in order to preserve party unity, which was in itself electorally desirable.

*MPs*
The Shadow Cabinet was generally centre–right and maintained a good relationship with the leader. The Parliamentary Party as a whole, however, suffered from low morale. It was vastly outnumbered by Government MPs. Additionally, some MPs faced de-selection by the hard left's local-level control of candidate selection and the leadership was unable to do anything.

*Membership*

The membership lost the party support in two ways: hindering change and acting in a way to bring the party into disrepute. Kinnock had to tread carefully with the trade unions (they remained a strong source of finance); the party's National Executive Committee (NEC); and the membership. The membership, or its most active section, continued to strongly resist the idea of a market orientation: Gould (1998b: 67) observes how, at the 1986 party conference, 'delegates voted to retain nearly all the policies which had lost them the 1983 election so dramatically'. Two particular groups within the membership lost the party support. The first was militant Labour. In the 1970s it permeated weak inner-city constituency Labour parties and then local councils. One notorious case was in Liverpool. The council refused to reduce services when its budget was cut by central government. The council consequently fell into debt and services had to be reduced anyway. The council attracted media attention by using a taxi, at tax-payers' expense, to hand-deliver redundancy notices to council-service workers. The second was the trade unions, linked to the miners' strike in 1984–85. The strike lost public support because its leader, Arthur Scargill, failed to ballot miners beforehand. Scargill also refused to compromise or condemn violence that occurred during the strike.

Kinnock responded to both problems with strong leadership. He refused to condone Scargill's actions. He also refused to back the action of militant councillors in London and Liverpool and succeeded in passing motions at the 1986 party conference to expel leading militants. Despite this, both gave the Labour Party a very negative image amongst voters. Militant occurrences led the party to be labelled 'loony left' by the opposition and the media. Furthermore, the party conference passed resolutions in support of the miners' strike that reinforced the perception that Labour was strongly linked to the unions. These issues also hindered further change in the party. Charles Clarke (quoted in Gould (1998b: 42)), one of Kinnock's key staff, explained that:

> It made it very difficult to open up other ideological challenges in the way that we wished to do. We were forced on to the defensive against the leftists. There was a national solidarity with the strike which people throughout the Labour movement felt, and it made it very difficult to promote other changes, both organisational and policy-based.

*Staff*

The Labour Party made effective use of staff and professionals. Larry Whitty was appointed as General Secretary of the Party in 1985. Whitty re-organised Labour headquarters and recruited new department directors. Kinnock drew on a number of advisers. For example, Charles Clarke became his Chief of Staff and Patricia Hewitt his Press Secretary. Clarke had previously been a parliamentary adviser, and Hewitt had been a public relations officer. The most notable appointment was Peter Mandelson as Director of Campaigns and Communications in October 1985. Mandelson's career had previously been in television as a producer with London Weekend Television. He brought valuable experience and a unique perspective on presentation and communication with the electorate via various media.

Under Mandelson's direction, the party's communications were transformed. He brought in Philip Gould, an experienced advertising consultant, to conduct an assessment of the state of the party's communications. Mandelson also asked Gould to co-ordinate the work of a new body, the Shadow Communications Agency (SCA), created in February 1986. The SCA brought together party figures with volunteer-professionals: members included planners and researchers from ad agencies, polling agencies and market research companies. Many of them were brought in through Mandelson's personal contacts. Members included Chris Powell, Peter Herd, Alan Tilly and Paul Leeves from Boase Massimi Politt (BMP), an agency which had a good reputation for eye-catching advertising. The SCA provided the party with a wealth of talent and experience, and its advice was well received by the leadership.

The one negative part of the SCA's work was that its influence expanded rather secretly: Gould (1998b: 57) recalls how 'although Neil Kinnock and Robin Cook knew we were working for Peter, only Mandelson knew the extent of our expanding communications empire'. Peter Mandelson's position was in an area that required major change; the state of Labour's communication efforts had, until 1983, been poor. Mandelson (BBC (1995)) recalls how, at the beginning:

> It was a bit like swimming through treacle ... I found myself constantly knocking my head against what seemed to be a brick wall of sort of total incomprehension of what I was saying. That things that were accepted in the outside as completely normal, natural and axiomatic were seen in the culture of the Party at that time as sort of really very odd and slightly threatening.

Over time, Mandelson's influence upon the party expanded which aroused suspicion from others. This was also due to his close relationship with the Party Leader. Mandelson's emerging control had the affect of making others within the top levels of the party feel unreasonably excluded.

*Constitution*
Kinnock tried to introduce the 'One member, one vote' principle for candidate selection but this was rejected by the 1984 party conference by

3,992,000 to 3,641,000 votes. Constituency delegates and trade unions were against the measure. This left MPs dependent on local activists rather than the whole membership.

*Symbols*
The party changed its symbol from a red flag to a red rose and launched it at the 1986 conference. This helped to remove the perception that Labour represented only the working class.

*Activities*
The presentational aspects of annual conferences became increasingly stage-managed, with the back-drop designed to suit television and senior party figures advised to dress smartly. But the policy decisions were against public opinion. Neil Kinnock's passionate speech against nuclear weapons at the pre-election conference in October 1986 inevitably increased attention to the party's unpopular defence policy.

*Policy proposals*
The manifesto was entitled *Britain Will Win* (see The Labour Party (1987)). It was produced after a much less contentious and far more organised process than in the past. Left-wing commitments from 1983 were reduced, for example:

- Economic proposals showed less reliance on state planning.
- The target-unemployment figure was reduced from zero to a one million reduction within two years of gaining government.
- Labour accepted the sale of council houses.
- Labour did not oppose British membership of the European Economic Community.

This did not, however, remove all the unpopular policies. Reducing unemployment to one million in two years was still an ambitious promise. And in other areas the party continued to move against public opinion. For example:

- Defence: the party's unilateralist policy on defence was retained after re-affirmation by a big majority at the 1984 party conference: a Labour Government would remove all weapons from British soil and thus de-commission Polaris and cancel Trident. This was despite the results of market intelligence which made it clear that it was unpopular. What the party did do was alter the presentation of the policy, focusing on how Labour would continue membership of NATO and increase its spending on conventional forces and was concerned with the strengthening Britain's real defences.

- Economy: Labour continued to promise expansion of state ownership and intervention in the economy. 'Half a million jobs' would be created by improving the public services. 'Another 360,000 new jobs and training places [would] be created.'
- A minimum wage would be introduced.
- Pensions for couples would be increased.
- The changes made by the Conservative Government for closed shops and secondary picketing would be restored.

Overall, the Labour Party's product was not designed to respond to voters' demands.

### Stage 3: Product adjustment

*Achievability*
Labour did not lay out the cost of its proposals. It did not explain how it would achieve its promises: for example the jobs section claimed that the party would decrease unemployment and create jobs, without discussing how.

*Internal reaction analysis*
Kinnock's style of leadership clearly took significant account of party views but, arguably, too much because responding to members was at the expense of reflecting voters' views.

*Competition analysis*
Labour's research identified that the party was strongest on social, caring issues, and this was where the Conservatives were weak. But it did not try to adjust its product accordingly. Competition analysis was used in the campaign but, here, the focus was on selling the party, not designing the actual policy.

*Support analysis*
Support analysis was limited. MORI identified over one hundred seats that Labour had to win, but information on these and marginal seats was not very detailed. Target marketing focused on its own supporters: soft and ex-Labour voters, together with Liberal/SDP supporters, rather than those it needed to gain to win the election.

### Stage 4: Implementation

The leadership may have taken on the need to respond to voter concerns, but the party as a whole did not accept the *idea* of becoming market-oriented, let alone exhibit market-oriented behaviour. The hard left of the party also continued to argue against any change in the manifesto. Conference often voted for motions that were not popular, such as the resolutions over the miners' strike and the defence policy. Party unity was higher than in the past but various sections of the party acted differently: to each other; to what was demanded by voters; and to the leadership line. Kinnock's own comments imply how he failed to take the whole party with him in his quest for electoral success. He (quoted in Shaw (1994: 50–1)) said he was:

> never sure the whole party was with me. I was always dragging it, inch by inch, advancing a little, fighting more, advancing. I had to choose my ground so carefully.

### Stage 5: Communication

The party's communications became more organised and professional during this period. The first step taken was to identify the problems in the existing system of communication and what should be changed. Mandelson drew on the independent audit which he commissioned Philip Gould to complete. The report (Gould (1985)), produced in December 1985, criticised the party for the command over communications being weakly organised and advised that:

- the power of the Director of Campaigns and Communications be increased;
- a Shadow Communications Agency (SCA) be set up;
- Labour should use the mass media to gain publicity, not simply rely on local party campaigning;
- research should be more integrated and focused on how to win votes.

Mandelson (1988: 11) contends that these objectives were broadly achieved by 1987.

The second step was to begin the party's communication effort, which started in advance of the actual election. Labour launched several 'mini-campaigns'. The first was called 'Jobs and Industry' and was launched in 1985. This was followed by 'Freedom and Fairness' in April 1986. Both were designed in response to the results of qualitative and quantitative research conducted by MORI and members of the SCA but did not necessarily increase electoral support. As Gould wrote about the first one in a letter to Peter Mandelson in November 1985 (quoted in Gould (1998b: 40)): 'I would think that there is a very good chance that it will prove much more effective in stimulating support at the grass roots and with party activists, than with projecting a message to the public at large.'

Another campaign called 'New Jobs for Britain' was inappropriate because, as Gould (1998b: 74) notes, it was launched 'against a background of a country basking in four years of sustained economic growth'. Joe Napolitan, who had been a political consultant to Walter Mondale in the USA, also advised Kinnock: for example he suggested he change his clothes so that he would look more like a Prime Minister.

### Stage 6: The election campaign

The election campaign was well planned and highly disciplined. Labour's performance was greatest in this Stage than any other of the marketing process, as would be expected from a Sales-Oriented Party. Planning began in early 1985. The Shadow Communications Agency (SCA) directed the actual campaign. There was a theme for each day that ran through all activities such as press conferences and photo opportunities. A Central Campaigner's unit established at Walworth Road helped co-ordination. Communication between different parts of the campaign organisation was high. Various daily and weekly meetings took place and feedback from the polls and the media was considered throughout. Candidates were briefed three times a day.

About half of the press conferences hosted by Neil Kinnock were held in London with the rest in regional centres. The leader and over forty senior party figures went on visits around the country. The party tried to ensure that every media region was visited each day by a notable politician. The location was chosen carefully 'to show Labour policies in action, while at the same time providing good interview opportunities, strong human interest and attractive, relevant pictures' (Hewitt and Mandelson (1989: 52)). The timing was also designed to suit television deadlines.

The first party election broadcast focused on Neil Kinnock, called *Kinnock: The Movie*. It took a biographical approach and presented a warm, caring image intended to extend to the party as a whole. It was made by Hugh Hudson, a former maker of TV commercials and now a film director. Labour's poll ratings experienced an increase immediately afterwards. Indeed, the campaign overall focused on Neil Kinnock. This responded to market intelligence by trying to improve the leader's standing. More generally, Labour attempted to focus on its own strengths and highlight opposition weaknesses. It argued that the Conservatives were authoritarian, would neglect the social problems facing the country and that proposals such as the poll tax were unfair. Advertising constantly criticised the Tory Party for not caring about groups such as the poor, sick and elderly. On the other hand, Labour's response to charges by the Conservatives that their proposals would cost an extra £35 billion was haphazard and ineffective.

The Labour Party's communication and campaigning were generally extremely professional. Mandelson (1988: 11) argued that the party responded positively to the introduction of 'modern marketing techniques'. But this was a Sales-Oriented Party approach. The party did not apply the market-oriented concept to its product. And as Mandelson (1988: 11) himself acknowledged, 'whilst absolutely necessary, good presentation and marketing by themselves are insufficient to ensure political success'. The Director of Campaigns and Communications could only control the presentation and communication of the party's behaviour: the party had to determine the behaviour itself. And the product itself was faulty: not even the most effective Sales-Oriented Party can make up for this.

### Stage 7: Election – the party's success in attracting support

Indeed, Labour's sales orientation had limited effect, as shown not just by electoral results but by public opinion.

*The general election*
Labour lost the election. It improved only slightly on the 1983 results, with 229 seats and 31.7 per cent of the vote. The party's own post-election analysis also revealed that what support it did attract was not because, but in spite of, the product design. Mandelson (1988: 11) noted that the top reasons given by voters for supporting Labour were that the party was seen as the best representative of the working class and they had always voted Labour. The foundations of this type of support were also likely to decline.

*Membership*
Membership fell further under Kinnock's leadership, from 295,344 in 1983 to 288,829 in 1987.

*Voter evaluations of party behaviour*
Labour had unpopular policies in areas of great importance to voters, such as unemployment and taxes (see Chapter 2 for further details). Kinnock received relatively low ratings as Party Leader: see Tables 4.1 and 4.2. Although he was seen as more likeable and caring, he was not seen as being the best potential Prime Minister or most likely to get things done.

**Table 4.1** *Best Prime Minister, July 1987*

*Question asked: Who would make the best Prime Minister?*

|          | %  |
|----------|----|
| Thatcher | 42 |
| Kinnock  | 31 |
| Owen     | 17 |
| Steel    | 10 |

*Source:* Gallup Political Index Report No. 323
(July 1987), p. 27, quoted by Heath *et al.* (1994: 130).
*Note:* n = 4,886.

**Table 4.2** *Voters' perceptions of the party leaders, 1987*

*Question asked: Would you describe Mrs Thatcher/Mr Kinnock as ...?*

|                            | Thatcher (%) | Kinnock (%) |
|----------------------------|--------------|-------------|
| Good at getting things done | 90           | 45          |
| Bad at getting things done  | 6            | 34          |

*Source:* BES (1987).
*Note:* n = 3,826.

76 per cent of respondents to the BES thought Labour was divided. Labour also faced a relatively united opposition which was generally perceived as capable of delivering. Labour was not seen to be capable of strong government: see Table 4.3.

**Table 4.3** *Party's capability of strong government, 1987*

*Question asked: On the whole, would you describe the Conservative/Labour Party as capable or not capable of strong government?*

|              | Capable (%) | Not capable (%) |
|--------------|-------------|-----------------|
| Conservative | 95          | 5               |
| Labour       | 36          | 64              |

*Source:* BES (1987).
*Note:* n = 3,826.

### Why Labour did not win: the failure of a sales orientation

Labour did not change its product sufficiently to attract enough votes to win the election. It only changed its communication: it was more like a

Sales-Oriented Party. Labour more or less retained the same pre-determined product design, but recognised that those whose support it needed to win the election would not necessarily vote for such a product. It then tried to persuade them that the party was right, and focused effort on selling. As O'Shaughnessy (1990: 2) notes, the quest for election:

> was not driven by any marketing concept: it was advertising devoid of the larger awareness that marketing brings, otherwise the Party would have attended more to the popularity of its 'products,' that is, its policies.

Gould (1998b: 81) supports this, admitting that Labour 'had modernised its communications, but not its policies or the Party itself, and the best communications professionals in the world could not rescue it'. In fact the focus on communication may have facilitated neglect of the product. As David Blunkett MP said (BBC (1995)) with regard to the Hudson broadcast, what Labour did was appeal 'to those around us in the media who would judge that our campaigning, that the Party political was a superb piece of presentation. It was. It didn't win us a single extra vote'. Furthermore and somewhat ironically, Labour's use of effective communication may also have constrained its future success: if the product is poor, it may be better to not convey it so well so that voters do not realise what the product is really like and are not so ready to reject it if it is not what they want.

### Why Labour could not adopt a market orientation by 1987

*The case for Kinnock's defence: obstacles against change*
Political marketing is not easy: it involves many difficult balancing acts and decisions and it is difficult for parties to adopt a market orientation in all aspects of their behaviour. Even if the leadership fully accepts the need for the party's behaviour to change, they may not be able to implement a new, more market-oriented product design. One reason, as suggested within the theoretical model, is internal party politics. As party leader Kinnock was determined to change the Labour Party, but implementing a market orientation proved highly difficult. Gould (1998b: 58) illuminates the difficulty faced in trying to move the party to a sales-oriented position, let alone a market orientation, as the work of the SCA grew:

> we had stepped into a morass, entering a party at war with itself at every level. The left-dominated NEC, which had shown little interest in campaigns and communications, in the past, saw us as a direct threat. Shadow Cabinet members were at best suspicious, at worst openly hostile. Labour had become so distanced from the public that we were going to have to fight the Party itself over every appeal to the voters.

Labour had, after all, been product-oriented only a few years ago. Not only were the party's existing policies unpopular but the organisational structure worked against changing them. This may explain why efforts during 1983–87 focused on changing the organisation rather than the product. Fielding (1995: 73) claimed that Neil Kinnock 'could not move ahead with reforming party policy as quickly as he might have liked'. Implementing a market orientation into the Labour Party was not easy. Nonetheless, the reality was that voters in the 1987 election did not make allowance for this.

*The case for attack: poor party management?*
The model takes account of these difficulties by noting the need for product adjustment and internal reaction analysis. It suggests that changes in policy need to be placed within or with reference to the party's traditional ideological framework. The leadership could consult the membership and MPs on how the party might change before it tells it to change. The implementation stage is also very important. As the model suggests, a party leadership intent on making the organisation more responsive to voters' demands will inevitably encounter some hostility and resistance. Firstly, just the idea of following rather than trying to lead public opinion can be controversial. Secondly, marketing often leads to a re-allocation of power within the party and the leader needs to be prepared for this and any resentment that might occur as a result. The leadership needs to try to ensure that important sectors of the party accept and understand the idea of a market orientation and the organisational and communication aspects of the implementation of marketing are crucial in this. Market intelligence needs to be disseminated widely, everyone in the party needs to be invited to contribute to ideas on how the party might behave and the leadership needs to create a feeling that members can contribute to the party's goals. This involves careful party management, which is not easy but vital for marketing to be implemented effectively.

Unsurprisingly, Kinnock did not use all these complex and subtle aspects of the model. His leadership lacked discussion with the membership, with power resting in the leader's office, rather than open discussion. Much of the work of the SCA was done in secret. The motion to adopt the red rose, for example, was carried out very cautiously. Peter Mandelson (quoted in Gould (1998b: 66)) explained how it was done at a Press and Publicity sub-committee NEC meeting. Mandelson gave a report and:

> said that we were introducing a new campaigning logo for the Party. We played it down, didn't say it was a change in corporate identity for the entire party, merely referred to it as a logo to use in our campaigns. They didn't know what a logo was or anything. I passed it round the committee. ... It

was all sort of 'yes, very good' and that was it and all agreed without anyone noticing.

Perhaps the change was made too quietly, however, for in the end when it came out at the 1986 party conference Gould (1998b: 66) notes how it came as a shock to the NEC: 'they hadn't really understood what we were up to'.

The beginning of marketing Labour's product rather than just its communications was therefore introduced through the back door. Even these small changes in the product were portrayed as changes in communication. A number of significant party figures were displaced in the move towards a sales orientation. There was a blurring of the design and communication of behaviour which should be kept separate. Such an approach is understandable and easier to manage in the immediate period, but laid problems for the long term. The party's internal culture worked against open change but this is a problem for the Labour Party in particular, not political marketing. It also relates to a general problem for party management and political leadership. Tony Blair did succeed where Kinnock had failed, proving it to be possible, albeit under circumstances where the party had lost further general elections. It depends upon the willingness of the party to change its behaviour to win an election: a factor occurring as a normal part of the democratic process rather than the use of political marketing.

Additionally, the movement to a sales orientation may have hindered the adoption of more market-oriented behaviour. Labour's use of political marketing in this period was simply changes in presentation, in advertising. This was not popular within the party. John Prescott for example, when discussing the introduction of the red rose as the party's symbol, said (BBC (1995)):

> I have a lot of criticisms to make of that ... because it seems to me that we were more caught up with image than substance. I've always been in politics to talk about ideas and how we change them. And whilst we were doing some of that, the greater attention had almost moved to winning by soundbites on radio and televisions, and the picture-spot and all those kind of things, and the rose was just part of that image.

Marketing, or any change, even when it was just the communications, therefore acquired negative association, particularly as some people gained more power in the party through the increased focus on selling. This may therefore have contributed towards creating obstacles against later moves to adopt a market orientation and hindered the party's ability to win the 1992 election.

## Summary

Whilst highlighting how not all parties use political marketing at all times, this further illustrates that a major party needs to become market-oriented in order to achieve electoral success. Although a Product-Oriented Party may be normatively favourable to some, it is not possible for a major party to adopt such an attitude and succeed in Britain today. Similarly, a Sales-Oriented Party, whilst exhibiting great ability in utilising the latest developments in technology, neglects attention to what really counts: the party's actual behaviour and potential effect on government and the people – substance over style. As Whyte (1988: 48–9) argued, 'whether the Labour Party will be more successful in future will depend on what changes in substance Mr Kinnock can bring about, rather than on a repackaging of their communications programme'. This argument did not go unheard within the Labour Party. Mandelson (1988: 13) conceded that: 'Next time ... we will need to get further in marketing the Party on the basis of our programme for government than our professionalism ... What we stand for and what we will actually do for people are the additional qualifications for success.' The next section will examine whether this was successful, by focusing on the 1992 general election.

## The limited effect of limited marketing: why Labour did not win in 1992

We have now effectively completed the building of the new model party ... The product is better, the unity is real, our democracy is healthier, our grass-roots more representative and the whole outlook now geared to the realities of government rather than the illusions of opposition. (Peter Mandelson, *Guardian* 16 February 1990)

Everything about an organisation talks. (Kotler and Levy (1969: 13))

We had every hope that Labour's weaknesses would drag them down. They were socialists, in a world that had turned against socialism; union-dominated when unions are demons from the past, and widely seen as a party that was still unable to be trusted on Europe, defence, and nationalism; led by a man whom it appeared the electorate neither trusted nor respected; and, most of all, a still thinly disguised party of tax and spending addicts. (John Wakeham (1995: 3))

The 1992 election result came as a surprise: the majority of political commentators expected a Labour victory or at least a Conservative loss. The polls predicted a hung Parliament, so it was somewhat unexpected. It caused much academic debate (see, for example, several chapters within Heath *et al.* (1994) for detailed discussion of why Labour lost). The question for this research is whether political marketing analysis can explain why the Conservatives managed to win again. Certainly, in terms of a market orientation, the parties were closer in this election than at any other and so this is the most difficult result to explain.

In the elections of 1979, 1983, 1987 and 1997 the contrast between the parties is significant enough to make it clear which one was most market-oriented. In 1979, the Conservative Party determined its behaviour to suit the electorate to a far greater extent than the Labour Party. The Conservatives engaged in far more comprehensive marketing intelligence and had a culture that aided a change in its behaviour to suit the findings. Their party organisation was clearly stronger than Labour's; they were was better funded, more clearly organised and there was more effective communication between the different components of the party. Their full-time constituency agents outnumbered Labour's by 346 to 70 and they spent an estimated five times as much as Labour on posters, press advertisements and party political broadcasts. The Tories were also more willing to use modern advertising techniques, in determining the leader's image, but also in their use of professionals, allowing Saatchi and Saatchi to get on with their job. The Labour leader dominated his party as much as he could, whilst Thatcher was much more willing to listen and heed views other than her own. More significantly, there was a stark contrast in popularity of their policies. Labour failed to be market-oriented and determine its proposals, let alone the rest of its behaviour, to suit the demands of the electorate.

In the 1983 election, the difference was even greater. The Conservative policies were far more in line with market opinion than were Labour's. Furthermore, the public believed they were more credible and that the party was more capable of governing and delivering them. Labour suffered from high levels of disunity and an unpopular leader, which contrasted strongly with the strong leadership and organisational coherence offered by the Tories. The dominant wing in Labour at the time of the 1983 election exhibited a product rather than a market orientation.

In the 1987 election, the Labour Party moved from a product towards a sales orientation, whilst the Conservative Party continued to offer a product which was broadly market-oriented. The election result was a rational response to the 'products' on offer. Labour also faced the problem of lacking credibility because of past behaviour: voters did not think it was fit to govern. The overall behaviour of the Conservatives was closer to a market orientation than Labour.

In 1997, the Labour Party was clearly the most market-oriented: indeed, its behaviour was the closest example of Market-Oriented Party ever seen in Britain. Labour conducted significant market intelligence, whereas the Conservatives neglected it. Labour designed its leadership,

148

MPs, membership nature and power, conferences, constitution, symbols and policies to suit voters, while the Conservatives had continued to push their existing design, despite failure to deliver on promises made in 1992. There is much evidence of target marketing by Labour, yet there is a striking lack of analysis of support by the Tories. The Conservative Party displayed public disunity while Labour's image was that of a strong, unified party ready for government. Conservative plans for the communication and campaign stages were haphazard, ever-changing and hindered by high turn-over of staff, but when it came to the election campaign Labour's work had already been done. The election result reflected the behaviour of the two parties.

During 1987–92, however, the Labour and the Conservative Party attempted to respond to voters' demands. Both engaged in the marketing techniques of market intelligence, communication and campaigning. The Labour leadership initiated an extensive review of all policy, changing at least parts of its behaviour to reflect electoral preferences. The Conservatives responded to the problems with Thatcher by a change in leader, recovering a sense of pragmatism towards the second half of the period. Nonetheless, detailed political marketing analysis reveals that overall Labour remained less popular on key parts of the product, such as the leader, certain policies and overall party unity and this chapter will show that the Conservatives remained the most market-oriented of the two.

### Labour

The third successive loss of a general election encouraged greater acceptance within the Labour Party of the need to respond to voter demands in order to win a future election. In marketing terms, the party attempted to move from a sales to a market orientation.

#### Stage 1: Market intelligence

Labour made extensive use of this stage of the marketing process. Firstly, it solicited substantial post-election market intelligence – a polling and demographic review about the party's declining electoral fortunes, called *Labour and Britain in the 1990s*, involving academics, economists and market researchers. This argued that problems were mainly due not to changes in society but to party behaviour.

This prompted further informal and formal market intelligence.

*Informal*

- A Policy Review which involved people from throughout the party (The Labour Party (1989: 5) and (1998: 1)).
- *Labour Listens* in 1987–88, a series of open meetings all over the country, although this was more an exercise in public relations. It enabled Neil Kinnock to claim that Labour had *shown* it was 'in touch with the values of the British people' (Labour Party (1990: 4)). It did not mean that it actually was.
- A centre–left think-tank was established in 1989 – the Institute of Public Policy Research – which also contributed to the policy review.

*Formal*

- Between November 1987 and April 1988, research was conducted on tax and benefits, which identified that voters were opposed to increased direct taxation.
- In 1990 NOP became Labour's main polling and survey agency; NOP conducted by-election polls and several studies of voters' attitudes in the run-up to the election.
- The party also used qualitative research and secondary analysis of existing material and focus groups to pre-test advertisements, policy and the Shadow Budget.
- Labour also spent £200,000 on intelligence during the campaign. NOP conducted daily surveys by phone, and a weekly panel. NOP also operated surveys in some marginal seats.

The influence of market intelligence on product design was, however, limited by opposition to change within the party. For example, according to Gould (1998b: 121–4) the party did not respond to the findings about tax. When the findings showing that around 70 per cent of those polled believed they would pay more tax under Labour were presented to the Shadow Cabinet, John Smith in particular rejected this, 'saying he wouldn't be lectured to by admen and pollsters'. When NOP identified that voters lacked trust in Labour's economic management, doubted how it would pay for its promises, felt that living standards would fall under Labour and that the party was against aspiration and advancement. Labour did nothing to address this.

One contributory factor to the limited effect of market intelligence may have been that the results of market intelligence were not widely disseminated. For example NOP reports went first to Philip Gould rather than all the party leadership. In another instance, Hewitt wrote a memo to the Campaign Team reporting the same findings from qualitative research, but Charles Clarke saw it and prevented it going to others. Problems with the leader were identified by market intelligence but Gould failed to present these results to Kinnock. Generally speaking, staff received results before politicians. Clearly the party made substantial, broad use of market intelligence but, as always, its effectiveness was constrained by its limited influence on the product design.

*Stage 2: Product design*

*Leadership*
Neil Kinnock continued to lack electoral appeal (see Tables 4.14 and 4.15). He did succeed in gaining more control over his party. He exercised increasingly strict party management over the Shadow Cabinet and front bench team. Those who were against change were isolated; the media were briefed in a way that discredited those who strayed from the favoured party line. For example, negative reports appeared in the press about Michael Meacher and Bryan Gould, both from the soft left. Both were later moved to lower positions within the party. This inevitably aroused some discontent within the party. Clare Short MP (BBC (1995)) recalls that:

> Under the Neil leadership, people around him misused the media and their contacts with the media to do over, and attack and undermine senior figures in the party who they were displeased with in some way ... I always thought it was disgraceful behaviour. Here was a leadership that was claiming it was wanting to reunite the party, using the media to attack senior levels of its own organisation.

It could be argued that this was done to ensure party unity and this is what voters wanted. Nonetheless the secretive way in which it was done remains open to criticism. It means that marketing was not an open process and the product design was never fully accepted within the party.

*MPs*
The leadership acquired greater control over candidate-selection, arguably to ensure that the MP aspect of the product was in line with voter demands. At the 1988 party conference, the National Executive Committee (NEC) obtained the power to intervene and determine the candidates for by-elections. It imposed its own candidate in the Liverpool Walton by-election in July 1991 and expelled two MPs, Terry Fields and David Nellist.

*Membership*
Kinnock began a process of changes in membership powers to increase the formal number and rights of the individual member but reduce the influence of activists. This responded to voters' demands by increasing individual-member democracy within the party, while at the same time eroding left-wing influence. The main changes were:

- The dependency of MPs to delegatory bodies in constituencies was reduced.
- The Constituency Labour Party vote at conferences was increased from 9 to 30 per cent.
- The party exercised more careful control over the membership, creating detailed definitions to enable exclusion if necessary, so that by 1992 the NEC had expelled over 100 members.
- Control over recruitment moved to the party's London headquarters.
- A campaign to increase membership was launched by Neil Kinnock in January 1989.

The opinions held by members remained out of line with public opinion, however. The results of a study of the Labour Party membership carried out in 1989–90 (Seyd and Whiteley (1992)) indicate that the majority of the party membership did not support many of the changes undertaken under Kinnock's leadership (see Table 4.4). The majority of members appear to have possessed an attitude more in line with a product orientation: over 60 per cent thought that 'the Labour Party should stand by its principles even if this should lose an election'.

*Staff*
The party's staff was increased, in terms of both the size and the range of professional expertise available. Its influence on party behaviour also increased. Neil Kinnock possessed capable staff within his own office, including Charles Clarke, Neil Stewart and Julie Hall (his Press Secretary). The Shadow Communications Agency (SCA) was co-ordinated by Philip Gould; it included senior party staff and professional experts. Jack Cunningham was Campaign Co-ordinator and also Chair of Labour's General Election Planning Group. Robin Cook was the 1992 campaign manager. The Directorship of Communications suffered from turnover, however, when Peter Mandelson left to take a safe Labour seat in Hartlepool in 1990. John Underwood became the new Director in July 1990 but felt undermined by his Deputy, Colin Byrne, who was closer to Mandelson and Kinnock. He resigned in July 1991 and David Hill took his place.

The expanding influence of certain officials also caused tension within the party. The relationship between the SCA and other parts of the party organisation was problematic. The SCA held meetings which Kinnock did not attend or were kept secret, excluding some senior party figures, while at the same time it became increasingly influential. Communication between key figures was therefore poor and there was some resentment between NEC members and party staff. Peter Mandelson was a particular source of discontent. The changes emanating from his advice aroused feelings of resentment from certain members. John Prescott (BBC (1995)) indicates how far Mandelson's influence extended beyond his specific

**Table 4.4** *Labour Party members: views on policy and organisation,*
*1989–90*

*Question asked: Next there is a set of statements about important political issues. We*
*would like to know if you agree or disagree with them. Please tick one box for each*
*statement: strongly agree, agree, neither, disagree, strongly disagree.*

| | Strongly agree (%) | Agree (%) | Neither (%) | Disagree (%) | Strongly disagree (%) |
|---|---|---|---|---|---|
| The production of goods and services is best left to a free market | 5.4 | 19.7 | 17.0 | 34.3 | 23.6 |
| The central question of British politics is the class struggle between labour and capital | 28.2 | 37.8 | 14.4 | 16.2 | 3.3 |
| The Public Enterprises privatised by the Tory Government should be returned to the public sector | 44.7 | 37.2 | 10.2 | 6.8 | 1.1 |
| Workers should be prepared to strike in support of other workers, even if they don't work in the same place | 15.4 | 45.1 | 18.1 | 14.6 | 6.7 |
| The next Labour Government should establish a prices and incomes policy as a means of controlling inflation | 24.9 | 39.2 | 16.4 | 14.8 | 4.7 |
| It is better for Britain when trade unions have little power | 3.5 | 9.6 | 13.3 | 44.6 | 29.0 |
| The next Labour Government should abolish private fee-paying education entirely | 3.5 | 9.6 | 13.3 | 44.6 | 29.0 |
| Further nuclear energy development is essential for the future prosperity of Britain | 3.5 | 8.9 | 8.2 | 35.8 | 43.7 |
| Constituency Labour Parties should have the exclusive right to select their own parliamentary candidates | 25.8 | 36.6 | 11.3 | 21.9 | 4.4 |
| The Labour Party should stand by its principles even if this should lose an election | 25.2 | 35.7 | 11.9 | 20.5 | 6.7 |

*Source:* Seyd and Whiteley (1992).
*Notes:* n = 5,065. These data were generated through a postal questionnaire, using a
two-stage systematic random sample of Labour Party members. Figures taken from
totals given in Appendix II of Seyd and Whiteley.

communication role to the design of actual behaviour:

> I think when you get very much caught up with the press and the media, people like Peter became extremely important as advisors in those areas. I thought he had extraordinary influence beyond what he should have exercised but I'm sure Peter would feel he was carrying out the job that he was expected to do. It's in that grey area of what you're doing for whom and who agrees it that we get these disagreements and the feelings of jealousy and the accusations of mythical power.

Indeed, Mandelson's departure occurred after a fraught period. John Underwood recalls (BBC (1995)) that Mandelson 'was in a sense a player in the game. He wasn't a neutral servant of the Party: he didn't claim to be, he didn't want to be . . . and therefore he tended to promote those people whose views he felt were in line with his own'. Hostility towards him increased during the summer of 1990 amidst disputes between other staff. David Hill (quoted in Gould (1998b: 107)), who became the new Director of Communications in July 1991, said when he took over, there was 'no sense of everybody running in the same direction. People didn't know who to trust. They had clearly in the previous year taken sides'. Informal greying or blurring of responsibility between staff and politician, adviser on communication and adviser on behaviour, clearly causes problems.

### Activities
Party conferences were designed to suit the electorate at large. The role they played in policy-making declined. There was little substantial debate. For example, the policy review report of 1989–90 was presented to conference to accept or reject as a whole, not one item at a time, reducing the chance for dissent. The rights of members to voice their opinion on party decisions was carefully controlled in order to prevent the party from appearing disunited to the wider electorate.

### Policy proposals
The party's final manifesto, launched on 18 March 1992, built on reports from the Policy Review (see The Labour Party (1988, 1989, 1990 and 1991)). It was called *It's Time to Get Britain Working Again* (see The Labour Party (1992)). Labour's policy commitments were most significantly altered in the areas of defence, the economy and its relations with the trade unions. The main changes were:

- a move away from state intervention; discarding public ownership as a major object of party policy: instead a policy to subject those industries already privatised to increased regulation and competition;
- the abandonment of the unpopular defence policy of unilateralism: instead, a promise to keep all nuclear weapons and stay in NATO;

- the revision of full employment as a goal;
- consideration of the end consumers of public services, aiming to improve their quality;
- a weakening of the party's traditionally strong relationship with the trade unions. A Labour Government would not simply repeal all union legislation enacted by Conservative Governments, but the party would continue to pursue good conditions and rights for workers;
- a more positive approach to Europe.

Labour's most unpopular policies were therefore removed, but this does not mean that all policies were market-oriented. During the review there was continual resistance to responding to results of market intelligence and the policies it produced reflected this. Traditional attitudes remained within the manifesto. Neil Kinnock's foreword is very negative, criticising every-thing the Conservative Government had done, combined with a vague assertion of Labour's values and visions. The opening to the first section is entitled 'Immediate action for national recovery' and speaks of fear and recession. It contends that a new Labour Government would be able to solve this, by creating a 'National Recovery Programme' and goes on to provide a list of extra investments it would make, which suggested a traditional socialist approach to managing the Government. For example (see the Labour Party (1992): Section One):

- Housing investment will generate jobs.
- Additional resources of at least £600 million will be available for investment in education.
- Additionally at least £1 billion will be available for investment in the National Health Service.

In some ways the party was responding to a general desire for greater state provision or action on problem areas. The BES indicates that a majority of voters wanted greater welfare provision: see Table 4.5.

**Table 4.5** *Voters' views on welfare benefits, 1992*

*Question asked: I want to ask about some changes that have been happening in Britain over the years. Please say whether you think it has gone too far, not gone far enough, or is it about right: the welfare benefits that are available to people today*

|  | % |
| --- | --- |
| Gone too far | 17 |
| About right | 37 |
| Not gone far enough | 46 |

*Source:* BES (1992).
*Notes:* n = 2,855. 'Gone too far' combines 'Gone much too far' and 'Gone too far';
'Not enough' combines 'Not gone far enough' and 'Not gone nearly far enough'.

General survey questions on voters' views also suggested that they wanted more Government spending in certain areas such as health and education: see Table 4.6.

**Table 4.6** *Voters' views on what Government should do, 1992*

*Question asked: Please say whether you think the Government should or should not do each of the following things, or doesn't it matter either way?*

|  | Should (%) | Does not matter (%) | Should not (%) |
|---|---|---|---|
| Spend more money to get rid of poverty | 92 | 2 | 5 |
| Put more money into the NHS | 92 | 3 | 4 |
| Spend more money on education | 92 | 3 | 3 |

*Source:* BES (1992).
*Notes:* n = 2,855. 'Should' combines 'Definitely should' and 'Probably should'; 'Should not' combines 'Probably should not' and 'Definitely should not'.

Nevertheless, Labour did not respond to these specific demands but looked at other areas. For example it:

• proposed that child benefit and old-age pensions would be increased;
• promised to introduce a minimum wage which was 50 per cent of median earnings.

Labour's Shadow Budget in March 1992, just before the election, confirmed the party's plans to increase the top rate of income tax. Unfortunately this pushed the tax issue high on the agenda. Labour arguably responded to the general feeling or area of concern amongst voters, but did not create the desired measure to deal with such problems. Labour also lacked governing competence, especially on the economy (see Tables 4.21 and 4.22). A majority of voters thought that a Labour Government would lead to an increase in taxes, inflation and strikes. Labour was also criticised for lacking a strong alternative to the Conservative product. The Policy Review removed Labour's most apparent weaknesses, but did so without creating any new strengths.

### Stage 3: Product adjustment

*Achievability*
Labour did not succeed in trying to make its product achievable. The policy review produced policies and spending plans that were only suitable to the economic conditions prevailing at time of writing. As Cook (1995: 17) conceded, by the time of the election in 1992 its plans were 'expensive'

and 'lacking in ... relevance' to the problems in 1992. The party needed
to produce policies that would be suitable for any conditions: not some that
would be rendered out of date within a matter of years. Labour was also
highly criticised by the Conservatives for failing to make it clear where the
money was coming from to pay for its spending pledges.

*Internal reaction analysis*
The Labour leadership tried to manage the party carefully. For example,
the defence policy was carefully designed to suit two strands of opinion: for
and against nuclear weapons. The majority of party activists believed in
unilateralism, but senior party figures argued that it needed to be abandoned because it was electorally unpopular. Labour qualified its new
commitment to keeping nuclear weapons by establishing a policy of 'no
first use' and cancelling the fourth Trident submarine. The Labour Party
(1989: 5) also claimed that many constituency parties 'discussed the
issues' and gave input into the policy review, but this is highly disputable.
The review process had been carefully controlled by the leader's office.
Kinnock tried to create groups with a political balance which would
produce the results he wanted. The drafting and final editing was done by
Kinnock and his staff. As already discussed, that some party figures were
sidelined using the media indicates that the leadership did not, ultimately,
take account of their views.

*Competition analysis*
Labour engaged in comprehensive and well-researched analysis of the
opposition for the election campaign. The Shadow Communications
Agency (SCA) gave various presentations that identified Labour's strengths
and weaknesses. Labour attempted to focus on its own strengths, such as
health, during the campaign. It created a special Party Election Broadcast
but this created a controversy that distracted from the issue.

*Support analysis*
The Shadow Communications Agency (SCA) made numerous presentations to the party leadership, identifying particular sections of the
electorate, such as the undecided and non-voters, whose support the party
needed to attract. The report *Meet the Challenge, Make the Change* (The
Labour Party (1989)) advocated policy positions to appeal to selected voter
groups: home buyers, upwardly mobile white-collar workers and professionals. Labour's General Election Planning group identified key seats the
party needed to win to gain control of the Government. Labour also developed a campaigning organisational structure that focused on key
marginals.

*Stage 4: Implementation*

The Labour Party's attitude to market-oriented political marketing was more positive than ever before. The main reason was the poor 1987 election results. Although many felt that the 1987 election campaign had gone well, there was a growing realisation that the party had not changed enough to win. Its organisational structure was also much more amenable to change: the leadership exercised significant control over the party and decision-making. This does not mean that all within the party accepted the changes, however. Even at the top level there was some resistance. This provoked tension between those who wanted to respond to voters' opinions and those who wanted to hold on to political convictions. This was also exacerbated by confusion and resentment arising from the change in power distribution away from politicians towards the staff. Although the Labour Party was more unified behind the product it had on offer than in past elections, changes had really only taken place at the top, not through all levels of the party. The views of the membership were certainly out of line with those of the leadership.

*Stage 5: Communication*

The Labour Party began to put effort and planning into its communications from July 1991 onwards but it was not overly successful. The party launched a summer campaign in 1991 called 'Ready for Government' to convey that it was capable of governing, but this did not receive much attention. The Government dominated the news agenda with foreign visits made by the Prime Minister. A new campaign called 'Secret Agenda' was then launched to suggest that the Tories would privatise health and education, responding to market intelligence that suggested this is what voters thought they would do. It was relatively effective, according to the polls. In early 1992, Labour launched a mini-campaign called 'Made in Britain', concerning its economic vision and policy of modernisation, rather than privatisation, but this may have served to reinforce the party's socialist or product-oriented history. It also attempted to attack the Conservatives' economic strategy but faced a battle over its own taxation plans. Labour tried to convey an image of economic competence: John Smith, the Shadow Chancellor of the Exchequer, met with businessmen on many occasions and the Shadow Budget was presented very formally.

*Stage 6: The election campaign*

Labour had gone through the marketing process relatively well but with inconsistencies, problems and with important aspects such as policy, leadership and membership remaining out of line with market demands. The campaign could have been very important, but in this Labour actually lost some of the sales-oriented status it had achieved in 1987. The campaign was generally well planned but possibly too inflexible and the organisation had many tensions and disputes within its personnel. Gould tried to respond to tensions by creating a series of meetings by a CAT (Campaign Advisory Team), chaired by Jack Cunningham, but these meetings were kept secret because he thought Walworth Road would object to it. Decisions the CAT made permeated the campaign subtlety without making it clear where they came from. Hewitt (quoted in Gould (1998b: 108)) recalls:

> We would have this secret meeting, then you would head down to Walworth Road for the official meetings. It was a joke. Parallel decision-making structures. You had a secret meeting structure with people brought in from the outside to compensate for the fact that the people on the inside couldn't do the job.

There were many other meetings and Hewitt and Gould's influence went beyond their formal role. They would argue this was necessary in order to prevent the campaign turning into chaos. Nevertheless, as Gould (1998b: 113–14) recalls, 'by the start of the election a campaign machine that had been brilliant in 1987 and strong in 1990 had weakened almost to breaking-point. . . . The campaign team was riven with suspicion bordering on paranoia; lines of command were confused; and the leader of the Party was isolated from his own campaign team'.

Labour tried to focus on one of its strengths, health, by creating a Party Election Broadcast about two girls with the same illness, put out on 24 March. One of these had private health-care; the other relied on the NHS and so had her operation delayed. The impact of the broadcast was hindered by the media's discovery of the identity of the girl on whom it had been based. Debate moved on to Labour's use of such a story. Consequently, the media focused on the circumstances behind the production of the broadcast rather than its actual content and message. The whole episode is now referred to as the 'Jennifer's ear saga'. Cook (BBC (1995)) suggests that the problem was in part due to a lack of party control:

> This was a clear example where presentation had got to the point that it was no longer under political control and where a whole broadcast had been prepared without the participation or the knowledge of the spokesperson involved. I firmly believe that it is important that yes, we use communication experts; yes, we use the skills of people who can put across our message more effectively than we can. But we have to remain in control of the message.

The campaign's last week was also damaged because Labour was exhausted, the Conservatives increased their effort, and then Neil Kinnock raised the possibility of electoral reform even though Labour had not worked out a policy on the issue. This damaged voters' perception of the party's general governing competence. Another event criticised was the Sheffield Rally, held on 2 April. It displayed the Shadow Cabinet as the future Government and made full use of presentational devices in a cele- bratory manner. Arguably, this was aimed more at Labour's internal supporters than the whole electorate but as Hill (1995: 37) contends: 'It concentrated the minds, not only of journalists and commentators, but of the wider electorate, which began to concentrate not on the nebulous prospect of a Labour victory, but, for the first time, on the reality of a Labour victory.' This would still mean that voters did not want Labour to win: the Labour Party's product was not sufficiently market-oriented. Indeed, Gould (1998b: 158) firmly contended that post-election polling made it clear that Labour: 'lost because people thought they had left the Party, and the Party had left them ... The electorate looked onwards and upwards ... Labour looked downwards ... if Labour was to have a chance of winning, it had to change completely'.

Hill (1995: 39) cites the party's behaviour as a barrier to voters supporting Labour. Canvassers found that voters 'felt that Labour was a party which was no longer in tune with them' (Hill 1995: 39). This indi- cates that the party lacked a market orientation: it was not responding to what voters really wanted. Policy still contained socialist elements and the party was perceived to have strong links with the trade unions. It could also be criticised for not offering anything new. David Lipsey (1992: 1) commented that: 'The concept of a party without ideas may have a certain appeal for image makers and politicians of the most pragmatic and least imaginative ilk. It has none for most people in the Party. ... Labour, they believe, must believe in something or it is nothing'.

### The Conservatives

The problems with Labour's behaviour therefore gave the Conservatives a chance to win, especially because they managed to maintain a market orientation and many of their traditional assets. Although in the early period there were problems, they recovered their sense of pragmatism towards the end by changing the Party Leader and responding to voter dissatisfaction. It could not be claimed that the Conservatives were a classic example of a Market-Oriented Party but overall it remained more market-oriented than Labour.

*Previous marketing – Stage 8: Delivery under John Major*

Conservative delivery was a mixture of problems and success.

*The poll tax*
The new leader, John Major, transformed the party's attitude to the problematic poll tax. The March 1991 budget increased grants from central government to local authorities in order to reduce poll tax bills. Major appointed Michael Heseltine to create a replacement local tax and in October 1991 the Government launched plans for a new council tax based on property value.

*The economy*
The Government experienced difficulty in responding to the economic situation. In August 1990, while Major was Chancellor of the Exchequer, the Government entered into the Exchange-Rate Mechanism (ERM), but was later forced to bow out under Major's premiership when a crisis emerged during the deep recession in summer 1992. Furthermore, the Government's response was easily criticised. Major's government firstly denied the problem, then it agreed there was a problem but said it would get better. When the problem continued, it attempted to deflect blame by pointing to the poor situation all over the world. Then, as time came closer to the election, it claimed that in any case it would be worse under a Labour Government. Sanders (1992: 198–9) argues that evidence suggests that voters did not view Major's Government as responsible for economic problems. In this respect it is arguable that the Conservatives did not really deliver, but were still able to gain more electoral support than the opposition.

*Europe*
Major built a more co-operative relationship with European leaders than Thatcher while at the same time resisting the loss of future control. He achieved a compromise at the Maastricht Summit in December 1991, whereby Britain would opt out of implementing the Social Charter and monetary union but retain the option to join at a later date.

*Other areas*
The Conservatives fulfilled several promises of further privatisation. Attempts were also made to introduce an internal market into the National Health Service. NHS hospitals could become trusts and doctors could apply for the right to allocate their own budgets. These changes were heavily criticised by Labour and polls indicated that the public was at the least unsure about them. In August 1990 Saddam Hussein seized Kuwait and

Britain entered into the Gulf War against him and succeeded in making him pull out. Major's handling of this crisis received broad public approval.

Delivery was therefore not a complete failure, but it was not going to win the election for the Conservatives either. They still had to go through the marketing process all over again.

## Stage 1: Market intelligence

The Tories conducted substantial market intelligence.

### Formal

* A big programme of qualitative market intelligence was commissioned in December 1989, run by Dick Wirthlin who had worked as a consultant on Ronald Reagan's presidential campaigns; in-depth, highly qualitative interviews were run with voters to discover their values; Harris carried out the work.
* Extensive polling of voter attitudes was conducted from October 1991 onwards.
* Harris was commissioned to conduct polls of marginal seats.
* £250,000 was spent on polls for the campaign: Harris conducted full-scale surveys; qualitative focus groups; weekly surveys; two 'quickie' surveys; surveys where Liberal Democrats were a threat; a one-off 800-sample survey in 10 West-Midlands marginals and qualitative studies with floating voters.
* Public polls were analysed.

### Informal

* Informal advice was sought from Gordon Heald, Head of Gallup, and Robert Worcester of MORI.
* A number of policy groups were set up just before Thatcher resigned, consisting of MPs and Conservative-supporting experts, to evaluate existing policy and suggest new ones. They submitted reports to Chris Patten and the No. 10 Policy Unit.
* Senior ministers were also invited to contribute to policy design.
* The Research Department also prepared 'vital background material' which was used in communication and campaigning.

The Wirthlin qualitative research was highly expensive and was ended in March 1991 without exerting much influence on party behaviour. The polling of voter attitudes revealed that nearly 80 per cent of people believed that Labour would raise taxes, which the Tories used in their product design and campaign.

*Stage 2: Product design*

*Leadership*

John Major, formerly Chancellor of the Exchequer, won the party election contest and so became Prime Minister. Major's background was more similar to those of ordinary voters: he was from Brixton, left school at sixteen, had been unemployed and had worked his way up through a career in banking and local politics. He was only forty-eight years old. Overall, though, John Major appealed to the public far more than Kinnock (see Tables 4.14–6 below). He was a huge electoral advantage for the Conservatives: it was almost as if, with Major becoming leader, the whole party or product had changed. His attitude towards Europe was much more conciliatory than Thatcher's. He built a good relationship with European leaders. His handling of the Gulf War and relationship with US President Bush and other allies established him as a good leader in a crisis. His style with regard to the party was also well liked. He formed his Cabinet carefully, including his former contenders in the leadership election. He was willing to listen to different views and criticism at Cabinet meetings. He encouraged them to think of their own ideas on policy; giving them greater autonomy to fulfil their position. Major also proved popular in the House of Commons.

*Membership*

The Conservative membership suffered a significant loss of morale during the implementation of the poll tax. Members came into direct contact with those badly affected by it. Calls came from the grass-roots and CCO for the Government to take action to reduce the levels of the bills, but this was rejected, although ultimately it proved necessary. The relationship between the leadership and the membership was further strained by the leadership contest in which Thatcher resigned. However John Major and Chris Patten worked carefully to reduce any division and Major quickly attracted the support of the membership.

*Staff*

Major made a number of changes to his staff once he became leader. Under John Major, the No. 10 Policy Unit became more influential in the design of policy. Major also appointed Chris Patten as Party Chairman. Patten already had experience working in CCO, he was very interested in communication and campaigning and also had experience writing manifestos. When Patten took control of CCO it had many problems: lack of funds, an advertising agency, a new policy design, electoral strategy and an election was just under two years away. In this context, Patten's Chairmanship was extremely successful, increasing funds, creating new Deputy Chairs to be able to spend more time in No. 10 building up close relationships with John Major and the Policy Unit and getting involved in the detail of Government policy. Patten appointed Shaun Woodward as Director of Communications. Woodward had relevant professional experience, as did other staff recruited in communication. A number of agencies were considered to do the advertising. Saatchi was re-appointed in 1991.

*Symbols*
The new Director of Communications, Brendan Bruce, created a new logo for the party in 1989. This was a torch and flame.

*Policy proposals*
The final manifesto was launched on 18 March 1992. It was called *The Best Future for Britain* (see The Conservative Party (1992)). The document was long: 30,000 words. It contained details of previous action, future promises and Labour's policies. It was drawn up by the No. 10 Policy Unit. The party did not want to change its policies completely: it wanted to indicate how different John Major was to Margaret Thatcher, without dismissing all Thatcher's achievements. The manifesto proposed:

- further privatisation: selling British Coal, local authority bus companies and parts of British Rail;
- the establishment of an Urban Regeneration Agency for cities;
- a rent-to-mortgage scheme for council tenants;
- reducing waiting times for the NHS;
- a Millennium Fund to increase the support given to the arts and heritage;
- increase in the tax threshold for inheritance tax;
- encouragement of private pensions;
- membership of the ERM to control inflation.

Not all these proposals were market-oriented. For example, Table 4.7 does not indicate support for further privatisation.

**Table 4.7** *Voters' views on nationalisation, 1992*

*Question asked: Are you generally in favour of more nationalisation or privatisation?*

|  | % |
| --- | --- |
| More nationalisation | 22 |
| More privatisation | 22 |
| Left as they are | 52 |

*Source:* BES (1992).
*Note:* n = 2,625.

The Tory manifesto could also be criticised for neglecting to respond to voter concerns about the public services and welfare provision or at least for greater government spending in certain areas (see Tables 4.5 and 4.6 above). Arguably, the party did respond to this but with a different solution to meet the ends, with the Citizen's Charter. This was Major's initiative, launched in July 1991 then re-launched in January 1992. It was intended to improve the quality of public and privatised services, by giving consumers more information about their rights, including the right of appeal and complaint. It was in response to growing voter dissatisfaction with public services.

### Stage 3: Product adjustment

*Achievability*
The manifesto was subject to discussion with ministers. For example, Norman Lamont cut out the proposal to abolish inheritance tax completely in order to ensure that the Conservatives' promises were achievable. They still presented themselves as the party of low tax. In their manifesto they claimed: 'We are the only party that understand the need for low taxation' and reiterated their commitment towards a basic income tax rate of 20p (The Conservative Party (1992): Section Two, Wealth and Ownership). At the same time they affirmed their commitment to the public services such as the NHS (National Health Service) and Education (see The Conservative Party (1992): Section Four: Opportunity for All and Section Six: Responsibility for Others). Nevertheless it is arguable that promises to further reduce tax and improve public services were not really achievable.

*Internal reaction analysis*
The leadership sought input from the party through the policy groups and the unit in the Cabinet office before the preparation of the manifesto. Francis Maude, Treasury Minister, also chaired meetings with ministers to ensure agreement on policy.

*Competition analysis*
The Conservatives turned their own weakness into a Labour weakness, by changing the argument about the state of the economy into an issue of probable economic competence, on which Labour would lose. They also attacked Labour on tax, claiming that it was the party of high tax increases. They attempted to co-opt traditional Labour strengths by trying to be more caring. Market intelligence identified that health was the biggest 'caring' issue. The Conservatives argued that they had increased spending on health and the NHS was in a good state, but Labour continued to lead on this issue. During the election campaign they announced

new spending pledges: a £3.5 billion spending package on defence, roads, health and welfare. They also announced the creation of a national lottery. These, and other moves, were partly in response to Labour becoming much stronger.

The Conservatives were also firmly aware of Labour weaknesses. John Wakeham (1995: 3) later recalled how Major's conviction that the Tories would win was 'born of evidence and analysis' and they 'knew that there was every chance of high spending and high-taxing Labour candidates losing votes'. Contrasting Labour policies were included within the manifesto. Party staff advised that senior figures should try to increase public awareness of the defence issue because this was a Conservative strength but also a clear difference with Labour. The insights gained from this competition analysis were used accordingly to inform communication and campaigning.

*Support analysis*
The Conservatives made good use of this stage, focusing on voters whose support they did not have but needed to win. Campaigning efforts were focused in the 100 most marginal seats. The campaign also used targeting in the communication stage, focusing on former Conservatives, voters who held positive perceptions of John Major but did not support the party and middle-aged C2 men.

### Stage 4: Implementation

The Conservative Party as a whole remained committed to marketing and in support of the need to change behaviour to suit electoral opinion. Thatcher's leadership moved away from this, but her downfall and the election of John Major showed that the party's MPs, at least, had not. Under Major's leadership the party re-gained some of the ground it had lost and started to appeal once again to the public. The party was also broadly united under Major (see Table 4.17 below).

### Stage 5: Communication

The Conservatives were extremely successful in using this stage of the marketing process. They engaged in communication well before the actual election. A No. 12 Committee was created in February 1991, made up of staff and senior party figures, became increasingly involved in general party communication and even met daily. In September 1991 staff visited the USA and those who had advised Presidents Reagan and Bush. They were particularly interested in the Reagan 1984 campaign, which had been fought in a recession. They discovered that the Reagan team had made greater use of the months before the campaign, in which they attempted to control the agenda through co-ordinated communications. On their return the UK staff therefore introduced a longer and more co-ordinated communication effort. Patten asked Andrew Lansley, Director of the Research Department, to prepare a strategy paper, drawing on discussions with ministers' political advisers and advice from the advertising agency Saatchi. This was considered by the No. 12 Committee, the No. 10 Policy Unit, and Cabinet, from which a paper of some fifty pages called *The Near Term campaign* was produced in mid-November, outlining a plan to control the agenda.

Senior party figures were also actively encouraged to think about the forthcoming election. In a paper to the Cabinet for 19 December 1991, Patten (quoted in Butler and Kavanagh (1992: 82)) wrote: 'It is a half-way house between customary activity and election conditions. . . . It means . . . adopting the election campaign imperative that each of us participates to the full in getting the Party's message across.'

The Prime Minister also tried to increase ministers' attention to the election. He ended each Cabinet meeting with an item to discuss the election without civil servants present. He encouraged ministers to seek and accept interviews with the media. Staff met with each Cabinet Minister between 29 November and 19 December to advise them on what to say and what to avoid, dependent on results from market intelligence showing whether the party was weak or strong on an issue.

The party was relatively successful in its communication effort. In mid-June 1991, a 'mini-campaign' was launched, called *Labour's Going for Broke Again* which attacked Labour's spending promises. This theme was played out in election broadcasts, posters, speeches and continued in the campaign. Another mini-campaign that attacked Labour's links with the unions and commitment to the European Social Chapter was launched in the summer. Various posters were launched that responded to the findings from market intelligence which suggested that voters believed that Labour would increase taxes. In January 1992, the poster entitled *Labour's Tax Bombshell* was produced. This pictured a World War II bomb, under which was the slogan 'You'd pay £1,000 more tax a year under Labour'. In February they launched one called *Labour's Double Whammy* under which was written '1. More Taxes, 2. Higher Prices.' The Conservatives also put considerable effort into communicating the argument that no matter how bad the economy was, it (and voters) would be worse under Labour. This enabled them to control the agenda in the months immediately preceding the formal election campaign. They pushed those issues on which they were strong, such as tax, economic policy and law and order, high on to the agenda. These were also Opposition weaknesses.

*Stage 6: The election campaign*

By the start of the formal election campaign on 13 March the Tories' message had already been well communicated. Chris Patten managed the campaign effectively. The Conservatives used the slogan 'You Can't Trust Labour'. This was displayed with the 'L' in Labour as a red learner-driver symbol. It was extensively pre-tested. Maurice Saatchi (quoted in Rosenbaum (1997: 159)) observed that the Conservatives: 'chose the learner symbol after the most comprehensive research every undertaken for a political slogan. Our focus groups concluded that Labour were inexperienced, incompetent, unqualified and had never passed the test.'

Posters were used most effectively: 4,500 were produced. The party re-launched those already created; the figure used for the poster 'Labour's Tax Bombshell' was increased to £1,250 and exhibited on 22 March. A positive message was sent out in the last five days of the campaign with the launch of a poster picturing John Major and some children, with the slogan 'The Best Future for Britain'. Posters were also placed as the backdrop for daily press conferences so that they would be conveyed via television news. Large press advertisements were taken out on 3 April.

The Conservatives exploited Labour weaknesses, especially how voters perceived them to be against aspiration. John Major made a speech in Manchester on 19 March, mimicking an earlier speech by Kinnock and warning voters of what might happen after a Labour victory: 'I warn you not to be qualified. I warn you not be successful. I warn you not to buy shares. I warn you not to be self-employed. I warn you not to accept promotion. I warn you not to save. I warn you not to buy a pension. I warn you not to own a home.'

John Major played a major part in the Conservative campaign. One party election broadcast attempted to convey the image of the 'common man', by featuring him going from Brixton to Downing Street. *Meet John Major* question and answer sessions were held between Major and Conservative-inclined voters. He also used a so-called 'soapbox' on which he stood to talk to people on the street during the campaign. Wakeham (1995: 7) contends that this 'capitalised on his popular personality'. It promoted the feeling that he was in touch with the ordinary voter (see also Woodward (1995: 35)). During the last week of the campaign the focus moved on to him.

Overall, the Conservatives in 1992 offered a product that was broadly market-oriented: a leader, John Major, who was popular, economic competence and low rates of direct taxation.

*Stage 7: Election – the parties' success in attracting support*

The results reflected the Conservatives' marginally greater degree of market orientation than Labour.

*The general election*
The Conservative Party won the 1992 election. They achieved 41.8 per cent of the popular vote and 336 seats, compared to Labour's 34.3 per cent and 271 seats. The majority in the House of Commons was 21. Conservative support was strong in the South of England, East Anglia and the Midlands; Labour in the North of England, Wales and Scotland. The Conservatives' success was therefore tempered by a loss of seats compared with the previous election and small majority. This partly reflects how although the party's degree of market orientation under John Major was significantly greater than Labour, the difference was not as substantive as in previous elections.

*Membership*
The membership drive attempted under Kinnock was not successful. Labour membership levels grew and then fell again in the 1987–92 period: see Table 4.8.

**Table 4.8** *Labour membership, 1987–92*

| 1987 | 288,829 |
|------|---------|
| 1990 | 311,152 |
| 1991 | 261,000 |
| 1992 | 279,000 |

*Source:* as for Table 1.2.

Furthermore, in their 1989–90 study of the Labour Party Membership, Seyd and Whiteley (1992: 89) reported a qualitative decline: a reduction in activity amongst the members surveyed. That activists arguably helped to attract external support for the party renders this an even bigger problem. The Conservative Party's membership levels halved in the 1987–92 period, from 1,000,000 to 500,000, reflecting the discontent at the lower level. It still remained higher than Labour.

*Voter evaluations of party behaviour*
The Conservatives had overall more popular policies, leadership, unity and governing competence. Table 4.9 shows how a majority of voters favoured the policies offered by the Tories.

**Table 4.9** *Party with best policies overall, 1992*

*Question asked: Taking everything into account, which party has the best policies?*

|  | % |
|---|---|
| Conservative | 46 |
| Labour | 37 |
| Liberal Democrat | 14 |
| Other | 2 |

*Source:* Gallup post-election survey, adapted from that quoted in Sanders (1992: 195).
*Note:* 'Don't knows' excluded from the percentage base.

The difference between the two was insubstantial, as reflected in more detailed analysis by a MORI panel survey: see Table 4.10.

**Table 4.10** *Best party policy on key issues, 1992*

*Question asked: I am going to read out a list of problems facing Britain today. I would like you to tell me whether you think the Conservative Party, the Labour Party or the Liberal Democrats has the best policies on each problem.*

|  | *Labour or Conservative better policy (% lead over the other)* |
|---|---|
| Defence | Conservative (27) |
| Law and order | Conservative (14) |
| Europe | Conservative (10) |
| Northern Ireland | Conservative (8) |
| Taxation | Conservative (5) |
| Managing the economy | Conservative (4) |
| Trade unions | Labour (3) |
| Education | Labour (14) |
| Public transport | Labour (15) |
| Housing | Labour (22) |
| Unemployment | Labour (24) |
| Health care | Labour (30) |

*Source:* MORI polls.
*Notes:* n = c. 1,000 or 2,000, surveys based on GB residents aged 18 +. Poll taken 23 March, except for transport which was taken 17–21 January and trade unions which was taken 30 March.

Sanders (1992: 194) argues that this nonetheless translated into votes: 'The overall percentage of respondents thinking that each of the major parties had the best policies broadly corresponds with the vote shares that the parties actually received.'

Voters' perceptions were much more ambiguous in 1992. Table 4.11 indicates that the issues which were most important to voters' decision on which party to support were those on which Labour scored more highly: health care, education and unemployment.

**Table 4.11** *Issues important to vote, 1992*

*Question asked: Which two or three issues will be most important to you in helping you to decide which party to vote for at the general election?*

|  | % |
| --- | --- |
| NHS/Health care | 59 |
| Education/schools | 48 |
| Unemployment/jobs | 38 |
| Inflation/prices | 20 |
| Tax cuts | 13 |
| Housing | 10 |
| Law and order | 8 |
| Defence generally | 6 |
| Interest rates | 6 |
| Pollution/the environment | 6 |
| AIDS | 6 |
| Immigration | 2 |
| EC/Common Market | 2 |
| Public transport | 2 |
| Rent/rates | 1 |
| Trade unions | 1 |
| Drugs | 1 |
| Foreign policy generally | 1 |
| Northern Ireland | 1 |
| Other | 21 |
| Don't know | 3 |

*Source:* MORI/*Sunday Times* Panel survey.
*Notes:* The MORI/*Sunday Times* Panel baseline consisted of a nationally representative sample of 1,544 adults aged 18+ in 65 constituency sampling points throughout Great Britain, first interviewed between 11 and 12 March 1992. Subsequently, 1,257 (81%) members of the original panel were re-interviewed on 18–20 March, 1,292 (84%) on 25–27 March, and 1,265 (82%) on 1–3 April. Re-interview responses were weighted by first-week voting intention. Figures shown are those taken on 1–3 April.

Table 4.12 indicates that the majority of voters also believed that the Conservative Party was the best to handle most key issues, such as Europe, taxation, law and order, inflation, defence and strikes, but Labour scored highly on the important issues such as health and education.

**Table 4.12** *Voters' perceptions of the best party to handle key issues, April 1992*

|  | Conservative best | Labour best |
| --- | --- | --- |
| Defence | 52 | 22 |
| Strikes | 48 | 30 |
| Europe | 46 | 26 |
| Inflation | 45 | 30 |
| Taxation | 42 | 31 |
| Law and order | 41 | 29 |
| Environment | 21 | 25 |
| Status of women | 23 | 38 |
| Education | 27 | 41 |
| Transport | 25 | 46 |
| Pensions | 29 | 47 |
| Homelessness | 20 | 48 |
| Unemployment | 26 | 48 |
| National Health Service | 25 | 51 |

*Source:* Gallup pre-election survey, 7–8 April 1992, adapted from that quoted in Sanders (1992: 209).

Table 4.13 shows how maintaining order in the nation, or the issue of crime, continued to be a most important issue: this was traditionally a Conservative strength and a Labour weakness.

**Table 4.13** *Voters' most desirable option, 1992*

*Question asked: If you had to choose from among the items below, which seems the most desirable to you?*

|  | % |
| --- | --- |
| Maintaining order in the nation | 42 |
| Fighting rising prices | 22 |
| Giving people more say in important political decisions | 12 |
| Protecting freedom of speech | 11 |

*Source:* BES (1992).
*Note:* n = 2,855.

Differences in the party's standing in terms of policies were therefore not outstanding but did lie in favour of the Tories overall. Clearer differences can be found in voter's response to the leaders. Both polls and the BES indicate that John Major was more popular: see Tables 4.14–4.16.

**Table 4.14** *Evaluations of party leader as potential Prime Minister, 1991–92*

*Question asked: Who would make the best Prime Minister?*

|  | Major (%) | Kinnock (%) | Ashdown (%) | Don't know (%) |
|---|---|---|---|---|
| January 1991 | 48 | 28 | 10 | 14 |
| March 1991 | 45 | 25 | 18 | 12 |
| June 1991 | 42 | 25 | 20 | 13 |
| September 1991 | 47 | 24 | 17 | 11 |
| December 1991 | 42 | 25 | 21 | 12 |
| January 1992 | 48 | 22 | 18 | 12 |
| 17–18 March 1992 | 42 | 24 | 17 | 17 |
| 7–8 April 1992 | 39 | 28 | 18 | 15 |

*Source:* Gallup Political Index/Newton (1992: 151).

In particular, as Table 4.15 shows, Major had strengths where the Conservatives were traditionally weak. For example, 74 per cent of respondents said he was caring (also a traditional Labour strength) and 80 per cent described him as moderate. At the same time he was seen as a strong leader: 71 per cent, compared with only 45 per cent who said Kinnock could be strong.

**Table 4.15** *Voters' perceptions of the party leaders, 1992*

*Question asked: Would you describe John Major/Neil Kinnock as ...?*

|  | Major (%) | Kinnock (%) |
|---|---|---|
| Extreme | 15 | 40 |
| Moderate | 80 | 52 |
| Looks after one class | 40 | 49 |
| Looks after all classes | 54 | 42 |
| Capable of being a strong leader | 71 | 45 |
| Not capable of being a strong leader | 24 | 50 |
| Caring | 74 | 75 |
| Uncaring | 20 | 18 |

*Source:* BES (1992).
*Note:* n = 2,855.

A MORI panel survey also found that more voters felt Major was the most capable of being Prime Minister: see Table 4.16.

**Table 4.16** *Most capable Prime Minister, 1992*

*Question asked: Who do you think would make the most capable Prime Minister – Mr Major, Mr Kinnock or Mr Ashdown?*

|  | % |
|---|---|
| Mr Major | 41 |
| Mr Kinnock | 32 |

*Source:* MORI/*Sunday Times* Panel survey.
*Notes:* The MORI/*Sunday Times* Panel baseline consisted of a nationally representative sample of 1,544 adults aged 18+ in 65 constituency sampling points throughout Great Britain, first interviewed between 11 and 12 March 1992. Subsequently, 1,257 (81%) members of the original panel were re-interviewed on 18–20 March, 1,292 (84%) on 25–27 March and 1,265 (82%) on 1–3 April. Re-interview responses were weighted by first-week voting intention. Figures shown are those taken on 1–3 April.

Another perspective is that although voters may not have approved of Thatcher's performance, they were willing to give John Major a chance. Furthermore, the Labour product was not liked. Although Labour's leadership made substantial efforts to take on a market orientation, not all policies were changed to suit public opinion. The party conducted market intelligence but did not respond to all the results. Despite all Kinnock's efforts to change Labour, it was still viewed by a majority of voters as divided. In contrast, 72 per cent thought the Tories were united: see Table 4.17.

**Table 4.17** *Party unity, 1992*

*Question asked: Would you describe the Conservative/Labour Party nowadays as united or divided?*

|  | United (%) | Divided (%) |
|---|---|---|
| Conservative | 72 | 28 |
| Labour | 33 | 67 |

*Source:* BES (1992).
*Note:* n = 2,855.

General feelings towards parties are indifferent between the parties, although Labour comes out as more caring: see Table 4.18. As already indicated, it is arguable that the Conservative leader's caring image made up for this.

**Table 4.18** *Voters' perceptions of the parties, 1992*

*Question asked: On the whole, would you describe the Conservative/Labour Party nowadays as . . .*

|                        | Conservative (%) | Labour (%) |
|------------------------|:----------------:|:----------:|
| Extreme                | 30               | 29         |
| Moderate               | 61               | 61         |
| Looks after one class  | 55               | 54         |
| Looks after all classes| 38               | 35         |
| Caring                 | 47               | 70         |
| Uncaring               | 42               | 17         |

*Source:* BES (1992).
*Note:* n = 2,855.

Voters' perceptions about living standards during 1987–92 suggest that the Government had failed to deliver. Table 4.19 shows that most (over 90 per cent) respondents in the BES felt that prices, unemployment and crime had increased. A majority felt that standards in education, health care and general living had fallen.

**Table 4.19** *Voters' perceptions of life under the Conservative Government, 1992*

*Question asked: Since the last general election in June 1987, would you say that [. . .] has increased or fallen?*

|                                       | Increased (%) | Stayed the same (%) | Fallen (%) |
|---------------------------------------|:-------------:|:-------------------:|:----------:|
| Prices                                | 96            | 2                   | 2          |
| Unemployment                          | 92            | 3                   | 4          |
| Crime                                 | 93            | 4                   | 2          |
| Taxes                                 | 53            | 16                  | 22         |
| The standard of the health and social services | 22   | 22                  | 51         |
| The quality of education              | 14            | 22                  | 51         |
| General standard of living            | 30            | 24                  | 43         |
| Own standard of living                | 34            | 37                  | 28         |

*Source:* BES (1992).
*Notes:* n = 2,855. 'Increased' combines 'Increased a lot' and 'Increased a little'; 'Fallen' combines 'Fallen a little' and 'Fallen a lot'.

Similarly, a majority felt that the economy had got weaker over the last year or so: see Table 4.20.

**Table 4.20** *Voters' perceptions of the economy, 1992*

*Question asked: Would you say that Britain's economy . . .*

|  | Got stronger (%) | Stayed the same (%) | Got weaker (%) |
|---|---|---|---|
| Over the last year or so has | 12 | 32 | 56 |
| Over the last ten years has | 34 | 21 | 45 |

*Source:* BES (1992).
*Note:* n = 2,855.

Nonetheless, despite this evidence of voter concerns, there is a possible answer: voters felt there were problems, but believed that the Conservative Party was the best party to deal with them. The BES indicates that nearly 90 per cent of respondents felt that the Conservative Party was capable of strong government in general, compared with only 41 per cent for Labour: see Table 4.21.

**Table 4.21** *Parties' capability of strong government, 1992*

*Question asked: On the whole, would you describe the Conservative/Labour Party nowadays as capable or not capable of strong government?*

|  | Capable (%) | Not capable (%) |
|---|---|---|
| Conservative | 87 | 13 |
| Labour | 41 | 59 |

*Source:* BES (1992).
*Note:* n = 2,855.

In particular, the Conservatives won the issue of economic competence. Although voters were not completely satisfied with the state of the economy, they believed that the Conservatives were still the best party to handle it: Labour would make the situation worse (see Table 4.22). Newton (1992: 134–5) puts forward an ironic explanation: 'it may even be that the worse the economy, the more the electorate was inclined to turn to the Conservatives, even though they were at least partially responsible for Britain's difficulties in the first place.'

**Table 4.22** *Evaluations of Conservative and Labour economic competence, 1991–92*

*Question asked: With Britain in economic difficulties, which party do you think could handle the problem best? The Conservatives under Mr Major or Labour under Mr Kinnock?*

|  | Conservative (%) | Labour (%) | Neither (%) | Don't know (%) |
|---|---|---|---|---|
| March 1991 | 53 | 29 | 9 | 8 |
| June 1991 | 42 | 38 | 13 | 7 |
| September 1991 | 45 | 29 | 17 | 10 |
| December 1991 | 45 | 31 | 15 | 9 |
| January 1992 | 44 | 29 | 17 | 9 |
| February 1992 | 44 | 30 | 17 | 9 |
| March 1992 | 43 | 31 | 17 | 9 |
| 7–8 April 1992 | 45 | 38 | 10 | 6 |

*Source:* Gallup Political Index; quoted in Newton (1992: 142).
*Note:* Figures based on between 4,923 and 12,670 interviews.

Combined with a more popular leader and higher party unity, the Tories had more general governing competence than Labour. Overall, therefore, the Conservatives were the more market-oriented and more successful in attracting support.

### Why Labour didn't win in 1992

Labour's product suffered in many ways. One is history: the idea that voters have long memories. In 1979 voters rejected the party for several reasons, one of them lack of delivery: the party's response to this was not to design a better, more achievable product, but to go the other way. In 1983 they created a product design which was perceived to be unachievable, thereby projecting not just an unwanted behaviour but a general attitude of non-responsiveness to the wishes of the majority of the electorate. This affected the party's reputation for a long time. In 1987, the dominant orientation of the party was to focus on selling: image, presentational, sound-bite politics which could be as unpopular as unwanted policies. Professionalisation led to displacement of party figures for new staff and the party only succeeded in communicating an unpopular product. Even though it is understandable why Labour failed to adopt a market orientation and one can sympathise with Kinnock's difficulties in managing his party, in doing so it not only lost in 1983 and 1987, but laid the grounds for missing a chance of victory in 1992. In 1992 the governing party had created voter dissatisfaction by significantly neglecting voters demands and the majority of commentators predicted that it was time for a change, but voters' opinion of Labour reflected its past behaviour as well as that after 1987. The party's resistance against adopting a market orientation between 1979 and 1987 therefore not only lost them those elections, but hindered their ability to move towards a market orientation later on.

Nevertheless, in 1992 Labour still failed to change the product enough, even after losing so many elections. Labour was also traditionally weak and seen as soft on crime, which as Table 4.23 indicates ran against the current of public opinion.

**Table 4.23** *Voters' views, 1992*

*Question asked: Please say whether you agree or disagree with each of these statements, or say if you are not sure either way:*

|  | Agree (%) | Not sure (%) | Disagree (%) |
|---|---|---|---|
| People who break the law should be given stiffer sentences | 80 | 11 | 8 |

*Source:* BES (1992).
*Notes:* n = 2,855. 'Agree' combines 'Strongly agree' and 'Agree'; 'Disagree' combines 'Strongly disagree' and 'Disagree'.

In terms of the Party Leader, Kinnock had significant weaknesses and Major strengths in traditionally weak Conservative areas: the Tory leader helped to shore up his party as a whole. Labour's product design was not completely implemented: the party suffered from relatively low party unity. The negative association expected with the Tories due to the poll tax seemed to disappear when Thatcher went. Although 65 per cent of respondents to the BES thought the tax was a bad idea, as Table 4.24 indicates, it had a somewhat ambiguous influence on voting in the 1992 election.

**Table 4.24** *Importance of the poll tax in vote decision, 1992*

*Question asked: When you were deciding about which party to vote for in the election, how important to you was the Government's handling of the poll tax? Was it...*

|  | % |
|---|---|
| Important | 52 |
| Not important | 48 |

*Source:* BES (1992).
*Notes:* n = 2,855. 'Important' combines 'Extremely important' and 'Important'; 'Not important' combines 'Not very important' and 'Not at all important'.

There were many tensions within Labour's organisation, a blurring of roles amongst staff, and secret meetings and planning which worked against the emergence of market orientation throughout the party. Market intelligence was not conducted and disseminated openly and as Gould (1998b: 90) argues 'was largely ignored' in the policy review. Gould (1998b: 114) said that although defence was changed, 'on trade unions, on public ownership and above all on tax and spending, essentially we were still stuck in the past'.

Labour needed to change further if it was to win in 1997. The party had mastered the art of communication, but it needed to pay even more attention to the product it was conveying, and more attention to the desires of the voters it was seeking to govern. The Conservatives on the other hand had once again succeeded in connecting with the essential aspects of what voters wanted. The Conservative success was not that secure: there were undoubtedly weaknesses in their product. They appeared to offer a new product with a new leader, reducing the feeling of 'time for a change' and showing voters how the party could respond when part of its product became unpopular. But they gained electoral support over the opposition because out of all the 'products' on offer, voters believed them to be offering a response that was the closest to what they wanted. It does not mean it was exactly what they wanted. This was reflected in the rise in voter dissatisfaction after the 1992 election already discussed in the previous chapter. From this point of view, the ultimate potential of political marketing, to create voter satisfaction (rather than simply help an individual party win an election) also depends upon the behaviour of the opposition. The greater the competition amongst parties to be market-oriented, the more likely it is that voters will receive, let alone buy, what they want.

However, the next chapter will examine a case where a party did follow the Market-Oriented Party model closely: Labour in 1997. Labour did not receive serious competition from the Tories between 1992 and 1997, but because of losing three previous elections, it was convinced of the need to be market-oriented. No longer would Labour struggle to respond to voter demands. It would become the King of all Marketers and attract substantial electoral support to match.

### Note

1  Unless otherwise stated directly within the text because of particular originality or primary nature, this chapter draws on the secondary empirical descriptive accounts of the time period listed below. Details of other works consulted and directly cited are in the full bibliography at the end of the book.

### Labour, 1983–87

Banker (1992), BBC (1995), Butler and Kavanagh (1988), Dunleavy with Ward (1991), Fielding (1995), Fielding (1997b), Gould (1985), Gould (1998b), Gould *et al.* (1989), Harrop (1987), Harrop (1990), Hewitt and Mandelson (1989), Kavanagh (1995), Kleinman (1987), Kotler and Levy (1969), Laczniak, Lusch and Murphy (1979), M. Smith (1992), Mandelson (1988), O'Shaughnessy (1990), O'Shaughnessy (1999), Punnett (1992), Rosenbaum (1997), Sackman (1996), Scammell (1994), Scammell (1995), Sharkey (1989), Shaw (1994), Webb (1992b, Webb (1994), Whyte (1988), Wring (1994–95), Wring (1996b, Wring (1997a).

### Labour and Conservative, 1987–92

Brown (1992), BBC (1995), Butler and Kavanagh (1992), Clemens (1983), Cook (1995), Crewe (1981), Croft (1992: 210), Fielding (1995), Franklin (1994), George and Rosamond (1992), Gould (1998b), Heath and Jowell (1994), Heath *et al.* (1994), Hill (1995), Hughes and Wintour (1990), Jun (1996), Kavanagh (1992), Kavanagh (1995), Kotler and Levy (1969), Lipsey (1992), Lipsey *et al.* (1989), Moon (1999), Newton (1992), Norton (1992), Pearce and Stewart (1992), Rosenbaum (1997), Sackman (1996), Sanders (1992), Scammell (1995), Seyd and Whiteley (1992), Shaw (1993), Shaw (1994), Wainwright (1987), Wakeham (1995), Woodward (1995), Wring (1996b).

---

**5**

---

# Blair and the New Labour design: a classic Market-Oriented Party?

Tony Blair's New Labour Party is the most recent and easily identifiable case of political marketing. During 1992–97 the Labour Party became a classic Market-Oriented Party. It was united in the desire to change all aspects of its behaviour in order to win the next election and followed the model with startling clarity. Full-scale market intelligence was conducted and many aspects of the product altered to suit voters' demands. It was not just a new campaign style, but changes in substance: policies of low tax and stricter measures on crime, a stronger leadership and constitutional reform. The new product was communicated so effectively that by the time of the election campaign the party had little to sell: voters already knew what they had to offer. Labour subsequently achieved substantial electoral success.

But the New Labour design is a problem. During the market-oriented process, Labour alienated traditional supporters and critiques contend it has lost all its ideology and beliefs and stands for nothing. It is almost as if someone has come along and ripped the party from its roots. This may show the limits of marketing political parties. Perhaps parties are not meant to act like businesses. In using marketing and changing the product like a company alters its product to suit its consumers, Labour asked for support on the basis of promised outputs. The party needs to deliver in government if it is to maintain its success, but if it is seen to fail in this regard not only are voters unlikely to excuse it, Labour has little traditional support to fall back on.

Detailed analysis will show, however, that Labour neglected important aspects of the marketing process for a Market-Oriented Party that might have prevented such problems. Blair did not give much attention to adjusting the product to suit internal support. The product was never properly implemented. All troubles were suppressed in the desire to win. Maybe New Labour is a false Market-Oriented Party: it is more a case of 'New Labour, New Danger'. The New Labour design will come toppling down like a House of Cards if another party with more time, which goes through the model with greater care, can replace it on much more solid foundations than New Labour can ever have. This chapter explores in detail the extent to which Labour followed the Market-Oriented Party model.[1]

## Stage 1: Market intelligence

Labour utilised every aspect of this stage.

### Post-election analysis

- The Fabian Society commissioned three detailed studies, focusing on 'swing' voters who had voted Tory despite being traditional supporters of Labour.
- Philip Gould conducted focus groups that showed how Labour was still not seen as having changed: see Box 5.1.

The research also showed that the party had to make clear and believable promises to voters or they would not be believed.

### Informal

- Six policy commissions were created to discuss policy ideas within the party; they produced reports that went to the National Policy Forum and the Party conference.
- A new Joint Policy Committee was formed with equal numbers from the NEC and Shadow Cabinet, together with representation from the party at European and local level.
- A new Institute of Public Policy Research on social justice and the welfare state was set up to find a way to reform welfare without increasing taxes.
- Labour gleamed advice from successful centre–left parties in other countries, such as Australia and the USA; Gould wrote a report on what the party should do in light of Democratic President Clinton's success; Tony Blair and Gordon Brown visited Clinton's advisers in January 1993.

### Formal

- NOP began a regular survey in November 1993.
- Stan Greenberg, President Clinton's pollster in 1996, and Gould were involved in this.
- Focus groups were used to pre-test proposed designs and throughout the campaign.

**Box 5.1 Results of post-election focus groups on Labour**

*1 Labour is judged by its past*

Phrases associated with the party are:

- Winter of Discontent
- union influence
- strikes
- inflation
- disarmament
- Benn/Scargill
- Brent/Islington
- miners' strike/three-day week

*2 Labour's values are negative, aimed at depriving people of:*

- wealth, in the form of taxes
- choice in education and health
- ownership, in the form of council houses

*3 Labour is hostile to:*

- people who have money/savings/even pensions
- people who want to start their own business; and
- people who want the best for their kids

*4 Labour is no longer the party of 'ordinary working people'*

People are saying,
'I've left the Labour Party and the Labour Party has left me.'
'It's obvious isn't it: the better you are doing, the more money you have got, the more likely you are to vote Tory. It's hardly surprising.'

*Source:* Gould (1998a: 5).

The response to Labour's draft manifesto *New Labour, New Life for Britain,* launched in 1996, was analysed afterwards, enabling it to remove anything that proved problematic before the production of the final manifesto in 1997.

*Stage 2: Product design*

*Leadership*
The Labour Party's move towards a market orientation was most evident under the leadership of Tony Blair. The leadership of his predecessor (John Smith) was cut short by death in May 1994; Blair was elected in July. Blair was a popular choice with voters. King (1998b: 201) contended that Blair 'might almost have been a product of computer-aided design. He was young. He was classless. He was squeaky clean'. He was a family man, centre–left and media-friendly. As such he appealed to those voters the party needed to attract to win the next election and his poll rating relative to other party leaders was strong (see Tables 5.6–5.8). More importantly, Blair believed that the party would not win unless it enacted significant changes in line with the findings from market intelligence. In order to do this, he increased and expanded his power as party leader. Senior party figures that voiced opinions against the party line were isolated from the media. Blair publicly reprimanded those such as Clare Short and some of the party's European MPs when they strayed from the party line. He called for strong discipline and unity throughout the parliamentary party and stretched this to include constituency parties and proposed parliamentary candidates. Not surprisingly, this leadership style was criticised as autocratic and Stalinist. It nonetheless concurred with market intelligence that showed that voters wanted strong leadership with a clear sense of direction.

*MPs*
Under the Blair leadership, the character of proposed candidates for the 1997 election was closely observed in an attempt to ensure that they would broadly follow the 'New Labour design'. A subcommittee of the NEC drew up short lists of candidates for by-elections, which then went to local party associations for consideration. The leadership even overruled some decisions made by local party organisations, as in the case of left-winger Liz Davis, selected for Leeds North East, who was de-selected by the National Executive Committee. MPs were also bound by the strict rule of unity imposed by the leadership; senior MPs most loyal to the leader were promoted and those more critical of the changes moved to lower positions. The Shadow Cabinet was also highly unified. MPs accepted the need for greater discipline in order to achieve the goal of electoral success.

*Membership*
Several changes were made to the membership to make it more market-oriented. Under Smith, members were given the right to vote in a leadership election. This provided greater participatory incentives but,

much like the changes made under Kinnock, this also helped the leadership because it downgraded the power of activists. Tony Blair also initiated
a new membership drive to both increase membership numbers and make
its social composition more representative of the electorate.

Market intelligence had shown how trade union power within the party
had in the past adversely affected their electoral support. Firstly procedural
changes were made:

- In February 1993 John Smith announced a proposal to end the unions'
  collective presence in the party.
- At the 1993 party conference John Smith passed resolutions that made
  trade union members join as individuals and parliamentary selections
  be decided by a 'one member, one vote' system.
- Union representation in the party's electoral college was reduced from
  40 to 33 per cent, bringing it into line with MPs and constituency
  parties.

Blair also worked to distance the party from the unions in non-constitu-
tional ways:

- He declared that unions could not expect special deals from the party if
  it did get into government.
- The financial dependence that Labour had on the unions was also
  reduced by replacing it with alternative sources of financial support.

*Staff*

Blair made substantial use of staff. He built up a small group of advisers, a
so-called 'inner circle'. In this group were Peter Mandelson, Kinnock's
former Director of Communications, and Philip Gould. Gould had professional advertising experience, conducted focus groups for Labour and had
also worked on the 1992 and 1996 Democratic Party campaign in the
USA. Blair recruited a new press secretary, Alastair Campbell, who had
been political editor for the *Daily Mirror*. Anji Hunter was appointed as his
personal assistant. Jonathan Powell took over administrative tasks in
Blair's office. Blair took their advice extremely seriously: the negative
consequence of this was that it made others in the party feel somewhat
sidelined. Blair's Policy Adviser was David Miliband. Miliband was from the
Institute for Public Policy Research and brought in intellectual experience
and contact with think-tanks such as Demos and Charter 88. Tom Sawyer
became General Secretary of the party and supported Blair in changing the
role of party conference and the NEC. There was much turnover at the
party's official Press and Publicity Department, however. David Hill was
Director of Campaigns, Elections and Media but left a few months after the
1992 election. He was replaced by Sally Morgan but she later moved to

Blair's office when he became leader. Joy Johnson, a BBC political editor, took on the post in July 1994 but left in February 1996 because she was constantly usurped by Mandelson and Campbell.

*Constitution*
Blair succeeded in changing Clause IV, section iv of the party's constitution in April 1995. It had been adopted in 1918 implied a party policy commitment to state ownership of the means of production: an unpopular position. The new clause confirmed a commitment to a market economy and stated that the Labour Party was a democratic socialist party. The reform was also symbolic and helped to convey to voters that the party was genuinely offering a new product.

*Activities*
Party conferences were well organised and stage-managed, to ensure they would appeal to the electorate at large. Debate was carefully controlled to ensure that the party appeared united.

*Symbols*
The slogan 'New Labour, New Britain' was launched at the 1994 party conference. The attachment of the word 'New' to 'Labour' was thereon continued, emphasising how the party had changed and was different from 'Old' Labour. At conferences the national flag was increasingly held up alongside the party's traditional red flag. Only one verse of the party's traditional song *The Red Flag* was sung at the party conference before the 1997 election, de-emphasising its traditional one-sector appeal.

*Policy proposals*
The Labour Party made significant policy change in order to make it more market-oriented. This continued the process initiated by Kinnock but also went much further. The key changes were that it:

• abandoned the unpopular call for higher income tax;
• abandoned plans to re-nationalise privatised industries;
• took a much more pro-business attitude;
• began to talk of reforming the welfare state instead of expanding it;
• became tougher on crime;
• presented itself as the party of aspiration.

The party made specific promises for how it would behave in government. Before the manifesto some promises emerged in pledges and statements. For example, in July 1996 it launched five pledges under the slogan 'New Life for Britain', about education, youth crime, NHS waiting lists, youth unemployment and fiscal prudence. Four months before the election Labour said it would stick to existing Conservative spending plans if it was to be elected for the first two years of a new Parliament. It also promised that it would not raise the basic and top rates of income tax. The final manifesto, entitled *New Labour because Britain deserves better*, was launched on 3 April 1997. This provided a ten-point contract with the people which built on those promises already made: see Box 5.2:

---

**Box 5.2 Labour's ten-point contract with the people, April 1997**

1 Education will be our number one priority, and we will increase the share of national income spent on education as we decrease it on the bills of economic and social failure.
2 There will be no increase in the basic or top rates of income tax.
3 We will provide stable economic growth with low inflation, and promote dynamic and competitive business and industry at home and abroad.
4 We will get 250,000 young unemployed off benefit and into work.
5 We will rebuild the NHS, reducing spending on administration and increasing spending on patient cases.
6 We will be tough on crime and the causes of crime, and halve the time it takes persistent juvenile offenders to come to court.
7 We will help build strong families and strong communities, and lay the foundations of a modern welfare state in pensions and community care.
8 We will safeguard our environment, and develop an integrated transport policy to fight congestion and pollution.
9 We will clean up politics, de-centralise political power throughout the United Kingdom and put the funding of political parties on a proper and accountable basis.
10 We will give Britain the leadership in Europe which Britain and Europe need.

*Source:* The Labour Party (1997).

---

Additionally the manifesto included a windfall tax on nationalised utilities which had most recently been privatised, responding to voters' concerns about the directors of these utilities making too much profit from privatisation. It attended to Scottish voters by making a commitment to major constitutional reform. Labour proposed to end the rights of hereditary peers to sit in the House of Lords, hold a referendum on devolution to Scotland and Wales, introduce a Freedom of Information Act and implement the European Convention on Human Rights. It also promised to set a national minimum wage (although no actual level was specified).

All these policies were carefully designed to respond to voters' demands.

They were not only popular but in the issue areas that voters considered most important.

*Stage 3: Product adjustment*

*Achievability*
The Labour Party's list of definite pledges that it promised to deliver on if elected was short and limited. It also included details on how it would achieve them. For example, pledge 3 was to cut waiting lists in the NHS, and this Labour claimed it would do by reducing the money spent on bureaucracy. With regard to the early pledges, Gould (1998b: 271) shows how it responded to market intelligence:

> Some people may be horrified that it required so much research to find out what people wanted, but they misunderstand. For election after election Labour has offered better hospitals, better schools, more jobs, but it has never been believed. The issue is not the promises, but *making the promises credible*. What research revealed was that the public wanted smaller, more concrete pledges, they wanted them costed and they wanted them presented in the form of an accountable contract. The result was more honesty, less fudge, more trust. Much of the media sneered, but it was the electorate who showed common sense and maturity, and I am glad they were consulted.

The party also took steps to limits its spending plans: the Shadow Chancellor Gordon Brown advised fellow Shadow Cabinet members to avoid further public spending commitments because Labour's 'tax and spend' image had lost it support in past elections. The commitment to existing government spending plans also helped to prevent this weakness emerging. In the introduction to Labour's manifesto, Tony Blair noted how people were 'cynical about politics and distrustful of political promises' and stated:

> That is why we have made it our guiding rule not to promise what we cannot deliver; and to deliver what we promise. (See The Labour Party (1997))

He also claimed that the party's proposed behaviour would be about 'telling the truth; making tough choices; insisting that all parts of the public sector live within their means'. Labour knew from its market intelligence that voters did not believe parties that made grand promises that did not seem achievable.

*Internal reaction analysis*
The leadership provided various mechanisms for greater participation within the Party. Blair took the case to reform Clause IV to the party and provided consultation mechanisms on the new wording. The leader sent

out a questionnaire to every local party branch, socialist society and affiliated trade union asking for opinions on Labour's aims and values, the results of which were published in *Labour's Aims and Values: The Consultation report* in 1995. Blair attended thiry-five meetings with party members throughout the country to put the case for reform. He balloted members on the proposed clause: members were asked for a yes or no to the new clause. 85 per cent voted yes. The new proposal was passed at a special conference held in London on 29 April 1995. The party made special attempts to increase the involvement of the ordinary member. Political education meetings were held across the country between 1994 and 1997, designed for new members, with small group discussions providing an opportunity to discuss party policies. The leadership also balloted the membership on the manifesto and achieved 95 per cent endorsement (The Labour Party (1997)).

Nevertheless, the changes Blair made to the party's product to increase its support in the electorate created significant dissatisfaction within the party, which even in the lead-up to the 1997 election had a particularly emotive potency and ideological depth. Blair was determined to ensure Labour became electable at all costs. In April 1995 he declared

> I did not come into this Labour Party to join a pressure group. I didn't become leader of this party to lead a protest movement. Power without principle is barren, but principle without power is futile. This is a party of government or it is nothing, and I will lead it as a party of government. (Quoted in Seyd (1998: 49)).

Although the leadership was undoubtedly aware of the views within the party, it did not adjust the product accordingly. Traditional supporters would always buy Labour's product, so Labour could neglect responding to their views and still achieve electoral success. Political marketing was used to win the election, but not to provide satisfaction first, at least on an internal level.

One example is Blair's proposal to change Clause IV. This was a surprise move, which was suggested but not implicitly stated in Blair's speech at the party conference on October 4 1994. The party's commitment to Clause IV had been endorsed by delegates the year before; the 1994 conference even argued that the 'objective of public ownership be fully incorporated into the Party's policies' (The Labour Party (1994: 199)). The clause may have only been symbolic, but this is precisely why some members objected to the change: the clause was of ideological, emotive importance, embodying what they had been fighting for during all their years of involvement in the party.

Despite Blair's efforts at consultation, he took on a product orientation with regard to the membership. He decided what should be done and argued the case for it. He could have asked the party in advance what they thought about whether the constitution needed to be changed, rather than argue the case after it had been decided. He might have gained more support this way. Instead dissatisfaction was created not simply because of the actual change but the way in which it was brought about. There were several indications of discontent. Thirty-two Labour MEPs took out an advert against its reform in the *Guardian* on 10 January 1995. Fielding (1995: 106) noted how 'Tony Benn compared Blair's proposal to revising the Ten Commandments: he did not intend this to be a compliment ... Arthur Scargill described Blair's speech as a declaration of war on the rest of the Party.' Were it not for the leadership's tough line on unity, no doubt there would have been many more.

On other occasions changes in policy, even complete reversals of past party commitments, were announced with little consultation with the rest of the party. One example is the decision that a Labour Government would hold a referendum on Scottish and Welsh devolution. Gordon Brown, the Shadow Chancellor, also encountered opposition to his proposed tough controls over public spending. Disputes occurred over issues such as job seekers' allowance, child benefit, minimum wage and state pensions. Brown was criticised by trade union leaders such as Bill Morris, John Edmonds and MPs Roy Hattersley, Roger Berry and Bryan Gould. Brown's policy, fully supported by Blair, nonetheless prevailed.

As already explained, parties cannot simply shed their history. Because parties are different to businesses, they must adjust the product to suit internal demands which include party ideology and traditions. Under Blair, the Labour Party changed so much that as Rose (1997: 751) notes, by 1997 it 'had fewer similarities with the party of Harold Wilson or Hugh Gaitskell than it did with the new Democrats of President Clinton, not a party in the textbook sense but a campaign apparatus with a single clear goal, electoral victory'. Clare Short's (1996) criticisms of Blair's approach a year before the 1997 election suggested that the leadership (or its advisers) had gone too far in abandoning the party's past:

> These people are making a terrible error. They think that Labour is unelectable, so they want to get something else elected, even though really it's still the Labour Party. This is a dangerous game, which assumes people are stupid. It gets to the point where you are ashamed of your own past ... They are saying 'Vote for Tony Blair's new Labour. We all agree the old one was absolutely appalling and you all know that most of the people in Labour are really the old one, but we've got some who are nothing to do with that, vote for us!'

Blair appeared to override Labour's traditional history. Butler and

Kavanagh (1997: 50) contend that he did not even try 'to present himself as a man of the left or as one who would try to balance the Party factions'. An old vanguard of the left of the party, Arthur Scargill, declared that 'on all fundamental issues that affect our lives and our society, new Labour has adopted policies that cannot be supported by those who call themselves socialists' (quoted in Seyd (1998: 49)). He split off from the Labour Party to form his own new Socialist Labour Party. Blair did not succeed in changing the party within its traditional framework as the model suggests parties need to.

*Competition analysis*
The Labour Party made various changes to its product, together with expending significant efforts in communication, to remove electoral weaknesses it had exhibited in previous elections. One example is the move made to distance the party from its historical link with trade unions. Blair made it clear that unions would have no special favours from a prospective Labour Government. The party's organisational changes also helped to convey a weakening of the relationship between it and the unions. This prevented the Conservatives from being able to argue that it was controlled by the old union barons. Another was the reassurance given to voters that the party would not increase income tax, addressing Labour's poor image in economic management. Labour also attempted to convey a pro-business attitude, launching a special business manifesto and sending the party leader to attending numerous meetings with businessmen. In the manifesto, it was argued that 'New Labour will be wise spenders, not big spenders' (The Labour Party (1997)). Table 5.1 indicates how the party was successful in removing many past weaknesses.

**Table 5.1** *Public perception of the Labour Party, July 1996*

|  | Agree (%) | Disagree (%) | Don't know (%) |
|---|---|---|---|
| Labour has become too extreme | 20 | 68 | 13 |
| Labour is the only party that can turn out the Government | 78 | 16 | 7 |
| Labour Party leadership is poor now | 22 | 66 | 12 |
| Labour is too split and divided | 32 | 56 | 12 |
| The economy would be in a worse state under Labour | 26 | 58 | 15 |
| Labour has a strong team of new young leaders | 57 | 22 | 21 |

*Source:* adapted from Gallup Political and Economic Index, Report No. 431, July 1996: 6, quoted by King (1998b: 203).
*Note:* n = not known.

In terms of the competition, many of the policy positions Labour moved to appeared extremely close to the Conservatives. It is almost as if the Labour Party examined the Conservative strengths, and took them for themselves. In the manifesto Blair admitted 'some things the Conservatives got right. We will not change them. It is where they got things wrong that we will make change' (The Labour Party (1997): Introduction). No longer did the party make all criticism of the opposition negative. Arguably this helped to make Labour's own promises and everything the leadership said more credible. Labour then exploited the remaining Tory weaknesses, which came into the open very easily. For example, they made the most of the headline news about huge wage increases for the directors of recently privatised utilities. Labour's more radical proposals on the constitution enabled them to create another potential Tory weakness. However Labour moved perhaps too far to the Conservatives, failing to differentiate the New Labour product from pragmatic Conservatism.

*Support analysis*
Labour made effective use of target marketing. It focused on gaining the support of voters in what Blair himself called 'middle income, middle Britain'. Changes in behaviour were designed to suit the demands of these voters, particularly 1992 Tory voters. Labour also engaged in targeted communications and campaigning through its key seats strategy called 'Operation Victory'. Two years before the election, the party created a task force to change 5,000 voters minds in 90 target marginal seats. The voters targeted were called 'switchers': those judged to be likely to change from supporting the other parties to Labour. Henig (1997: 5–6) reported how these voters were identified eighteen months before the election, through questions asked by telephone to establish the party identification, intended vote and other characteristics of electors. This information was then used to create categories of voters, creating smaller target groups. The most important of these were the switchers but also first-time voters seen as weak identifiers; Labour supporters who did not always vote; and Liberal Democrat voters in 1992 who preferred Labour to Conservative. This information was then used in the campaign.

### Stage 4: Implementation

Blair accepted the idea of marketing and was convinced that the party had to change, responding to findings from market intelligence and using them to show to others in the party. His decisive leadership style helped to ensure the product design would be implemented, whatever the attitude of others in the party. Blair assumed a superior role to the NEC. His strong leadership imposed unity on all levels of the party and resulted in a successful implementation of the product design. More importantly, the response of voters as measured by polls suggests they accepted the party had changed and was unified (see Table 5.10).

However these assertions are in need of qualification. Such unity may not be long-lasting, based as it was on the desire for electoral success. The extent to which the new product design was accepted by the party is questionable. Implementation was achieved superficially, but perhaps only because of the desire for electoral success and strict leadership control. Blair's leadership style also led to criticism. Clare Short (1996) referred to Blair's advisors as 'people who live in the dark'. Marketing was not an open, integrated activity: as under Kinnock's leadership, it became tied to a small group of people close to the leader and centre of power.

### Stage 5: Communication

The party's communications strategy was extremely tightly run and disciplined. A new communications centre was created in Millbank Tower in Westminster, where the party began to lease two floors from the autumn of 1995. All key staff were moved there. Only party headquarters remained at Walworth Road in South London. Communications were designed to project images and receive reports that would depict the party in a light favourable to the demands of the electorate. Peter Mandelson became Chair of the General Election Planning group in 1995 and Shadow Minister for Election Planning in 1996. Around eighty staff worked under his direction, striving to put the party's message across in a positive way. Mandelson had clear access to and the support of Tony Blair and also worked closely with Alastair Campbell. Campbell designed a strategy to improve Labour's relationship with the popular press, including newspapers traditionally favouring the Tories. In particular, Blair worked to win favour with media-tycoons such as Rupert Murdoch, who owned the *Sun*, *The Times*, the *Sunday Times* and the *News of the World* and made a trip to Australia in July 1995 to address executives of *News International*, telling them that Labour had changed. Labour also projected itself as a party that would be economically competent in government, creating photo-opportunities between Blair and business entrepreneurs such as Richard Branson. The *Sun* and the *News of the World* endorsed Blair in the first week of the election campaign.

The media were fed positive stories and if any section of the media produced a report that was deemed to be unreasonably negative, party officials would often contact it and complain. Campbell also spoke directly to editors to reassure them that Labour had changed and could be trusted. Significant effort was also put into ensuring that a unified party line was projected. Shadow Cabinet members were reprimanded or punished if they stepped outside the party line. Together with the party's launch of five pledges and a mini-manifesto in 1996, this meant that the product design had been well communicated to voters before the election campaign even began.

## Stage 6: The election campaign

The campaign was not particularly striking. Labour simply reiterated what it had already been saying during the communication stage. Organisationally, it was carefully planned and tightly run, directed from the party's rooms at Millbank Tower in an open plan office area modelled on the 'War room' idea implemented by the US Democratic Party in 1992. Mandelson was general election campaign manager and Brown in charge of campaign strategy. There were over 200 staff working on the campaign and communication between them, key party figures and candidates was constant. The operation at Millbank was 24-hour; Blair was able to stay in touch whenever he went on tour.

Task-forces were created, each with a separate role to play. One was a rebuttal unit was created to deal with attacks from the opposition which used a £300,000 database system called Excalibur. Another of these task-forces was created to run Labour's 'Operation Victory,' the campaign in the ninety targeted seats. This unit was extremely important because the campaign used target marketing at both a national and local level and focused on the key seats wherever possible. A smaller unit was left to deal with non-key constituencies. Labour had already reduced its past weaknesses of tax and the economy: now it fought on its strengths: education, health and jobs. When problems did arise, the party appeared ready to deal with them. Conservative claims of a tartan tax due to Labour's Scottish devolution plans prompted Blair to argue the referendum would also ask voters about the tax-raising powers of a devolved Parliament. Labour announced a new measure in the last week: a popular initiative to spend funds from the National Lottery on health and education.

The campaign was clearly informed by market intelligence, especially that on 'switchers'. Cavass reports were sent to Gould. Advertising was handled by Boase Massimi Politt (BMP) which had close ties to the party: many BMP personnel had worked for Labour in past elections. Advertising was designed to suit findings from qualitative and quantitative research and the target audience of 'switcher' voters in marginal seats. Posters reinforced the pledges, using simple statements like 'Class sizes will be smaller' or criticised the Tories, with adverts saying '22 Tax increases since 1992'. The party's first election broadcast focused on portraying Labour as the 'party of business' which would also help to convince voters that it could handle the economy. Blair provided more photo opportunities than press conferences through his visits to sixty constituencies.

Labour's product was far more market-oriented than the Conservatives and as the theory predicts there was little need for selling. In an interview on election night on BBC 1, Alastair Campbell was asked 'Why, though, do you think you've won, what was it about the campaign – did you do so well, did the Conservatives do so badly – what was it?' He replied 'Well, I don't know whether the campaign in the end made that much difference'. As Lancaster and Massingham (1993: 12) explain, if a market-oriented organisation 'has applied the concept and techniques of marketing, i.e. identified consumer needs, produced appropriate products, priced, pack- aged, promoted and distributed the product correctly, then consumers should want to buy the product rather than the firm having to rely on intense selling'. By the time of the 1997 election, the Labour leadership had changed all aspects of the party's behaviour to suit findings from market intelligence and ensured that this change permeated all levels of the party to a considerable degree.

*Stage 7: Election – the party's success in attracting support*

Labour's market-oriented behaviour, especially in constrast to the more product-oriented attitude of the Tories, yielded substantial support from the public.

*The general election*
Labour won the election with a swing from the Conservatives of over 10 per cent, attracting 43.2 per cent of the popular vote and 419 seats with a majority of 179. The party also took seats normally considered unwinnable by any party other than the Conservatives and attracted a wide base of support, in terms of geographical distribution and social and age groups. Labour was also perceived as a party of all classes: see Table 5.2.

**Table 5.2** *The Labour Party's representation of class, 1997*

*Question asked: Regardless of how you voted today, do you think that the Labour Party is good for one class or good for all classes?*

|  | Labour Party (%) |
| --- | --- |
| Good for one class | 31 |
| Good for all classes | 69 |

*Source:* Kellner (1997: 622), from a BBC/NOP exit poll, 1 May 1997.

*Membership*
Under the leadership of Tony Blair, membership numbers rose from around 280,000 in 1993 to 400,000 by the 1997 election.

*Voter evaluations of party behaviour*
Labour produced popular policies in vast majority of areas: see Table 5.3.

**Table 5.3** *Best party policy on key issues, 1997*

*Question asked: I am going to read out a list of problems facing Britain today. I would like you to tell me whether you think the Conservative Party, the Labour Party or the Liberal Democrats has the best policies on each problem.*

| Policies | Labour or Conservative better policy (% lead over the other) |
|---|---|
| Health care | Labour (32) |
| Public transport | Labour (25) |
| Unemployment | Labour (24) |
| Housing | Labour (24) |
| Pensions | Labour (20) |
| Education | Labour (19) |
| Trade unions | Labour (18) |
| Protecting the natural environment | Labour (6) |
| Animal welfare | Labour (6) |
| Law and order | Labour (1) |
| Taxation | Labour (1) |
| Europe | Conservative (1) |
| Constitution/devolution | Conservative (2) |
| Managing the economy | Conservative (7) |
| Northern Ireland | Conservative (8) |
| Defence | Conservative (14) |

*Source:* MORI polls.
*Notes:* n = c. 1,000 or 2,000, surveys based on GB residents aged 18 +. Poll taken 8 April.

The priorities given by voters are displayed in Table 5.4. These indicate how Labour not only had popular policies, but they were in areas important to the way people voted, such as health care and education.

Voters chose which party they expected to make things better in Britain. An analysis of a BBC-commissioned NOP exit poll by Kellner (1997: 622) indicated that 57 per cent of voters expected Labour policies to make things better in Britain, whereas 49 per cent believed Conservative policies would make things worse (see Table 5.5).

**Table 5.4** *Issues important to vote, 1997*

*Question asked: Looking ahead to the next general election, which, if any, of these issues do you think will be very important to you in helping you to decide which party to vote for?*

|  | % saying |
|---|---|
| Health care | 68 |
| Education | 61 |
| Law and order | 51 |
| Unemployment | 49 |
| Pensions | 39 |
| Taxation | 33 |
| Managing the economy | 30 |
| Europe | 22 |
| Housing | 22 |
| Protecting the natural environment | 20 |
| Public transport | 18 |
| Northern Ireland | 12 |
| Defence | 12 |
| Animal welfare | 10 |
| Constitution/devolution | 7 |
| Trade unions | 9 |
| Other | 2 |
| Don't know | 2 |

*Source:* MORI polls.
*Notes:* n = c. 1,000 or 2,000, surveys based on GB residents aged 18 +. Poll taken 8 April.

**Table 5.5** *Voters' evaluation of expected party performance post-1997*

*Question asked: If Labour/the Conservatives win the election, do you think that, overall, Labour/Conservative policies will make things in Britain a lot better, a little better, no difference, a little worse or a lot worse?*

|  | Labour policies (%) | Conservative policies (%) |
|---|---|---|
| Better | 57 | 31 |
| No difference | 11 | 19 |
| Worse | 33 | 49 |

*Source:* Kellner (1997: 622), quoted from a BBC/NOP exit poll, 1 May 1997.
*Notes:* n = not known. 'Better' combines those saying 'A lot better' and 'A little better'; 'Worse' combines those saying 'A lot worse' and 'A little worse'.

In terms of the party leaders, Blair received higher overall ratings as measured by opinion polls (see Table 5.6). He was also viewed as the best Prime Minister (see Table 5.7) and when asked more specific questions voters also perceived him to have more favourable characteristics (see Tables 5.8 and 5.9).

**Table 5.6** *Leader approval ratings, 1994–96*

|  | Blair (%) | Major (%) | Ashdown (%) |
|---|---|---|---|
| Aug–Dec 1994 | 41 | 16 | 14 |
| 1995 | 42 | 17 | 13 |
| 1996 | 39 | 19 | 14 |

*Source:* Denver (1998: 40) from *Gallup 9000*.

**Table 5.7** *Best Prime Minister, 1997*

*Question asked: Who would make the best Prime Minister: Tony Blair, John Major or Paddy Ashdown?*

|  | % |
|---|---|
| Tony Blair | 65 |
| John Major | 19 |
| Paddy Ashdown | 16 |

*Source:* BES (1997).
*Note:* n = 3,376.

**Table 5.8** *Images of party leaders, October 1996*

|  | Blair (%) | Major (%) |
|---|---|---|
| Understands the problems facing Britain | 34 | 21 |
| A capable leader | 33 | 19 |
| Has got a lot of personality | 33 | 5 |
| Rather inexperienced | 27 | 9 |
| Down to earth | 22 | 16 |
| Has sound judgement | 19 | 11 |
| Tends to talk down to people | 11 | 18 |
| Out of touch with ordinary people | 9 | 47 |
| Rather narrow minded | 7 | 21 |
| Too inflexible | 7 | 19 |

*Source:* Denver (1998: 42), from MORI.
*Note:* Respondents had to choose whether the above statements suited Major and Blair.

**Table 5.9** *Qualities of party leaders, 1996*

|  | Blair (%) | Major (%) |
|---|---|---|
| Caring/not caring | +65 | +9 |
| Tough/not tough | +25 | −49 |
| Effective/not effective | +38 | −46 |
| Can/cannot be trusted | +25 | −18 |
| Competent/not competent | +61 | −17 |
| Winner/loser | +56 | −33 |
| Firmly in charge/not firmly in charge | +27 | −60 |
| Decisive/indecisive | +40 | −36 |
| Likeable/not likeable as a person | +57 | +20 |
| Listens/does not listen to reason | +44 | +2 |
| Likely/not likely to unite the country | +20 | −67 |

*Source:* Denver (1998: 42), from *Gallup Political and Economic Index*, Reports No. 427, 431.
*Notes:* Sample taken from June for Blair and from March 1996 for Major. Respondents were asked whether the positive or negative statement applied to the leader: the figures are the negative choices (%) subtracted from positive choices (%).


Labour was also more united: the exit poll on May 1 1997 showed that a clear majority (66 per cent) of voters thought that Labour was a united party, contrasted sharply with 84 per cent who thought the Conservatives were divided (see Table 5.10).


**Table 5.10** *Voters' perception of party unity*

*Question asked: Regardless of how you voted today, do you think that the Conservative/Labour Party is united or divided?*

|  | Conservative Party (%) | Labour Party (%) |
|---|---|---|
| United | 16 | 66 |
| Divided | 84 | 34 |

*Source:* Kellner (1997: 622), from a BBC/NOP exit poll, 1 May 1997.


The Labour Party as a whole was also seen as moderate and good for all classes by the vast majority of respondents to the 1997 BES. It was also seen as capable of strong government and a party that keeps it promises, indicating it had general governing and delivery capability (see Table 5.11).

**Table 5.11** *Voters' perceptions of Labour, 1997*

Question asked: On the whole, would you describe the
Labour Party nowadays as . . .

|                                        | (%) |
| -------------------------------------- | --- |
| Capable of being a strong government    | 92  |
| Moderate                               | 82  |
| Good for all classes                   | 80  |
| A party that keeps its promises         | 72  |

*Source:* BES (1997).
*Note:* n = 3,376.


### New Market-Oriented Party = 'New Labour, New Danger'?

I've seen so many failures based on the idea 'give up everything and you'll win', you give it up, and you don't win, then people say we didn't give up enough, so we're going to give up even more, and I think that is the tragedy of the Labour Party since . . . 1974; it hasn't appeared to stand for anything. People aren't fools, they see that, so they say better the devil we know. I think we'll get into power but we'll not make much of it. (Tony Benn MP, BBC (1995))

I think it's been a painful process; a painful withdrawal from hope and ideal- ism. It may or may not have been necessary. I don't believe that it was, and I think we have simply given up, and we will secure power but I don't think we'll make much of it and we will, as soon as the voters recover their confi- dence in the Tories, be removed in order to make room for the real thing. (Bryan Gould, BBC (1995))

The New Labour design is the closest example yet of a Market-Oriented Party in Britain. Yet there were quickly signs of problems for the party in government. These were however predictable even before the election, given that Blair did not follow the model completely. He neglected the more subtle aspects of marketing, such as the internal analysis part of Stage 3. In many ways Blair failed to carry his party with him when changing it to suit voters and perhaps changed it too much. It is as if the party was left behind. The consequences of this can now be seen in two ways: by looking at the party's internal support and externally in the electorate at large.


#### 'New Labour, New Danger': flimsy external support

The are two ways to examine this. The first is to re-analyse the support Labour gained in 1997, which is not as strong as it might first appear; the second is to cover the fortunes of the party since getting into office. This is within the context of a new electoral market as discussed in Chapter 1. Sanders (1998: 222) noted that the nature of new market 'contains an important warning to New Labour. What was so easily won so comprehensively in 1997 could be just as easily lost in 2001 or 2002 if Labour fails to please the huge numbers of floating voters who now exist'.

*The 1997 result re-analysed*
Indeed, focus groups conducted by the media discovered that voters remained as critical of Labour as they were of John Major and the Conservatives. Analysis of opinion polls in a slightly different way also suggests that support for Labour's policies vis-à-vis the Conservatives was not as strong as first thought. As Roger Mortimore of MORI noted (in direct correspondence with the author), 'since 1995 MORI have asked an extra question, on which of the issues on the list the respondent thinks will be very important in determining his/her vote'. Data for 'best party policy' and 'issues important to vote' were shown in Chapter 4 but these can also be correlated. As Mortimore explained, 'this makes the battery of questions more powerful, as we can analyse separately which is viewed as the best party on each issue by those thinking it important': see Table 5.12.

**Table 5.12** *Best party policy on issues deemed important, 1997*

*Questions asked: Looking ahead to the next general election, which, if any, of these issues do you think will be very important to you in helping you to decide which party to vote for? [and then, if issue cited as important] I would like you to tell me whether you think the Conservative Party, the Labour Party or the Liberal Democrats has the best policies on each problem.*

| Policies | Labour or Conservative better policy (% lead over the other) |
|---|---|
| Housing | Labour (37) |
| Public transport | Labour (37) |
| Health care | Labour (38) |
| Unemployment | Labour (38) |
| Trade unions | Labour (35) |
| Education | Labour (23) |
| Pensions | Labour (25) |
| Animal welfare | Labour (13) |
| Protecting the natural environment | Conservative (1) |
| Law and order | Conservative (2) |
| Northern Ireland | Conservative (9) |
| Taxation | Conservative (15) |
| Europe | Conservative (19) |
| Constitution/devolution | Conservative (21) |
| Managing the economy | Conservative (22) |
| Defence | Conservative (30) |

*Source:* MORI polls.
*Notes:* n = c. 1,000 or 2,000, surveys based on GB residents aged 18 +. Poll taken 8 April. This was based on respondents who mentioned the issues as important first.

This indicates that the Conservatives' policy on Europe was much more favourable than previously suggested and that the Tories hold better policies on more (eight as opposed to five) issues. Table 5.13 then shows the differences between this and that purely for best party policy. This provides further indication that the second measure shown above yields results more favourable to the Conservatives.

**Table 5.13** *Best party policy compared with best party policy on important issues, 1997*

*Questions asked: Looking ahead to the next general election, which, if any, of these issues do you think will be very important to you in helping you to decide which party to vote for?; I would like you to tell me whether you think the Conservative Party, the Labour Party or the Liberal Democrats has the best policies on each problem.*

| Policies | Labour or Conservative better policy (% lead over the other) | Labour or Conservative better policy (% lead over the other) |
|---|---|---|
|  | *Measure I: best party* | *Measure II: best party by issue important* |
| *Increase in Conservative advantage* | | |
| Managing the economy | Conservative (7) | Conservative (22) |
| Europe | Conservative (1) | Conservative (19) |
| Constitution/devolution | Conservative (2) | Conservative (21) |
| Defence | Conservative (14) | Conservative (30) |
| Northern Ireland | Conservative (8) | Conservative (9) |
| *Change from Labour advantage to Conservative* | | |
| Law and order | Labour (1) | Conservative (2) |
| Taxation | Labour (1) | Conservative (15) |
| Protecting the natural environment | Labour (6) | Conservative (1) |
| *Increase in Labour's advantage* | | |
| Health care | Labour (32) | Labour (38) |
| Education | Labour (19) | Labour (23) |
| Unemployment | Labour (24) | Labour (38) |
| Pensions | Labour (20) | Labour (25) |
| Housing | Labour (24) | Labour (37) |
| Public transport | Labour (25) | Labour (37) |
| Animal welfare | Labour (6) | Labour (13) |
| Trade unions | Labour (18) | Labour (35) |

*Source:* MORI polls.
*Notes:* n = c. 1,000 or 2,000, surveys based on GB residents aged 18 +. Poll taken 8 April. This was based on respondents who mentioned the issues as important first.

The figures alter with the second analysis. The Conservatives' position increases significantly, although Labour also increases its advantage on a number of issues. Arguably, this measure captures more useful information for parties: it is only when an issue is important to a voter that their opinion of a party's policy on it will be influential. Clearly this raises issues in how to measure support although they are outside the scope of this research. Unfortunately MORI did not use this type of questioning for elections prior to 1997. If it continues to pursue this line of questioning then some interesting results may be found. But certainly Labour's support, although appearing substantial, is open to change.

*Support since 1997*
Following their election in 1997, the Labour Party and Tony Blair (see Table 5.14) in particular has attracted extremely high levels of popularity (see King and Jones (1998), for example). This is congruent with the closeness of their behaviour to the model.

**Table 5.14** *Evaluations of party leader as Prime Minister, January–February 1999*

*Question asked: Who would make the best Prime Minister?*

|  | Blair | Hague | Ashdown |
| --- | --- | --- | --- |
| January 1999 | 54.5 | 13.4 | 17.3 |
| February 1999 | 52.6 | 11.8 | 18.2 |

*Source:* Gallup Political Index/*Daily Telegraph*, 5 March 1999.

Historically speaking, the Labour Government did very well in the mid-term elections in so much as the usual substantial dip in support did not occur. This reflects the theory that argued that a Market-Oriented Party will be better placed to attract support at all phases of the electoral cycle.

Again, however, a political marketing analysis offers a different perspective and suggests that 'New Labour, New Danger' may in fact have more relevance (even if more for Labour itself than voters at large) than first thought. Labour often discusses voters' needs, almost as if identification of demands is a substitute for responding to them. Sparrow and Turner's qualitative research already indicated future problems in 1999. Using focus groups, they suggested (1999: 17) that there was:

> a changing mood towards new Labour and the Blair leadership. A growing view is that Labour has 'done very little'; 'has not lived up to their promises'; and has been 'disappointing'. At worst, the Party often appears 'sanctimonious', 'arrogant', and even 'devious'. Increasingly, Labour is seen as 'full of

what they are going to do' without actually doing anything. Despite many policy initiatives, the problem for Labour is that voters are comparing their performance with their own idiosyncratic personal expectations born out of the promises which they saw Labour giving during the 1997 election campaign. Image is seen to predominate – 'they're all gloss ... whatever the next soundbite is'; 'they're nicey-nicey' and 'plasticky'. On policies the notion of 'government by stealth' has certainly caught on – 'you get a bit with one hand and it's taken back by the other'; 'it's all in the small print'; 'sneaking it through the back door'.

These negative feelings, which came from traditional Labour voters in 1997, and Tory and Liberal Democrat voters who have considered voting Labour, also began to permeate opinions of Blair himself because he is so closely connected with the New Labour design. Sparrow and Turner accepted the high ratings of satisfaction Labour still had in quantitative polls, but suggested that their qualitative research could 'be picking up on a change of perception which only later will translate into quantitative poll findings' (1999: 18). Political marketing analysis does the same. A report from the Labour Party itself based on its private polls, leaked to the *Independent* newspaper warned that 'the Party's huge lead in the opinion polls masks the fact that people are turning against the Government because they believe it is failing to deliver its 1997 general election promises ... William Hague ... has made a modest recovery as Mr Blair's popularity declines'. It detected 'real shifts behind the headline voting intention figures' and suggested 'a drift downwards in many of the image ratings, notably on arrogance, being in touch and keeping promises'. The biggest threats to the party's continued success were said to be 'non-delivery on health and education'.

A year later, these predictions of a loss in Labour's support have begun to show in quantitative polls. In January 2000 Dunleavy (2000) argued that Labour could not take the outcome of the next general election for granted. He contended that the polls overestimated Labour's support. Labour's support as measured by lower elections – by-elections; council; local government; the devolved legislatures in Scotland and Wales; the European Parliament – had fallen. This, and failure to deliver by Labour, meant that the party could not assume an easy win. In 2000 month after month produced journalistic reports that showed a fall in Labour's poll lead over the Tories. Additionally Labour's own qualitative research is showing problems for Blair. In May 2000 a report from the Labour adviser Philip Gould was leaked (see Leppard *et al.* (2000) for further detail). It revealed that Labour's focus groups showed high dissatisfaction with the Government. This was especially true of pensioners, who were only given a 75p increase per week in state pension. Furthermore the research found that the Opposition leader, William Hague, was attracting switcher voters (Tories who had supported Labour in 1997) back. But even loyal Labour voters showed signs of significant dissatisfaction because living standards were worse while education and the health service had not improved. There have also been a number of other events that indicate falling support. One prime example is the election for the London Mayor, a new position created by New Labour. After failing to be selected as the Labour candidate, arguably due to the way Labour ran the election, an old left-winger, Ken Livingstone, stood as an independent after calls from the public to do so. He succeeded in winning the election, which was an embarrassment for the Government. This was an indication of the discontent at the grass roots and more widely amongst London voters with Labour. Paul Flynn, MP for Newport West (quoted on BBC online, 5 May 2000):

> Labour's had a good kicking, because we have lost contact with our own members and supporters, who either stayed at home or voted for other candidates. We must learn the message from devolution, in London and in Wales. The Labour control freakery has tried to impose candidates and it has failed. We need a little bit of humility. Let's have an end to control freakery.

In June 2000 Blair was even slow hand-clapped by the Women's Institute, normally a fairly sedate and traditional organisation, after giving a speech seen as being nothing more than a party advertisement. Signs of voter dissatisfaction with the New Labour design continue to emerge. Satisfaction trends with the Labour Government and Blair show a downward slope (see MORI polls). On 20–22 July 2000, MORI conducted a telephone survey of 1,011 British adults aged over 18 and asked if they were satisfied or dissatisfied with the way that Tony Blair was doing his job as Prime Minister. 49 per cent said satisfied, 45 per cent dissatisfied. Table 5.15 shows more detailed signs of discontent. For example, 57 per cent of respondents did not think he had kept his promises.

**Table 5.15** *Tony Blair's performance as Prime Minister, July 2000*

*Question asked: Since becoming Prime Minister in May 1997, do you think Tony Blair has or has not ...?*

|  | Has (%) | Has not (%) | Don't know (%) |
| --- | --- | --- | --- |
| Kept his promises | 36 | 57 | 7 |
| Kept taxes down | 29 | 62 | 9 |
| Improved the NHS | 30 | 64 | 6 |
| Improved education | 42 | 42 | 16 |
| Stood up for Britain in Europe | 49 | 40 | 11 |
| Introduced policies to support the family | 45 | 43 | 12 |

*Source:* MORI telephone survey, 20–22 July 2000.
*Note:* n = 610.

In July 2000 there were two leaked memos from the party. The first was written by Blair himself, which indicated that he knew he was seen as 'out of touch with gut British instincts' on crime, asylum, defence and the family. Another memo from Gould indicated further voter disatisfaction evident in his focus group research. Extracts included the following comments:

- Our current situation is serious. There is absolutely no room for complacency.
- There is currently now a chance that our majority will fall dramatically, following the pattern of 1945 and 1964.
- We are outflanked on patriotism and crime; we are suffering from disconnection; we have been assailed for spin and broken promises; we are not believed to have delivered; we are believed by a huge margin to be slowing down rather than speeding up.
- The New Labour brand has been badly contaminated. It is the object of constant criticism and, even worse, ridicule. Undermined by a combination of spin, lack of conviction and apparent lack of integrity, manifested by the Mayoral process.
- We lack confidence in power. We have no proselytising press to rely on. We lack politicians genuinely in tune with the people. (How many ministers, for example, genuinely want to be tough on crime?)
- We need to get back in touch.

Furthermore, MORI stated that all their polling found the same results (report by Roger Mortimore 'Two leaks', 21 July 2000). Labour is still successful but the quality of support is weak and overall it can easily fall.

### Leaving the party behind: discontent in the grass roots

Even a few months into the new Government it was clear that there was significant potential for future problems within the party. There has been significant evidence of discontent amongst internal supporters. Various papers presented at the 1999 Political Marketing and EPOP conferences indicated problems with regard to the new procedures operated for elections to the European Parliament, the Scottish Parliament and Welsh Assembly. The influence extended by the national party leadership over the selection of the leadership candidate for the Welsh Assembly aroused significant discontent among Labour Party activists. When asked about this at the 1999 Political Marketing Conference, Philip Gould conceded that the issue was not handled well. Election procedures for all candidates to the Scottish Parliament and Welsh Assembly have also been criticised. The two new legislatures are not appearing to fulfil the promise of devolved, 'post-Westminster' politics (Greenstein 1999). Wilson and Croft's

(1999) analysis also presents qualitative evidence of discontent amongst party members in Wales during campaigning for local councils, the Welsh Assembly and the European elections. Similarly the selection procedures for the London Mayor were open to criticism as trying to ensure that the New Labour's Governments chosen candidate would win.

Consideration of the party's membership also suggests potential problems and confirms early speculation (Lees-Marshment (1997)) that the party would lose membership support in the long term. This is evident on two levels. The first relates to the alienation of more traditional members. In the lead up to the 1997 election and since, there have also been numerous journalistic reports about how 'Old Labour' members are dissatisfied with the way the party has changed and have even left because of it. Wilson and Croft's (1999) preliminary analysis also suggests problems in the relationship between party members and the 'political hierarchy in the Labour Party' in Wales. Wilson questioned Gould about the role of members at the 1999 Political Marketing Conference. Gould's response was to say that he and the party leadership believed in members; their role was to take the message out to the public and upwards through the hierarchy of the Labour Party; and the party's 'processes try to involve party members in both'. The second is apparent from a study of Labour's membership conducted in 1997 after the general election (Whiteley and Seyd (1998)). This suggests that members who joined after Tony Blair became leader are much less active and attached to the party. Numerous journalistic reports have also contended that such new members have failed to renew their membership and activists are leaving the party. This reflects the limited application of marketing to the membership. It also means that the foundations of Labour's support have been eroded, and it is even more crucial that they satisfy those voters whose support it obtained on the basis of promised outputs.

### Key to success: Stage 8: Delivery

The key to Labour's long-term electoral success will therefore be delivery. External support was gained on the basis of a promised product. If it is to retain this support it needs to deliver this product. It does not matter that delivery is hard in today's political system. People voted for Tony Blair because he promised to improve their daily lives in health, education and crime. He even gave specific pledges they will now expect him to meet. As Fletcher (1997) said of 'New Labour TM':

> While cynics believe you can fool all the people all the time if you go about it cleverly enough, it ain't quite so. The public gains its impression of brands both through advertising and through using them. They trust Kellogg's and Marks and Spencer because they've know them for a long time, and they've

almost certainly never been let down by them. Advertising can enhance and bolster that trust, but if Kellogg's tasted like crunchy bird droppings and Marks' underpants disintegrated in situ, all the advertising in the world wouldn't persuade people to trust them.

The Labour Government has been focused on delivery since getting into office. The Party's 1997 manifesto argued: 'we have promised only what we know we can deliver' (The Labour Party (1997)). They knew they must ensure that this is true: it must go all the way through the marketing process. At the end of his first speech as Prime Minister, outside Downing Street, Tony Blair declared: 'enough of talking – it is time now to do.'

Since getting into government Labour politicians frequently discuss their record on delivery. The party copied business and started to issue an annual report on its delivery of its promises (see newspaper reports on the 1998 edition such as Jones (1998), The Labour Party (1999: 3–7) and The Labour Party (2000)). At the back of these reports are feedback forms for people to fill in. The 1999 edition showed some of those from the year before, one of which stated: 'I want to say I am very impressed. I can't recall ever experiencing a government asking for feedback from the general public, without there being the stimulus of a general election. I think it's wonderful that you have reported back and that you are asking for comments.'

Aside from listing their achievements in relation to their promises, the Government also admitted to failing to deliver on some aspects: an approach which is arguably more believable (and perhaps more honest). The party also sent out a consultative survey one year into government which asked respondents to assess how well they thought Labour had done in meeting their ten pledges (The Labour Party (1998)). Another indication of the primacy being given to delivery was the Labour Party web-site in the summer of 1999, which took the reader straight to a page listing their successes, such as offering referendums on devolution in Scotland and Wales (see Box 1.1 in Chapter 1). The 99/00 report (see The Labour Party (2000)) is perhaps more like a pre-election manifesto, but on-line (www.pm.govuk) further detail was added, including a list of the 177 manifesto commitments and government progress on each one in detail.

It is at the time of writing too early to make full assessment of how Labour has delivered so far: or more importantly, what voters think about their delivery. In its 1999 annual report, it claimed to be on course with respect to its five main pledges and to have kept 90 others, with 85 on course and only two yet to be tabled (The Labour Party (1999: 7)). Labour has delivered on constitutional reform, with the introduction of devolution in Scotland and Wales and the removal of hereditary peers from the House of Lords. It may also meet specific pledges, such as reducing health service waiting lists and class sizes. But it remains to be seen whether, in voters' eyes, it will have delivered its more general claims to improve the health service and education. Table 5.15 above indicated signs of trouble: the majority did not think Blair had kept taxes down or improved the NHS.

New Labour is at present a highly successful and strong organisation. The party may respond to problems: it has continued to conduct market intelligence in government. According to Seyd (1999: 390–1) it established a 'party into power' project which acknowledged the lack of debate and direct participation at party conferences. It has introduced 'members only' sessions at the annual party conference from which the television cameras are barred, so as to ensure members get a chance to air their views but it does not lose the party support from voters at large. Policy forums have also been created to provide greater participation. Labour is, as Gould (1999) contended, advantaged by a relatively weak opposition: the Conservatives have continued to attract low levels of support since the 1997 election.

But it remains possible to hypothesise that if Labour experiences major problems in delivery (or at least voters' perceptions of it), if membership discontent intensifies and translates into non-turnout or votes for the Liberal Democrats, if signs of discontent amongst the public with Labour's approach increases and the opposition offers an effective alternative, Labour's support could collapse like a pack of cards. To make a difference to a general election results would require an effective opposition and Labour appears to dismiss the Tories. The Conservative heavy losses in the 1997 election provides simple justification for this attitude. However, surely the election was also a lesson in how no party, not even New Labour, can afford to be complacent. The tale of the Tories in 1997 is a potent reminder that in the current electoral market a party in government must continue to be responsive to changes in society if it is to remain in power. This is a sober lesson which 'New Labour' must learn quickly if it is to continue its success. Furthermore, as the next chapter will show, Conservative Party behaviour since then suggests that Labour's dismissal of its prospects is unwise, if understandable. Since the 1997 election, the Tories have transformed their attitude towards voters and engendered organisational reform and a *Listening to Britain* market intelligence exercise. Competition in Britain's electoral market is high. For the first time ever, both major parties are following the Market-Oriented Party model. They both want to offer voters what they want, the question is who can deliver this. With voters more critical and open to offers the market is more open. In many ways, the real party has only just begun.

### Note

1 Unless otherwise stated directly within the text because of particular originality or primary nature, this chapter draws on the secondary empirical descriptive accounts of the time period listed below. Details of other works consulted and directly cited are in the full bibliography at the end of the book.

Baker *et al.* (1999), BBC (1995), Blair (1997), Blumler, Kavanagh and Nossiter (1996), Broughton (1999), Butler and Kavanagh (1997), Crewe, Gosschalk and Bartle (eds) (1998), Denver (1998), Farnham (1996), Fielding (1995), Fielding (1997a), Fletcher (1997), Gould (1998a), Gould (1998b), Gould (1999), Greenstein (1999), Henig (1997), Jun (1996), Kavanagh (1997), Kellner (1997), King (1998a), King (1998b, King and Jones (1998), Lancaster and Massingham (1993), Lees-Marshment (1997), McSmith (1998), Norris (1997b), Norris (1998a), Norris (1998b), Powell (1998), Rose (1997), Sanders (1998), Seyd (1998), Seyd (1999), Seyd and Whiteley (1992), Short (1996), Shrimsley (1999), Sopel (1995), Whiteley (1998), Whiteley and Seyd (1998), Whiteley, Seyd and Richardson (1994), Wilson and Croft (1999), Wring (1994–95).

# 6

# The party's just begun

British political parties use political marketing to win elections. Specifically, they become Market-Oriented Parties. They conduct market intelligence to identify and understand people's demands: both their needs and wants. They then design a product, including leader, policy and organisation, that responds to these demands, but is also one that they can deliver in government, is believable and is adjusted to suit internal views within the organisation. They also take into account the nature of the competition and the support they have or need to win an election. The product design is then implemented throughout the party and then communicated to voters on a daily basis over a number of years leading up to an election. The actual election campaign is then almost superfluous to requirements but provides the last chance to convey to voters what is on offer. If the party is the most market-oriented of its main competitors, it then wins the election.

At other times parties may move towards traditional politics and become more product-oriented; simply arguing for what they think is right. This does not win a general election, however. Similarly, Sales-Oriented Parties, the type most commonly associated with political marketing, can produce well-organised and professional election campaigns. But a Sales-Oriented Party can never really get to the heart of the British people. As Britain's electoral market will no longer vote for a party simply because their family supported them in the past, it will also not warm to snappy advertising and clever slogans, or sound-bites and spin-doctors. This is not enough for the British electorate. If politics is to do anything for the people of this country, it must deliver what they need and want, not just discuss political ideologies remote from their everyday lives.

Political marketing, at least its market-oriented kind, has the potential to do this. We may have a long way to go before a full political marketing revolution takes place and we see the NHS, education service, Parliament itself as well as the civil service take on a market orientation not just in themselves but working together with Market-Oriented Parties so that as a whole the UK political system is continually responding to the public's needs. But nevertheless the potential is there.

This chapter will explore future developments in British party marketing, consider marketing in other countries, and discuss the normative implications of marketing political parties. It will also indicate how marketing might be applied to non-party organisations, before reaching an overall conclusion about political marketing.

## Marketing British parties

Although at times parties opt for a sales or product orientation, it is only when they are market-oriented that they stand a chance of winning the election. At least, the more market-oriented they are, the more likely it is they will win. Obviously the nature of the competition is important. If the opposition is product-oriented, a party may win against it without being market-oriented: a sales orientation and more effective advertising may be enough to attract greater electoral support. The trend in Britain currently is towards the Market-Oriented Party model and so the competition to be the most market-oriented is increasing. Political marketing is a new development and, as already explored in the previous chapter, even Tony Blair's New Labour Party, which is the closest example of a Market-Oriented Party, did not fit the model completely. Indeed, Labour's use of political marketing potentially placed it in a very weak position in the long term.

Nonetheless, since the 1997 election, political marketing has been taken a step forward. Both parties are competing to be the most market-oriented. Labour is focusing on delivery and continuing to conduct market intelligence. The Tories have transformed their attitude towards voters and engendered organisational reform and a 'Listening to Britain' market intelligence exercise. Indeed, since William Hague became leader in July 1997 he has consistently voiced cognisant desires to make the behaviour of the Conservative Party more responsive to voters' demands. In February 1998, he launched 'The Fresh Future', claiming that the 'Conservative Party is changing. Changing our institutions and our structures; changing the way we involve our members and changing our culture ... We are changing the way we do business' (Hague (1998a)). Although the new leader has suffered from extremely low levels of popularity, the interesting aspect of his leadership is that while taking the Tories through the marketing process he has taken more care with the stages such as internal analysis and implementation that Blair neglected. This suggests that in the long term the Conservative Party may emerge the more market-oriented of the two parties.

The Conservative Party has engaged in significant market intelligence. It has used formal research, commissioning polling of voters' opinions, including focus groups on former Tory voters. Informally, it initiated internal discussion about public perception of the party and its MPs, and the decline in membership (see The Conservative Party (1997b) and Archie Norman (1998)), culminating in a White Paper on reform (The Conservative Party (1998a)). In July 1998, the Party launched 'Listening to Britain'. This consisted of an extensive series of meetings where politicians listened to audience discussion (see The Conservative Party (1998–99)): there were over 1,400 meetings with over 250,000 people involved (Francis (2000)). This most notably reflected the market-oriented concept: Hague (1998c) argued that the exercise was 'about the whole party reconnecting with people'. Rachel Francis from the Listening to Britain Unit explained that the meetings were held 'at three levels: those meetings organised at constituency level: meetings which are organised county wide and key theme meetings organised by the Listening to Britain Unit which are usually attended by the Leader' (Francis (1999)). The Party sent 650 copies of a highly detailed manual (The Conservative Party (1998b)) to all its constituency associations to advise and encourage them to hold such meetings (Francis (2000)). Andrew Lansley, Director of the programme, explained that: 'The rationale behind it was to get in touch with the electorate; to extend our regular contact beyond members/election times and to obtain practical policy ideas and to change the culture of the Party' (Lansley (1999)). A representative from Central Office or the constituency attended each meeting and made notes on the discussion (Francis (1999)), from which *Listening to Britain: A Report* by the Conservative Party (Conservative Party (1999c)) was produced (Francis (2000)). This report identified key voter concerns in detail. For example, it discussed education, but more specifically concerns about too much paperwork for teachers, falling basic standards and too much government interference. Clearly this type of activity helps the party to re-connect with voters and be more responsive to suit their demands. Furthermore constituency parties continue to hold these type of meetings even now in order to understand local concerns and also to invite feedback on the Party's developing policies (Francis (2000)).

The Tory product has been put together in response to results from this market intelligence, although with some limitations. Although no one from the Tory Party would be sensible to admit it, because of the poor reputation gained by them between 1992 and 1997, they were unlikely to win the next election whatever they did. Strategy is therefore designed with the time frame of two electoral cycles in mind. The leader, William

Hague, who was elected leader in July 1997, is a substantial weakness in its product as far as external support is concerned because voters do not rate him highly. However his leadership and significant party management skills have significant benefits: he is the sort of leader the party needs in the first electoral cycle to implement the foundations for a market orientation. Changes he has introduced can remain in place even when or if either his public standing improves or the Tories elect a different, more voter-friendly leader. Policies have been gradually developed during the time the Tories know they have. This enables greater thought, creativity and chance to achieve acceptance and implementation throughout the party rather than have market-oriented policies imposed from on high.

Indeed, the most important changes Hague has made to the product are organisational, constitutional and cultural: subtle, internal changes that do not increase ratings in the public opinion polls but nevertheless lay the foundations for the party to emerge the most market-oriented in time. Hague initiated full-scale constitutional reform of the Conservative Party. The party adopted a new framework and organisational structure (see The Conservative Party (1998a)) which facilitated a market orientation in other aspects of the product.

For example, changes have been made to increase the numbers and involvement of members (see The Conservative Party (1998a)). Voting rights were given to individual members for electing the party leader and candidate-selection. A national membership base was created to enable the leadership to communicate with party members. A Conservative Policy Forum was created to increase the opportunity for members to discuss policy and in April 1999 a Conservative Network was launched. The network offers a social and political programme of events, information and training and was designed to encourage young, professional people into the Party (Buscombe (1998)). New activities were introduced to promote membership participation. The National Conservative Convention was established to meet twice a year, with representation from all parts of the party. A new Committee on Conferences was created to ensure 'that the Party Conference debates topical issues ... [and] the Conference is open to as many Party members as possible' (The Conservative Party (1998a)).

The leadership has also sought to impose due influence over the party's MPs and candidates. An Ethics and Integrity Committee was established to investigate misconduct amongst MPs. Hague demoted those who were negatively associated with the previous Tory Government. The party also acknowledged the need to attract more women and ethnic minority candidates (see The Conservative Party (1998a) and Hague (1999)). Archie Norman, then the party's Chief Executive and a well-known business manager, said that they were 'working with head-hunters to try and encourage people from all professions to go into politics' (quoted by

Sylvester and Thomson (1998)). Norman also altered the structure and organisation of CCO, even knocking down walls to create an open-plan office design to encourage communication (see Sylvester and Thomson (1998) and Norman (1999a)).

Policy is in continual development, but there are a number of mechanisms feeding market intelligence, including reports from the 'Listening to Britain' exercise, feedback from Constituency parties and MPs into the policy design process. At the 1999 Party Conference a preliminary framework of policies was launched in *The Common Sense Revolution* (The Conservative Party (1999d)). Since then, other initiatives, such as a tough line on immigration and a proposed increase in pensions, have been launched, all of which appear to be in response to voter concerns, especially those with which the Labour Government is not perceived to be effective in dealing. Indeed a leaked report from the Labour adviser Philip Gould in May 2000 (see Sparrow (2000) and Leppard *et al.* (2000) for further detail) noted that focus groups perceived Hague to be 'speaking for the mainstream majority' and he was attracting switcher voters (Tories who had supported Labour in 1997) back. It should also be noted that the party has continued to conduct market intelligence on its policies. Stuart Hogue, a campaign officer in CCO, handled feedback (about 100 items a week) via leaflets and the web-site on the Common Sense Revolution (Hogue (2000)). At the local level the party also conducted a 'Common Sense Survey' which canvassed opinions about five pledges made by the Tories (Hogue (2000)). Nevertheless the party will obviously need to produce clear and popular policy responses to the enduring issues of health and education.

The most interesting aspect of Hague's marketing is that there is greater indication of behaviour that follows Stage 3 of the marketing process model: Product Adjustment. For example, organisational changes occurred after substantial consultation between the leadership and the rest of the party through a working party, circulation of documents, a questionnaire to all constituency associations and a ballot of members on the White Paper (see The Conservative Party (1998a)). The leadership is attempting to introduce changes in policy within the party's ideological framework (see Hague (1998a and b)). In an interview by the BBC at the 1998 Tory Party Conference, Lady Buscome (Vice Chairman, Development) argued that 'we are genuinely wanting to become a much more inclusive party; we're out there, we're listening … But … unlike the Labour Party, we haven't changed our principles. Our principles are there and they're strong'. The focus is on changing the policies, not the party's ideology, to suit voters' needs. There have also been significant efforts made at the local level, with 'Common Sense Revolution' meetings being held, shoring up traditional support before moving onto the wider electorate (Hogue

(2000)). This approach to marketing the party will aid implementation. Peele (1998: 141–3) argued that the culture of the Conservative Party had already changed a year after the 1997 election. All the changes described will take time to have an effect. It always takes time for rhetoric to become reality and institutional changes in organisational structure to change behaviour. For example, measures undertaken to attract new members and candidates from a wider background will take years to affect the overall character of the party's membership and MPs. The crucial point is that they have been put in place.

Furthermore, Hague's use of political marketing is interesting for this study. It differs from his predecessors' in many ways. Although under Thatcher the Conservatives used market intelligence to inform their policies, it failed to influence the organisation. Hague has responded to the decline in membership and other problems in the party by enacting substantial organisational reform. Political marketing has been used to influence all aspects of the product, not just policy. Compared with Blair, the use of market intelligence by Hague has been much more open and widespread: he solicited intelligence about the party itself before, during and after engaging in organisational reform. This facilitated greater internal analysis and the reforms themselves have laid the foundations for the emergence of a market orientation at all levels. Changes to membership participation and conference activities hold the potential to enable greater debate within the party. Hague has not tried to impose complete unity amongst the Parliamentary Party. Although the Tory leadership has taken measures to encourage a wider variety of candidates, constituency associations retain their autonomy. Hague also stands more chance of taking his party with him on the quest to become market-oriented. The Conservatives have used political marketing more carefully to ensure that the party responds to voter concerns but without disregarding its traditional principles. Hague has succeeded in gaining broad, if not universal, support for reform at all levels of the party. This is in contrast to Kinnock, who had to fight every step of the way to implement any change. As he said himself, he was 'never sure the whole party was with me. I was always dragging it, inch by inch, advancing a little, fighting more, advancing. I had to choose my ground so carefully'. There are some signs of discontent within the Tory ranks (see Strafford and Ball (2000) and The Charter Movement (2000)) but Hague has still been able to succeed in a shorter time period.

Overall, therefore, the Conservative Party has turned around from behaviour which not only neglected to pay attention to voter opinions but appeared equally dismissive of the need to do so, to that which at least aims to respond to voters' demands. Only a few years since the party was thrown out of office in the 1997 general election, it had a new leader determined to make it market-oriented, staff and organisation and had engaged in substantial market intelligence which was being used to develop new policies. Clearly the electorate will judge the party as it is, and has been, and as such it remains in a poor position in the short term. The party also faces the obstacle of a poor reputation for marketing in the period 1992–97. Like a business which earns a bad reputation for delivery, the Conservatives will need time to override this. Indeed, Hague (1998c) acknowledged that it would take time for the party's new approach to have an effect:

> When you're rebuilding a party from a heavy defeat that we suffered last year, you've got to go through certain phases.
>
> You have to go through that first phase where people say, the cynics say, the critics say, 'oh they lost so badly you know they could never recover, they could never turn that around'. And we've had to go through that over the last year.
>
> And then you go on into the second phase, which is coming next, probably just about to begin. Where they say 'okay, so you're improving things, you know, but you'll never improve things quickly enough'. And we have to go through that.
>
> And then you have to go on into the third phase, where they say 'OK, you're improving things quickly, but you'll never manage to keep it up, you know'.
>
> And it's only then, that you go into the fourth phase when they say 'we always knew you were going to succeed, we always knew you were going to rebuild the Conservative Party'.

There is also the factor of the opposition: as long as Labour remains the most market-oriented and delivers on its promises, the opportunity for the Tories to win an election against it is limited. It would nonetheless be a mistake to dismiss everything Hague has done on the basis of present opinion-poll ratings. Marketing, like elections, is cyclical. After any election the party will be able to begin the process again, but with many aspects already completed successfully. Attention can then be focused on those neglected, in time for the next election. The Conservatives are in a strong position to become the most market-oriented in time, because they have gone through the marketing process in greater depth than any other party. The most significant point arising from this discussion is nevertheless that both major parties in Britain are focusing on responding to voters' concerns and using political marketing to do this. The real competition and drive to become a Market-Oriented Party will now begin.

## Marketing parties across the world

Parties in other countries also use political marketing. The USA is one notable example. Ronald Reagan, who became Republican President in

1980, engaged in marketing. He conducted formal market intelligence, took the advice of professionals, and broadly designed the product on offer to suit the majority of the electorate. He promised to reduce the power of government, in particular the large state from FDR's 'New Deal', reduce income tax, reduce the cost of government, eliminate federal deficit by 1984 and create general economic prosperity. He also offered strong leadership, especially on foreign affairs, arguing that defence expenditure would be increased to make the USA safe. In terms of strategy, the Republican team engaged in competition analysis. It picked out competition weaknesses: the weakness of Carter on defence; and focused on its own strengths, especially in the second election when it highlighted the first-term record of economic recovery, increase in defences, and increase in national pride. In terms of support analysis, Reagan had the support of the south and west, so focused efforts on industrial heartland – states of Michigan, Illinois and Ohio. Communication and campaigning were well organised, with close links to the rest of the party, the campaign was planned well in advance, communications were used to control the agenda and were well co-ordinated. Reagan was pictured in a library-like setting with 'Can Do, America' imagery. He was successful in winning two presidential elections. Furthermore, he attracted broad support: as well as the more traditional Republican white middle-class professional males, he gained votes from blue-collar workers, and those in the suburbs and sunbelt for example.

Indeed, British politicians have often gone to their US counterparts for ideas. The Conservative Party visited the USA in 1991 to gain advice from the Reagan campaigns for the 1992 British general election. Labour built on the experiences of centre-left parties in Australia and the United States in the lead-up to the 1997 election. Blair's adviser, Philip Gould, worked on the successful Clinton/Democratic Presidential campaign in 1992. Gould wrote a report on what the party should do in light of Democratic President Clinton's success and Tony Blair and Gordon Brown visited Clinton's advisers in January 1993. William Hague visited the Canadian Conservatives and US Republicans in February 1999.

Indeed, many would think that the USA is the world leader in political marketing. More detailed comparison, however, suggests that market-oriented political marketing in fact has greater potential in the UK. Work by Ingram and Lees-Marshment (1999–2000) which compared Bill Clinton and the Democratic Party in the 1992 presidential election and Blair's Labour Party in 1997 found, unsurprisingly, that Clinton undoubtedly used elements of marketing in his bid to win the presidential election, in terms of broad policy objectives as well as the expected area of influence in communication and campaigning. Clinton used focus groups and surveys to test his image and campaign themes. His election as presidential candidate was aided by the changes the Democratic Party made to its primary procedures and schedules to give moderate-to-conservative candidates, who would appeal to the wider electorate, a greater chance of winning. Clinton himself appealed to voters because he was relatively young, a family man, and came from a humble background. His policy pledges were designed to appeal to target middle-class voters and traditional Democrat supporters, particularly the policies on the economy and healthcare. He nonetheless avoided making big spending plans and attempted to make his policy plans more detailed and achievable in response to market intelligence which showed that voters did not want vague promises. For example, the campaign team developed a detailed economic plan which scaled back a number of Clinton's spending pledges and other promises to make them more feasible. With regard to the competition, they focused on the economy that was a weakness for Bush, and addressed the issue of the federal deficit to attract supporters from the third-party candidate, Ross Perot, who had placed it on the campaign agenda. Clinton engaged in continual communication and made good use of marketing techniques. He used experienced and professional staff, operated a 'war room' in Little Rock and launched adverts such as the *Man from Hope* biography which sought to show the positive side of Clinton's character. Clinton appeared on non-political but popular media, such as MTV and the *Arsenio Hall Show*. The campaign was also targeted, with less money spent in states where Clinton's support was strong and more in those where he was weaker but needed to gain to become President.

Nevertheless there are significant differences between Clinton and Blair which reflect the systemic differences between the two countries. Clinton did not make as detailed a set of promises as Blair. He did not apply marketing to the 'whole party' because the leader cannot control the rest of the party, as in the UK. The party notion and structure are different in the USA. American parties are much looser organisations, and do not have such centralised structure, notion of membership or ideology. Election campaigns are more candidate-centred: the focus is on the candidate not their party; their product their own image, character and policy pledges rather than party behaviour and policy platforms. Another key difference was delivery. Clinton successfully won the election, indeed, he won with 370 electoral votes in thirty-two states, and saw the Democrats maintain control of both the House and Senate. The result put a Democrat in the White House for the first time since 1980 and ended twelve years of divided government, thereby raising the prospect of more co-operative relations between the Presidency and Congress. But delivery was mixed and problematic. He succeeded in passing a deficit reduction plan in Congress, but did little on improving economic performance and health care reform did not even come to a vote. He failed on his key election pledges even if he succeeded in other areas. In

1994, arguably as a result of these failures, the Democrats experienced major losses in the 1994 mid-terms, and the Republicans took control of both houses for the first time in forty years. This made it even more difficult for Clinton to control what happened in Congress. Ingram and Lees-Marshment (1999–2000) would argue that this was due to the nature of the governing system. American Presidents are bound to find it difficult to deliver on their policy promises because they have only limited influence on Congress and although compromise may produce outputs the process of compromising alters policies so much they no longer fulfil election promises. Labour at least has a greater chance of delivering, with more control over Parliament and its party. Systemic features substantially condition the scope, focus and application of political marketing. Although marketing techniques may initiate in the USA, comprehensive political marketing of a product which is not just communicated but delivered is more likely to occur in countries like Britain.

Political marketing is also undoubtedly used in countries other than the USA. In Canada, following their heavy defeat in 1992, the Ontario Conservatives initiated a listening exercise similar to that of Hague's. Indeed, the Tories' latest slogan to capture their new set of policies, a 'Common Sense Revolution', was first used there. The research by Bauer *et al.* (1996) indicates that German parties have or are attempting to apply a market orientation to their membership. Indeed, various studies of party membership both in Britain and elsewhere suggest that parties are doing this (see, for example, Seyd (1999), Scarrow (1998)). That by O'Cass (1996) and Dann and Dann (1998), however, suggests a lack of political marketing by major parties in Australia, but not necessarily a lack of demand for it. Baines *et al.* (1999) have studied the activity of political consultants in Europe and Harris *et al.* (1999) marketing (albeit with a focus on the campaign side) in Sweden.

The comparative study of political marketing therefore needs to take account of the institutional and cultural differences of other nations. Such differences include the structure of government, constitutional arrangements, separation of powers, type of legislature and electoral system. For example, if a country possess a proportional electoral system, it could mean that parties are more likely to promise things they cannot deliver, because after the election, in order to get into power, they have to compromise on the product they originally offered. Butler and Collins (1994: 23) cited an example of the Irish Labour Party in the 1992 general election. They claimed it 'used its considerably increased parliamentary representation to support a Government party which had suffered significant reversals. Many Labour supporters had anticipated a rainbow coalition of former opposition parties, and subsequent debate took on a bitter note'. Alternatively, such a system may foster smaller parties with a smaller market to which they can more easily be responsive and maintain a market orientation.

Where society is remarkably different to that in Britain, political marketing, or at least a market orientation, may not be as necessary to ensure party survival and we would not expect it to be used. Marketing is concerned with the relationship between the organisation and its market: thus research needs to take into account the nature of society and its effect on politics. A country which still has clearly defined political cleavages, for example, might be less likely to use marketing in the way the British parties have. A Product-Oriented Party may be more appropriate in some circumstances, as the empirical observations made by Allan Leonard's (1998) paper on the Alliance Party in Northern Ireland suggest. The societal changes outlined in Chapter 2, which are viewed in this research as being behind the rise of political marketing in Britain, have not occurred in all countries and thus Market-Oriented Party behaviour would not be expected. Other differences may be in the party system and governmental system and indeed, as indicated in Chapter 2, the nature of party itself.

Comparative research also needs to be in the CPM (Comprehensive Political Marketing) category to reach its full potential. It also needs to be conducted using theoretical foundations to prevent cursory, misleading conclusions about political marketing. One case that is commonly cited as an example of political marketing which also raises criticisms of the field is Silvio Berlusconi's *Forza Italia!* which won the 1994 election in Italy. Closer analysis of this case (for empirical details see Buffachi and Burgess (1998: 176–86 and 191–228)) using the CPM-framework established in this book reveals that this is an example of poor political marketing. Although, as Buffachi and Burgess argue, the common explanations of this new party's success as 'time for a change' and 'Berlusconi's control of the mass media' can be rejected, their conclusions that the formation of the party 'was, above all, an exercise in political marketing' (1998: 183) are in need of qualification. Firstly, Berlusconi's behaviour was partly that of a Sales-Oriented Party and, secondly, he made many promises which were not achievable. Once in government he also took on a product-oriented attitude: Buffachi and Burgess (1998: 191) explain that he developed a 'belief that the people had bestowed him a right to govern undisputed', he resisted criticism from the Opposition and failed to deliver (1998: 202–13). There is also the need for more than a superficial summary in order fully to appreciate marketing in other countries. For example, it may be that marketing is more effective at the local level in the USA. Like this study of Britain, detailed empirical investigation covering a long time-period is necessary to enable a subtlety of understanding as to not only whether parties use political marketing, but to what extent; how and why they do not; and the consequences of this.

## Marketing with a difference: different parties, goals and systems

Political marketing can also be applied to parties with different goals and under different systems. In Britain, for example, an interesting area of research would be the Liberal Democrat Party. Conversations with key party figures and the presentation by David Walter (1999), Director of the Liberal Democrat's Media Communications in 1999, indicate that the Liberals also engage in political marketing of a market-oriented nature. Indeed, some of their comments suggest that the Liberals may have the most mature political marketing approach to politics. The party's focus on building up support at the local level and in certain geographical areas may pay huge dividends in the long term. It holds the potential to build up loyal support and a reputation for delivery which, if it were possible to transfer this to the national level, could pay substantial electoral dividends. The main obstacle is the party's status as a third party and all the barriers this entails, despite its own assertions that it has moved from being a party of protest to a party of power because of its co-operation with the Labour Government. This is why the theoretical constructs embodied in this research need to be adapted to suit the position of a different type of party but, in this case, allowing for consideration of how to make the complex move from a minor to being perceived by voters as a major party. Research might also consider identifying and analysing Product-Oriented Parties. A Product-Oriented Party can have an important role to play in society, in terms of placing new issues on the agenda and political education and discussion. These aspects could also be considered across countries.

Additionally, the British political system holds much potential for change, given the move towards devolution and the possibility of altering the electoral system. These will not mean that political marketing will no longer be possible, but it may have to be used differently. Devolution raises many questions for political marketing and at this stage it is completely open to debate as to whether it will make marketing easier or more difficult. It could hold the potential for more effective and responsive institutions, better able to deliver because of the focus on a smaller level and region. On the other hand, it could make things more complex for the national parties: when questioned, Philip Gould (1999) conceded that devolution might make delivery more difficult for New Labour.

## Political marketing and democracy

Political marketing is clearly an important phenomenon in politics today. Marketing political parties in particular, however, arouses much normative criticism. There are many possible objections to the rise of both sales-

and market-oriented political marketing, but also some answers. The debate cannot be resolved here, but it can be begun.

Political marketing is often viewed as causing behaviour amongst political elites that will only be successful in the short term and neglects the real needs of the people. Smith and Saunders (1990: 298) note how people fear that marketing will cause a scenario 'where politicians increasingly focus on narrow, short term issues because they are popular, whilst leaving the more critical longer term, strategic planning to become a hostage to fortune'. Marketing could stop parties taking unpopular but arguably necessary decisions, because they pay so much attention to current public opinion. Critics of political marketing see it as responsible for politicians following fads in public opinion and neglecting the real needs of the population.

This may be how politicians sometimes behave, but this is not due to them using political marketing. The objective of political marketing is to ensure the organisation achieves its goals. If a party wishes to obtain electoral support for more than one election, it must determine its behaviour to obtain support in the long term. If politicians act to ensure success in the short term, rather than addressing the long term problems of the people, it is the short term goal-focus of the politicians that is the problem, not political marketing. Similarly, political marketing is often seen as aiding populism, but Smith and Saunders (1990: 298) argue that the perspective of populism is short-term and is in fact rooted in the selling era. If a party kept switching issues or offered inconsistent or impracticable product designs (Smith and Saunders (1990: 299) give the example of reduce taxation and increased public spending and thus 'voodoo economics') it would destroy the party's credibility.

From a policy point of view, the short-term nature of support the Market-Oriented Party attracts may not be sustainable through the enactment of long-term measures and thus may hinder the development of long-term yet arguably more effective policies. The argument is that some policies need more than one term of office, maybe even decades, to achieve successful implementation but they may not prove popular in the short term. If parties become sophisticated enough, it may be possible for them to calculate it worth taking a decision that will be unpopular in the short run in order to achieve success and support in the long run. This is also a general dilemma for democratic politics, rather than political marketing itself.

The rise of a Market-Oriented Party nonetheless raises important normative questions, because the basic idea of a market orientation is to follow, rather than lead, voter demands. It implies that conviction politics is over: this appears to confirm the prediction, made with some fear, by a political correspondent in the 1960s (quoted by Rose (1967: 219)) that:

The real risk is that we are moving towards the day when market research, opinion poll findings ... will be crudely and cold-bloodedly used to govern party strategies in government and out. When that day comes ... the point of politics will not be the conviction of politicians about the rightness of their principles, policies or beliefs. The point of leadership will not be to lead, but to follow the crowd.

That day has indeed arrived in Britain. It therefore raises the objection that political parties should not simply follow voters' demands: in politics, it is better to stand for what you believe and argue your case. The majority may not always be right. The minority or elite may have knowledge and understanding that the majority does not. This is against elite theories of democracy.

For example, Scrivens and Witzel (1990: 11) noted how 'asking the general population to vote effectively on certain subjects raises a number of complex issues ... the general public may hold views which are considered by policy makers to be unacceptable in society'. The political elite are better qualified to make decisions about what the people need and should be given. As Smith and Saunders (1990: 298) explain, 'pandering to the prejudices of the majority might herald a tyranny of the ill-formed. Capital punishment, forced repatriation and other lowest common denominator issues could become important if marketing research showed a short-term benefit in courting them'. Traditionally, British representative democracy held that politicians are elected as representatives not delegates (see Smith and Saunders (1990: 298)). Thus, as Edmund Burke said, 'I am here to represent your interests, not your desires'. This reflects the tradition within some parties such as the Labour Party which, as McLean (1987: 58) explained, 'has always been more ambivalent about marketing than the Conservatives' because it believed that 'it is not necessarily right to take voters' preferences as exogenous'.

These objections therefore relate to views about the nature of democracy and also the notion of a Product-Oriented Party and the behaviour of the Labour Party in the 1983 election (see Chapter 3). As already noted, there is a natural tension in the party arena between the politics of conviction and winning elections. This tension has always existed to an extent and has not simply arisen because of the use of political marketing. Lock and Harris (1996: 29) observed the objections to political marketing and how one argument was 'a somewhat atavistic longing for the good old days when politics was about real issues, before the soundbite, the spin doctor and the marketing message. Unfortunately for those steeped in such nostalgia, such images of an innocent political past are more myth than reality'. Opinions vary about the nature of democracy. Walsh (1994: 68), for example, argues that:

It is perfectly possible to argue that people want something, and that it might produce some beneficial results, but that it would be wrong to do it. The central questions of politics, the nature of punishment, the organisation of health and education, foreign relations and the formation of law cannot be settled on the basis of consumers' expression of wants. Politics is irre-deemably a moral undertaking and what is efficient comes second to what is right or good for the social community.

Similarly, Hodder-Williams (1970: 96–7) argued: 'There is something distasteful in the thought of British politics degenerating into a competition between two groups of electoral manipulators, each eager to attract at any price the support of that section of the electorate without ideological conviction.' John Smith in the Labour Party rejected responding to market intelligence about raising income tax before the 1992 election, saying (quoted by Gould (1998b: 124)): 'All we have in politics is our integrity, and if we lose that we lose everything. Neil's changed so much, I can't change at all.' Nonetheless, Neil Kinnock conceded (on the 1987 election) (BBC (1995)) that: 'You cannot have policies, that however appealing they are to you, are completely alien to a very substantial section of the popu-lation.'

Rose's study in the 1960s found that politicians generally did not engage in market-oriented behaviour, but also found an early opinion on the side of market-oriented politics from a 'veteran party official' (1967: 225):

I never ceased to be astounded by how relatively little politicians are guided in their actions by a calculus of electoral effect. I used to be rather impressed by this – men of principle little deflected from the course of righteousness as they see it by crude political considerations. Now I am not so sure, not least because on so many questions the *genius populi* seems so often to be more right than the principles of politicians.

Indeed, it can be argued that political marketing makes parties more democratic by rendering them more responsive to voters' demands. Political marketing is concerned with how organisations respond to peoples' needs. There remains room for leadership: political marketing identifies the demands of voters but it is still up to parties and politicians to design the policies to meet those needs. It is not the same as direct or delegatory democracy. It is still within the boundaries of democracy to suggest that elites are there to represent the people and thus need to be concerned with what they want. Political marketing can help this: it makes parties and the political elite more responsive to voters. Party decline, combined with party adaptation in the form of the Market-Oriented Party, can help to make parties govern better because they no longer have support guaranteed.

225

Perhaps the debate about political marketing simply raises the long-standing questions about the nature of democracy: delegatory or representative, majoritarian etc. As Scammell (1999: 739) contends, 'regardless of the ethics of its application, marketing necessarily transforms relationships between parties and voters and leaders and party members'. Political marketing might, at first glance, suggest a move to delegatory democracy, which can be criticised in many ways. One point is what voters' attitude will be towards parties when they understand what parties are doing in using political marketing. Tony Blair has already attracted criticism for leading by focus groups: as one comment on the British Politics Group e-mail discussion list was:

> Blair is a bit of a ditherer. One cannot imagine him saying in the style of Teddy Roosevelt, 'I have no idea what the British people think. I only know what they should think'. Rather it is, 'I don't know what the British people think, but some focus groups and surveys will soon tell me, and I will know what I think'.

Another example is Palmer (1998) who claimed that New Labour was 'a populist Government, whose policies are driven by polls, focus groups . . . [and] the next logical step is to re-introduce the death penalty for murder'. In particular, the use of focus groups by Labour has become and area of concern and comment. Additionally, since getting into government Labour created a 'People's Panel', described by Moon (1999: 174) as 'a research exercise designed to provide a constant form of monitoring reaction to the government's new initiatives'. The Government has also commissioned other polls. These are all at the tax-payer's expense, yet the results have not been made public. The revelation of this created a controversy at the beginning of September 1999 (see Ward (1999)) and the Conservatives have criticised it as Labour Party market intelligence funded by the public purse (see Moon (1999: 174)). The use of marketing intelligence has become an issue in itself (see Sparrow and Turner (1999) and Gould (1999)).

Worcester (1998) defends the use of opinion polls. He argues (1998: 72) that the lesson for politicians is: 'Listen, and listen hard to public opinion. The polls during the last parliament and the Wirral South by-election result were warnings to the last Tory government, and they failed to heed the message.' Defending Labour's use of focus groups, Gould (1998b: 326) argues that: 'With the exception of 'spin-doctors' no campaign phrase has ever been imbued with a greater air of nonsensical mystique than 'focus groups'. Their importance in modern politics is that they enable politicians to hear directly the voters' voices.'

Political marketing as used by political parties suggests more of a consolidation of representative democracy. Leadership is still important, because politicians need to judge and debate about how best to meet voters' demands. A Market-Oriented Party seeks to meet voters' needs and demands, but there remains room for discussion as to the best way to do this. Representative democracy and Market-Oriented Party behaviour can go together. Political parties still perform their functions as aggregators of interest and mediators of demands: political marketing simply helps them perform these more effectively under changed circumstances. Voters, like any consumers, seek the ends of party behaviour. As Day *et al.* (1979: 256) observe, people 'seek the benefits that products provide rather than the products per se. Specific products or brands represent the available combinations of benefits and costs'. Market intelligence identifies the problem to be solved: political elites judge how best to meet it. They may utilise the experiences and values of voters in designing solutions, but some judgement is still required. There may be less debate about what to deliver, but more on how and which party is more able to deliver. In terms of the solution, or policy therefore, although there may be broad agreement between parties there will still be room for debate about the fine details. As Peter Lilley, the then Tory Deputy Party leader, argued:

> Listening to Britain . . . is about the Conservative Party listening to the people of Britain . . . it is not about writing the next manifesto by opinion polls. Nor does it mean abandoning our principles . . . A car company developing its next model will consult and listen to its potential customers about transportation needs. But it won't ask them to design the engine or tell them the principles of engineering. Likewise, we should listen to people about their needs and concerns. But we must then develop policies to meet those needs based on the basis of Conservative principles. Our listening exercise is about identifying practical problems and applying Conservative principles to them. (Lilley (1998))

Politicians increasingly listen to voters to gain guidelines and feedback about what works; what does not; what needs improving; because no one person can understand everything about a country, but some mediation and balancing of demands is necessary. At the 1999 Political Marketing Conference Philip Gould was asked how far a party could go in being populist. Gould claimed that the country was not owned by journalists but by everyone, and rejected the idea that politicians knew best. There needed to be a dialogue between users and runners in order to provide the best services. There was a need for balance between political leadership and listening to people. The 'era of producer politics has gone'. This type of attitude is not populist in the academic sense, but is simply concerned with responding and listening to voters. Another question asked how a party could interpret demands and queried whether there was a need for ideas from politicians also. Gould agreed, and said 'people don't know of course all of the answers' but parties had to listen to people: they 'need to be having ideas and moving ahead'.

Furthermore, responding to voters' demands does not mean that parties will always follow polls. If they focus on the ends, they may in fact enact policies which although unpopular at first achieve the ends voters want in the long term. Danny Finkelstein (1998: 14), for example, highlights privatisation as a useful case-study – British Telecom (BT) and British Rail (BR) – and notes that they were both quote unpopular when first proposed, but:

> BT's privatisation, though unpopular as an individual policy, actually contributed something to Margaret Thatcher's popularity. The reason is that voters understood its purpose – to help cure the British disease – and were prepared to support policies they did not much like very much in order to further a purpose they did like. When BR privatisation began voters hadn't the same clear understanding of its purpose and so it was simply and straightforwardly unpopular.

At this stage it is therefore by no means certain that political marketing will reduce democracy and there are suggestions it may even enhance it. In their overview of the research conception of political marketing, Dermody *et al.* (1999; presentation rather than the paper) postulated the 'dream' that political marketing could in fact put the philosophy, democracy and idealism back into politics, by highlighting the need for politicians to serve better those they seek to represent and reduce the discontent and disillusionment generated through election after election of grand promises which are never lived up to in government. Gould (1998b: 328) argues that:

> The public want leaders who lead, they want governments that tough it out. But they also want to be heard. Of course, governing with principles and yet in a continuous dialogue with the voters is complicated. The electorate is more demanding and is right to be so. It is up to us to meet the new challenge. I do not just see focus groups and market research as campaigning tools; increasingly I see them as an important part of the democratic process: part of a necessary dialogue between politicians and people, part of a new approach to politics.

Another quote from Stan Greenberg, an American pollster whom Gould interviewed on 2 July 1998 (quoted by Gould (1998b: 333)), echoes these views about the use of market intelligence:

> It doesn't need defending. It is part of the democratisation of modern elections. Just as governments have changed, just as parties have changed, campaigns have changed. Democracy has changed. The institutions that used to be effective in mediating popular sentiment have atrophied … Politicians have always used various instruments to try to judge where the public stood. And now polls and focus groups are the best available means.

This does not necessarily mean the end of passion within politics. In fact it can be argued that more Product-Oriented Party behaviour is anti-democratic. Gould (1998b: 19), discussing the 1983 election, suggests that Labour had failed in its representative role; it 'had not merely stopped listening or lost touch: it had declared political war on the values, instincts and ethics of the great majority of decent, hard-working voters'. Similarly, defending later changes in the Labour Party, Tom Sawyer (quoted in Gould (1998b: 88)) told the Fabian Society in June 1988 that:

> We want to win the next General Election. And to anyone who says this is crude or unprincipled, I say that to put Labour into government, into a position where we can put our principles into practice, is the most sophisticated and principled aim that the Party could have.

There are clearly many points of view to be considered when assessing the normative significance of political marketing. This book, not surprisingly, would side on the positive side: that market-oriented political marketing makes parties more responsive to people which is ultimately the point of democracy. But clearly this debate is one that has only just begun and has some way to run before reaching a satisfactory conclusion, if that will ever be possible.

### The political marketing revolution

Political marketing can also be applied to other areas of politics: to local government, Parliament, the civil service, public policy, the public services and even the media. These would have different products, markets and goals and research would need to adapt the theoretical framework before conducting empirical study. Nonetheless political marketing holds the potential to provide a new set of analytical tools and concepts which can be applied to many areas: it is an exciting development for political science. Indeed, given the focus of Market-Oriented Parties on delivery, marketing perhaps needs to be applied to policy legislation and implementation. Political parties themselves, such as New Labour, are paying increased attention to the delivery part of the political process. This is understandable when it is now so important to their ability to attract support. There is no point in parties offering to meet voters' demands, asking for support on this basis, if the systems of implementation are ineffective. Research could draw upon the marketing literature which studies non-profit organisations generally, but consider and integrate the substantial political science research on policy formulation, design, networks and implementation. This could be analysed in conjunction with the concepts of marketing. These include the need to conduct market intelligence and general feedback from users and the need to implement a design which takes into account the costs (and so involves the Treasury), organisations (the civil service), institutions (the legislature which needs to pass the legislation) and so on; all with the perspective of responding to the organisation's 'market'. Another area of focus within this might be particular public services (see, for example, Christy and Brown (1999), Butler and Collins (1995) and Walsh (1994)). Research might also look at local government, examining for example the use of market intelligence by local councils. As Kotler and Levy (1969: 15) argued in their seminal article on broadening the concept of marketing:

> The [marketing] concept of sensitively serving and satisfying human needs ... provides a useful concept for all organisations. All organisations are formed to serve the interest of particular groups: hospitals serve the sick, schools serve the students, governments serve the citizens, and labour unions serve the members ... Marketing is that function of the organisation that can keep in constant touch with the organisation's consumers, read their needs, develop 'products' that meet these needs, and build a program of communications to express the organisation's purposes.

The other aspect to this is that the rise of political marketing may lead to changes in the governance of Britain. For example, the New Labour Government introduced a new approach to the public services at the local government level called 'best value', at least in part because it wishes to ensure that services are delivered effectively. Being market-oriented, it knows the importance of delivery to its success and therefore seeks to influence other governmental arenas. The marketing of parties may stimulate the marketing of public services but also the systemic nature of policy implementation, therefore including public administration and different levels of government. The development of political marketing in one area may lead to changes in other parts of the political system, altering the overall picture of how Britain is governed.

## Conclusion

Political marketing is making politics more responsive to its market: political organisations, such as political parties, are identifying the needs and wants of those they seek to serve and attempting to meet these demands. Political marketing is not about manipulation: rather than changing voter demands, it is concerned with responding to them. It has important potential with regard to the representative function of a political system and democracy in general.

Political marketing has helped British parties adapt to challenges in their environment and serve the people. Currently both major parties in Britain are attempting to respond more effectively to voter concerns. Neither is resting on support via political socialisation: each is concentrating on how best to make the system of government best serve the needs of voters, even if only to win elections. Political marketing is an answer to party decline and will help reduce voter dissatisfaction. Gould (1998b: 272) noted of Labour's pledges:

> The pledges have established a new pattern which will not be broken: hard, concrete accountable promises that are, effectively, a binding contract with the electorate; manifestos not just agreed by a few politicians in smoke-filled rooms but agreed by the party. *This is the way of the future, it is the way trust in politics will be restored.* (My emphasis.)

Similarly, Stuart Hogue, a Conservative Party Campaign Officer, said (Hogue (2000)) that 'with any product: you have to know what people want to be able to design something to satisfy and benefit people ... that's where the true value of government comes from'. Throughout this century, political parties have changed their behaviour in response to changes in their environment to ensure their survival. Political marketing is simply the most recent development. As Duverger (1954: 427) argued:

> The real way of protecting democracy against the toxins that it secretes within itself in the course of its development does not lie in cutting it off from modern techniques for organising the masses and recruiting leaders ... but in diverting these to its use, for they are in the last resort mere tools, capable no doubt of being used for good as well as for evil. To refuse to use them is to refuse to act.

Political marketing, far from being about 'designer politics' or manipulation, is about creating voter satisfaction and politicians actually delivering what they say they will. It does not mean that politicians have no role to play, or that there is no room for passion in politics. Although people such as Philip Gould and Peter Mandelson, and even Tony Blair, may be criticised for the way they have changed the Labour Party, this does not mean that they or their Conservative counterparts now changing the Tory party do not care. They are trying to find a more modern and effective way to fulfil those passions and desire to represent the people under different conditions. Before the 1997 election Tony Blair was interviewed as part of a BBC programme on the Labour Party and said (BBC (1995)):

> I am never in any doubt as to what the Labour party has to do in order to become a viable left-of-centre party of government again; I'm never in any doubt about that. I mean, I know it sounds arrogant to say it, but to me the values and principles of the Labour Party are what brought me into the Labour Party. You know, the belief in a strong and decent, cohesive society

as necessary for the betterment of the individual; the belief in social justice – the need to combat the social and economic evils around us, but the means of achieving those have got to be different in today's world.

Parties still fulfil the same functions as they did when the Mass Party Model was prevalent, such as representation, socialisation and aggregation of interests, but they do so in a different way. It is a new way of behaving under changed electoral conditions: it is about party adaptation rather than party decline. Ultimately, its success will depend not on theoretical concepts or models, but on the behaviour of the politicians. If used well, it holds much potential, not just in helping parties find electoral support and a new role in the political system, but in helping government and political elites respond to the people and continue to play a vital role in modern democracy. The pressure on the two major parties currently is intense. They compete to convince voters that they are the most Market-Oriented Party, capable of delivering what the people want. It is the voters who will ultimately decide which one is best, at the next general election. The market is open, the competition high, and the players fighting to win. In other words, *The party's just begun.*

# Bibiliography

Anderson, Paul F. (1982), 'Marketing, Strategic Planning and the Theory of the Firm', *Journal of Marketing*, 46, 15–26 (Spring).

Arndt, Johan (1978), 'How Broad should the Marketing Concept Be?', *Journal of Marketing*, 42:1, 101–3 (January).

Baines, Paul, Fritz Plasser and Christian Schuecher (1999), 'Investigating the Operationalisation of the Political Marketing Concept: A Comparison of US and Western European Consultants and Party Managers', Paper presented at the Political Marketing Conference, Bournemouth University (15–16 September).

Baker, David, David Seawright and Dominic Wring (1999), 'Panelism in Action: Labour's 1999 European Parliamentary Candidate Selections', Paper presented at the EPOP (Elections, Public Opinion and Parties) Conference, University College Northampton (17–19 September).

Ball, Stuart (1998), *The Conservative Party since 1945*, Manchester University Press.

Banker, Steve (1992), 'The Ethics of Political Marketing, the Rhetorical Perspective', *Journal of Business Ethics*, 11, 843–8.

Bartels, R. (1974), 'The Identity Crisis in Marketing', *Journal of Marketing*, 38, 73–6 (October).

Bauer, Hans H., Frank Huber and Andreas Herrmann (1996), 'Political Marketing: An Information-Economic Analysis', *European Journal of Marketing*, 30: 10–11, 159–72.

BBC (1995), *The Wilderness Years*, Television programme (December).

Behrens, Robert (1980), *The Conservative Party from Heath to Thatcher: Policies and Politics 1976–79*, Saxon House.

Bell, Tim (1982), 'The Conservatives' Advertising Campaign', Chapter 2 in Robert M. Worcester and Martin Harrop (eds), *Political Communications: The General Election Campaign of 1979*, George Allen and Unwin.

Blair, Tony (1997), First speech as Prime Minister.

Blake, Robert (1985), *The Conservative Party from Peel to Thatcher*, Methuen.

Blumler, J., D. Kavanagh and T. Nossiter (1996), 'Modern Communications versus Traditional Politics in Britain: Unstable Marriage of Convenience', Chapter 2 in David L. Swanson and Paolo Mancini (eds), *Politics, Media, and Modern Democracy. An International Study of Innovations in Electoral Campaigning and Their Consequences*, Praeger.

Bogdanor, Vernon (ed.) (1984), *Parties and Democracy in Britain and America*, Praeger.

Bowler, Shaun and David M. Farrell (eds) (1992), *Electoral Strategies and Political Marketing*, Macmillan.

Broughton, David (1999), 'After the Welsh Assembly Elections of May 1999: the Debut of Disillusion?', Paper presented at the EPOP (Elections, Public Opinion and Parties) Conference, University College Northampton (17–19 September).

Brown, Andrew J. (1992), 'The Major Effect: Changes in Party Leadership and Party Popularity', *Parliamentary Affairs*, 45: 4, 518–27.

Brownlie, D. and M. Saren (1992), 'The Four Ps of the Marketing Concept: Prescriptive, Polemical, Permanent and Problematical', *European Journal of Marketing*, 26: 4.

Buffachi, Vittorio and Simon Burgess (1998), *Italy since 1989: Events and Intepretations*, Macmillan.

Burch, Martin (1986), 'The Politics of Persuasion and the Conservative Leadership's Campaign', Chapter 2 in Ivor Crewe and Martin Harrop (eds), *Political Communications: The General Election Campaign of 1983*, Cambridge University Press.

Buscombe, Peta (1998), *Statement: Hague launches new Network for Young Professionals*, Information from the Conservative Party (24 April).

Butler, David (1996), 'Polls and Elections', Chapter 9 in Lawrence LeDuc, Richard G. Niemi and Pippa Norris (eds), *Comparing Democracies: Elections and Voting in Global Perspective*, Sage.

Butler, David and Dennis Kavanagh (1980), *The British General Election of 1979*, Macmillan.

Butler, David and Dennis Kavanagh (1984), *The British General Election of 1983*, Macmillan.

Butler, David and Dennis Kavanagh (1988), *The British General Election of 1987*, Macmillan.

Butler, David and Dennis Kavanagh (1992), *The British General Election of 1992*, Macmillan.

Butler, David and Dennis Kavanagh (1997), *The British General Election of 1997*, Macmillan.

Butler, Patrick and Neil Collins (1994), 'Political Marketing: Structure and Process.' *European Journal of Marketing*, 28: 1, 19–34.

Butler, Patrick and Neil Collins (1995), 'Marketing Public Sector Services: Concepts and Characteristics', *Journal of Marketing Management*, 11.

Butler, Patrick and Neil Collins (1996), 'Strategic Analysis in Political Markets', *European Journal of Marketing*, 30: 10–11, 32–44.

Butler, Patrick and Neil Collins (1998), 'Public Services in Ireland: A Marketing Perspective.' *Working Paper*, Department of Public Administration, National University of Ireland, Cork, No. VII (August).

Byrd, Peter (1986), 'The Labour Party in Britain', Chapter 3 in W. E. Paterson and A. H. Thomas (eds), *The Future of Social Democracy*. Clarendon.

Cannon, Tom (1996), *Basic Marketing: Principles and Practice*, Cassell.

Carman, J. (1973), 'On the Universality of Marketing', *Journal of Contemporary Business*, 2: 4.

Charter Movement (The) (2000), Informal discussion with members of the Charter Movement Committee and the author (29 July).

Christy, Richard and Jill Brown (1999), 'Marketing in the Public Services,' Chapter 6 in Sylvia Horton and David Farnham (eds), *Public Management in Britain*, Macmillan.

Clemens, John (1983), *Polls, Politics and Populism*, Gower.

Conservative Party (The) (1979), Party Manifesto.

Conservative Party (The) (1983), Party Manifesto.

Conservative Party (The) (1987), *The Next Moves Forward*, Party Manifesto.

Conservative Party (The) (1992), *The Best Future for Britain*, Party Manifesto.

Conservative Party (The) (1997a), *You Can Only be Sure with the Conservatives*, Party Manifesto

Conservative Party (The) (1997b), *Our Party: Blueprint for Change*, The Conservative Party.

Conservative Party (The) (1998a), *The Fresh Future: White Paper on Organisational Reform*, The Conservative Party (February).

Conservative Party (The) (1998b), *Listening to Britain Constituency Manual*, The Conservative Party (July).

Conservative Party (The) (1998–99), *Listening to Britain: List of Events*, Correspondence from Conservative Central Office (July–May).

Conservative Party (The) (1999a), *Speak out: Your say on tomorrow's challenges: Listening to Britain*, A Conservative Party Leaflet.

Conservative Party (The) (1999b), *Heartland: The Conservative Party Magazine*, The Conservative Party (October).

Conservative Party (The) (1999c), *Listening to Britain: A Report by the Conservative Party*, The Conservative Party (Autumn).

Conservative Party (The) (1999d), *The Common Sense Revolution*, The Conservative Party (Autumn).

Cook, Robin (1995), 'The Labour Campaign', Chapter 5 in Ivor Crewe and Brian Gosschalk (eds), *Political Communications: The General Election Campaign of 1992*, Cambridge University Press.

Cousins, L. (1990), 'Marketing Planning in the Public and Non-profit Sectors', *European Journal of Marketing*, 24: 7, 15–30.

Cowley, Philip (1997), 'The Conservative Party: Decline and Fall', Chapter 3 in Andrew Geddes and Jonathan Tonge (eds), *Labour's Landslide: The British General Election 1997*, Manchester University Press.

Crewe, Ivor (1981), 'Why the Conservatives Won', Chapter 9 in Howard R. Penniman (ed.), *Britain at the Polls, 1979 – A Study of the General Election*, AEI Studies.

Crewe, Ivor (1992), 'Class Dealignment', Chapter 3.2 in D. Denver and G. Hands (eds), *Issues and Controversies in British Electoral Behaviour*, Harvester Wheatsheaf.

Crewe, Ivor, Brian Gosschalk and John Bartle (eds) (1998), 'Introduction', in *Political Communications: Why Labour won the General Election of 1997*, Frank Cass.

Croft, Stuart (1992), 'The Labour Party and the Nuclear Issue', Chapter 14 in M. J. Smith and J. Spear (eds), *The Changing Labour Party*, Routledge.

Crowther-Hunt, Lord and A. Peacock (1973), 'Royal Commission on the Constitution 1969–73', *Memorandum of Dissent*, 2 HMSO.

Curtice, John and Roger Jowell (1995), 'The Sceptical Electorate', Chapter 7 in Roger Jowell, John Curtice, Alison Park, Lindsay Brook and Daphne Ahrendt with Katarina Thomson (eds), *British Social Attitudes: The 12th Report*, Gower.

Dalton, Russell J. (1988), *Citizen Politics in Western Democracies: Public Opinion and Political Parties in the United States, Great Britain, West Germany, and France*, Chatham House.

Dalton, Russell J. (1996), 'Political Cleavages, Issues, and Electoral Change', in Lawrence LeDuc, Richard G. Niemi and Pippa Norris (eds), *Comparing Democracies: Elections and Voting in Global Perspective*, Sage.

Dalton, Russell J. and Manfred Knechler (eds) (1990), *Challenging the Political Order: New Social Movements in Western Democracies*, Polity.

Dann, Susan and Stephen Dann (1998), 'The Failure of Mainstream Political Marketing as a Contributing Factor in the Success of One Nation in Queensland', Paper presented at the Political Marketing Conference, University of Cork, Ireland (17–19 September).

Day, George S., Allan D. Shocker and Rajendra K. Srivastava (1979), 'Customer-Oriented Approaches to Identifying Product-Markets', *Journal of Marketing*, 43, 8–19 (Autumn).

Delaney, Barry (1994), 'Commentary: Political Marketing', *Contemporary Record*, 8: 1, 44–8 (Summer).

Delaney, Tim (1982), 'Labour's Advertising Campaign', Chapter 3 in Robert M. Worcester and Martin Harrop (eds), *Political Communications: The General Election Campaign of 1979*, George Allen and Unwin.

Denton Jr, Robert E. (ed.) (1992), 'Primetime Politics: The Ethics of Teledemocracy', Chapter 6 in *Ethical Dimensions of Political Communication*, Praeger.

Denver, David (1994), *Elections and Voting Behaviour in Britain*, Harvester Wheatsheaf.

Denver, David (1998), 'The Government That Could Do No Right', Chapter 2 in Anthony King (ed.), *New Labour Triumphs: Britain at the Polls*, Chatham House.

Dermody, Janine, Kevin Moloney and Richard Scullion (1999), 'What is Political Marketing and What Might it Be?', Paper presented at the Political Marketing Conference, Bournemouth University (15–16 September).

Deschouwer, Kris (1996), 'Political Parties and Democracy: A Mutual Murder?', *European Journal of Political Research*, 29: 3, 263–78.

Downs, Anthony (1957), *An Economic Theory of Democracy*, Harper and Row.

Drucker, Peter F. (1973), *Management: Tasks, Responsibilities, Practices*, Harper and Row.

Dunleavy, Patrick (2000), 'Slippery Polls', *Guardian* (31 January).

Dunleavy, Patrick (with Hugh Ward) (1991), Chapter 4: 'Economic Explanations of Voting Behaviour' and Chapter 5 'Party Competition – The Preference-Shaping Model', in *Democracy, Bureaucracy and Public Choice: Economic Explanations in Political Science*, Harvester Wheatsheaf.

Duverger, Maurice (1954), *Political Parties*, Methuen and Company.

Evans, Eric J. (1997), *Thatcher and Thatcherism*, Routledge.

Evans, G., A. Heath and C. Payne (1999), 'Class: Labour as a Catch-All Party?', Chapter 5 in Geoffrey Evans and Pippa Norris (eds), *Critical Elections: British Parties and Voters in Long-term Perspective*, Sage.

Evans, J. R. and B. Berman (1994), *Marketing*, Macmillan.

Farnham, David (1996), 'New Labour, the New Unions and the New Labour Market', *Parliamentary Affairs*, 49: 4, 584–98.

Farrell, David M. (1996), 'Campaign Strategies and Tactics', Chapter 6 in Lawrence LeDuc, Richard G. Niemi and Pippa Norris (eds), *Comparing Democracies: Elections and Voting in Global Perspective*, Sage.

Farrell, David M. and Martin Wortmann (1987), 'Party Strategies in the Electoral Market: Political Marketing in West Germany, Britain and Ireland', *European Journal of Political Research*, 15, 297–318.

Fielding, Steven (1995), *Labour: Decline and Renewal*, Baseline.

Fielding, Steven (1997a), 'Labour's Path to Power', Chapter 2 in Andrew Geddes and Jonathan Tonge (eds), *Labour's Landslide: The British General Election 1997*, Manchester University Press.

Fielding, Steven (1997b), *Socialism and Society since 1951*, Manchester University Press.

Finkelstein, Daniel (1998), 'Why the Conservatives Lost', Chapter 2 in Ivor Crewe, Brian Gosschalk and John Bartle (eds), *Political Communications: Why Labour Won the General Election of 1997*, Frank Cass.

Fiorina, Morris P. (1981), *Retrospective Voting in American National Elections*, Yale University Press.

Fletcher, Winston (1997), 'Trusty as Underpants', *Guardian* (23 October).

Foxall, G. (1989), 'Marketing's Domain', *European Journal of Marketing*, 23: 8, 7–22.

Francis, Rachel (1999), Letter about listening to Britain, correspondence with author (18 May).

Francis, Rachel (2000), Interview between Rachel Francis (Listening to Britain Officer, The Conservative Party) and the author (11 April).

Franklin, Bob (1994), *Packaging Politics: Political Communications in Britain's Media Democracy*, Edward Arnold.

Franklin, Mark N (1985), *The Decline of Class Voting in Britain: Changes in the Basis of Electoral Choice 1964–1983*, Clarendon.

Gallagher, Michael, Michael Laver and Peter Mair (1995), *Representative Government in Modern Europe*, McGraw Hill.

Garner, Robert and Richard Kelly (1998), *British Political Parties Today*, Manchester University Press.

Gavin, Neil T. and David Saunders (1997), 'The Economy and Voting', *Parliamentary Affairs* 50: 4, 631–40.

George, Stephen and Ben Rosamond (1992), 'The European Community', Chapter 12 in M. J. Smith and J. Spear (eds), *The Changing Labour Party*, Routledge.

Gould, Philip (1985), *Report on Labour Party Communications* (18 November).

Gould, Philip (1998a), 'Why Labour Won', Chapter 1 in Ivor Crewe, Brian Gosschalk and John Bartle (eds), *Political Communications: Why Labour Won the General Election of 1997*, Frank Cass.

Gould, Philip (1998b), *The Unfinished Revolution: How the Modernisers saved the Labour Party*, Little Brown.

Gould, Philip (1999), 'Spinning and Winning', Presentation at the Political Marketing Conference, Bournemouth University (15–16 September).

Gould, Philip, Peter Herd and Chris Powell (1989), 'The Labour Party's Campaign Communications', Chapter 8 in Ivor Crewe and Martin Harrop (eds), *Political Communications: The General Election Campaign of 1987*, Cambridge University Press.

Grant, Nick (1986), 'A Comment on Labour's Campaign', Chapter 8 in Ivor Crewe and Martin Harrop (eds), *Political Communications: The General Election Campaign of 1983*, Cambridge University Press.

Greenstein, Rachel (1999), 'Incestuous Institutions: Political Parties and the Media's Coverage of the 1999 Scottish Elections', Paper presented at the EPOP (Elections, Public Opinion and Parties) Conference, University College Northampton (17–19 September).

Gwin, John M. (1990), 'Constituent Analysis: A Paradigm for Marketing Effectiveness in the Not-for-profit Organisation', *European Journal of Marketing* 24: 7, 43–8.

Hague, William (1998a), *The Fresh Future*, Statement provided by Conservative Central Office (16 February).

Hague, William (1998b), *The Fresh Future*, Speech at The Fresh Future Launch Conference, Information from the Conservative Party (28 March).

Hague, William (1998c), Opening Speech, Conservative Party Conference (6 October).

Hague, William (1999), Interview: *On the Record*, BBC (14 March).

Hall, Dave, Rob Jones and Carlo Raffo (1996), *Business Studies*, Causeway.

Harmel, Robert and Kenneth Janda (1994), 'An Integrated Theory of Party Change', *Journal of Theoretical Politics*, 6: 3, 259–87.

Harris, Phil (1996), 'Editorial', *European Journal of Political Marketing*, 30: 10–11, 18–20.

Harris, Phil, Andrew Lock and Terese Neivelt (1999), 'Perceptions of Political Marketing in Sweden: A Comparative Perspective', Paper presented at the Political Marketing Conference, Bournemouth University (15–16 September).

Harrop, Martin. (1986), 'Voting and the Electorate', in H. M. Drucker *et al.* (eds), *Developments in British Politics*, Macmillan.

Harrop, Martin (1990), 'Political Marketing,' *Parliamentary Affairs*, 43: 3, 277–91

Harrop, Martin (1997), 'The Pendulum Swings: The British Election of 1997', *Goverment and Opposition*, 32, 305–19.

Heath, Anthony and Richard Topf (1987), 'Political Culture', Chapter 3 in Roger Jowell, Sharon Witherspoon and Lindsay Brook (eds), *British Social Attitudes: The 1987 Report*, Gower.

Heath, Anthony and Roger Jowell (1994), 'Labour's Policy Review', Chapter 11 in Anthony Heath, Roger Jowell and John Curtice with Bridget Taylor (eds), *Labour's Last Chance? The 1992 Election and Beyond*, Dartmouth.

Heath, Anthony, Roger Jowell and John Curtice (1994), 'Introduction', Chapter 1 in Anthony Heath, Roger Jowell and John Curtice with Bridget Taylor (eds), *Labour's Last Chance? The 1992 Election and Beyond*, Dartmouth.

Heath, A., R. Jowell, J. Curtice, G. Evans, J. Field and S. Witherspoon (1991), *Understanding Political Change*, Pergamon.

Henig, Simon (1997), 'Labour's Target Seats Strategy', Paper presented to the EPOP (Elections, Public Opinion and Parties) Conference, the University of Essex (26–28 September).

Hewitt, Patricia and Peter Mandelson (1989), 'The Labour Campaign', Chapter 5 in Ivor Crewe and Martin Harrop (eds), *Political Communications: The General Election Campaign of 1987*, Cambridge University Press.

Hill, David (1995), 'The Labour Party's Strategy', in Ivor Crewe and Brian Gosschalk (eds), *Political Communications: The General Election Campaign of 1992*, Cambridge University Press.

Hilton, Steve (1998), 'The Conservative Party's Advertising Strategy', Chapter 5 in Ivor Crewe, Brian Gosschalk and John Bartle (eds), *Political Communications: Why Labour Won the General Election of 1997*, Frank Cass.

Himmelweit, H., P. Humphreys, M. Jaegar and M. Katz (1993), *How Voters Decide*, Academic.

Hodder-Williams, Richard (1970), *Public Opinion Polls and British Politics*, Routledge and Kegan Paul.

Hogg, Sarah and Jonathan Hill (1995), *Too Close to Call: Power and Politics – John Major in No. 10*, Little Brown and Company.

Hogue, Stuart (2000), Interview between Stuart Hogue, a Campaign Officer, The Common Sense Revolution, The Conservative Party and the author (11 April).

Hooley, Graham, James E. Lynch and Jenny Shepherd (1990), 'The Marketing Concept: Putting Theory into Practice', *European Journal of Marketing*, 24: 9, 7–24.

Hotelling, Harold (1929), 'Stability in Competition', *Economic Journal*, 30.

Houston, F. (1986), 'The Marketing Concept: What it Is and What it Is Not', *Journal of Marketing*, 50, 81–7 (April).

Hughes, C. and P. Wintour (1990), *Labour Rebuilt: The New Model Party*, 4th Estate.

Hunt, Shelby D. (1976), 'The Nature and Scope of Marketing', *Journal of Marketing*, 40, 17–28.

Ingram, Peter and Jennifer Lees-Marshment (1999–2000), 'The Anglicisation of Political Marketing: How Blair Out-marketed Clinton', unpublished work-in-progress.

Jaworski, J. B. and K. A. Kohli (1993), 'Market Orientation: Antecedents and Consequences', *Journal of Marketing*, 57, 53–70 (July).

Jones, George (1998), 'We've Set a Cracking Pace, says Blair', *Daily Telegraph* (31 July).

Jones, Nicholas (1997), *Campaign 1997: How the General Election was Won and Lost*, Indigo.

Jun, Uwe (1996), 'Inner-Party Reforms: The SPD and Labour Party in Comparative Perspective', *German Politics*, 5: 1, 58–80 (April).

Katz, R. S. (1990), 'Party as Linkage: A Vestigal Function?', *European Journal of Political Research*, 18, 143–62.

Katz, Richard S. and Peter Mair (1995), 'Changing Models of Party Organisation and Party Democracy: The Emergence of the Cartel Party', *Party Politics*, 1: 1, 5–28.

Katz, Richard S. and Peter Mair (eds) (1994), *How Parties Organise: Change and Adaptation in Party Organisations in Western Democracies*, Sage.

Kavanagh, Dennis (1982), *The Politics of the Labour Party*, George Allen and Unwin.

Kavanagh, Dennis (1987), *Thatcherism and British Politics – The End of Consensus?*, Oxford University Press.

Kavanagh, Dennis (1992), 'Private Polls and Campaign Strategists', *Parliamentary Affairs*, 45: 4, 518–27.

Kavanagh, Dennis (1995), *Election Campaigning: The New Marketing of Politics*, Blackwell.

Kavanagh, Dennis (1997), 'The Labour Campaign', *Parliamentary Affairs*, 50: 4, 533–41.

Keith, Robert J. (1960), 'The Marketing Revolution', *Journal of Marketing*, 35–8 (January).

Kellner, Peter (1997), 'Why the Tories were Trounced', *Parliamentary Affairs*, 50: 4, 616–30.

King, Anthony (1981), 'Politics, Economics and the Trade Unions, 1974–1979', Chapter 2 in Howard R. Penniman (eds), *Britain at the Polls, 1979 – A Study of the General Election*, AEI Studies.

King, Anthony (1998a), 'The Night Itself', Chapter 1 in Anthony King (ed.), *New Labour Triumphs: Britain at the Polls*, Chatham House.

King, Anthony (1998b), 'Why Labour Won – At Last', Chapter 7 in King (ed.), *New Labour Triumphs: Britain at the Polls*, Chatham House.

King, Anthony (1999), 'Hague the Scapegoat for Unpopular Tories', *Daily Telegraph* (3 September).

King, Tony and George Jones (1998), 'Labour Breaks All Records with Year of Success', *Daily Telegraph* (1 May).

Kirchheimer, Otto (1966), 'The Transformation of the Western European Party Systems', Chapter 6 in Myron Weiner and Joseph LaPalombara (eds), *Political Parties and Political Development*, Princeton University Press.

Kitchselt, Herbet (1990), 'New Social Movements and the Decline of Party Organisations', Chapter 10 in Russell J. Dalton and Manfred Knechler (eds), *Challenging the Political Order: New Social Movements in Western Democracies*, Polity.

Kleinman, Philip (1982), *The Saatchi and Saatchi Story*, Weidenfeld and Nicolson.

Klingemann, H. D., R. I. Hofferbet and I. Budge (1994), *Parties, Policies and Democracy*, Westview.

Kohli, Ajay K. and Bernard J. Jaworski (1990), 'Market Orientation: The Construct, Research Propositions, and Managerial Implications', *Journal of Marketing*, 54, 1–18 (April).

Koole, Rund (1996), 'Cadre, Catch-all or Cartel? A Comment on the Notion of the Cartel Party', *Party Politics*, 2: 4, 507–23.

Kotler, Philip (1972), 'A Generic Concept of Marketing', *Journal of Marketing*, 36, 46–54 (April).

Kotler, Philip (1977), 'From Sales Obsession to Marketing Effectiveness', *Harvard Business Review*, 67–75 (November–December).

Kotler, Philip (1979), 'Strategies for Introducing Marketing into Non-profit Organisations', *Journal of Marketing*, 43, 37–44 (January).

Kotler, Philip and Alan R. Andreasen (1991), *Strategic Marketing for Non-profit Organisations*, Prentice-Hall.

Kotler, Philip and Sidney J. Levy (1969), 'Broadening the Concept of Marketing', *Journal of Marketing*, 33: 1, 10–15 (January).

Labour Party (The) (1979), *The Labour Way is the Better Way*, Party Manifesto.

Labour Party (The) (1983), *The New Hope for Britain*, Party Manifesto.

Labour Party (The) (1987), *Britain will win with Labour*, Party Manifesto.

Labour Party (The) (1988), *Social Justice and Economic Efficiency: First Report of Labour's Policy Review for the 1990s*.

Labour Party (The) (1989), *Meet the Challenge, Make the Change: Final Report of Labour's Policy Review for the 1990s*.

Labour Party (The) (1990), *Looking to the Future*.

Labour Party(The) (1991), *Opportunity Britain: Labour's better way for the 1990s*.

Labour Party (The) (1992), *It's Time to get Britain Working Again*, Party Manifesto.

Labour Party (The) (1994), *Report of the Annual Conference*.

Labour Party (The) (1997), *New Labour Because Britain Deserves Better*, Party Manifesto.

Labour Party (The) (1998), *Shaping our Future: A Consultative Survey on the Future of Britain* (June).

Labour Party (The) (1999), *The Government's Annual Report 1998/1999*, The Stationery Office.

Labour Party (The) (2000), *The Government's Annual Report 99/00*, The Stationery Office.

Laczniak, Gene R., Robert F. Lusch and Patrick E. Murphy (1979), 'Social Marketing: Its Ethical Dimensions', *Journal of Marketing*, 43, 29–36 (Spring).

Lancaster, Geoff and Lester Massingham (1993), *Essentials of Marketing*, McGraw-Hill.

Lansley, Andrew (1997), 'The Future of the Conservative Party', Presentation at the Elections, Parties and Opinion Polls Conference, Essex University (September).

Lansley, Andrew (1998), *Statement: A Unique Event in Conservative Party Policy-Making*, Information from the Conservative Party (1 October).

Lansley, Andrew (1999), Letter about Listening to Britain, Correspondence with author (9 June).

Laver, Michael (1997), *Private Desires, Political Action*, Sage.

LeDuc, Lawrence, Richard G. Niemi and Pippa Norris (eds) (1996), *Comparing Democracies: Elections and Voting in Global Perspective*, Sage.

Lees-Marshment, Jennifer (1997), *The Extent and Limits of Political Marketing: the case of the British Labour Party 1987–1997*, unpublished M.A. thesis, Department of Government, University of Manchester.

Lees-Marshment, Jennifer (1999), 'Broadening the Concept of Marketing: How to Market a Political Party', *Working Paper Series* Number XI, Department of Government, University College Cork (July).

Lees-Marshment, Jennifer and Stuart Quayle (2001), 'Empowering the Members or Marketing the Party? The Conservative Reforms of 1998', *The Political Quarterly* (forthcoming).

Leonard, Allan (1998), 'Think Different: Vote Alliance – Political Marketing in a Cross-Community Party in Northern Ireland', Paper presented at the Political Marketing Conference, University of Cork, Ireland (17–19 September).

241

Leonard, Dick (1981), 'The Labour Campaign', Chapter 3 in Howard R. Penniman (ed.), *Britain at the Polls, 1979 – A Study of the General Election*, AEI Studies.

Leppard, David, Paul Nuki, Gareth Walsh and Michael Prescott (2000), 'Secret Memo shows Labour Fear of Hague', *Sunday Times* (28 May).

Levitt, Theodore (1960), 'Marketing Myopia', *Harvard Business Review*, 45–56 (July–August).

Lilley, Peter (1998), Statement on Listening to Britain, Information from the Conservative Party (14 July).

Lipow, Arthur and Patrick Seyd (1996), 'The Politics of Anti-Partyism', *Parliamentary Affairs*, 49: 2, 273–84.

Lipsey, David (1992), 'The Name of Rose', *Fabian Pamphlet*, 554 (July).

Lipsey, David, Andrew Shaw and John Williamson (1989), 'Labour's Electoral Challenge', *Fabian Research Series*, 352 (April).

Livingston, William S. (1981), 'The Conservative Campaign', Chapter 4 in Howard R. Penniman (ed.), *Britain at the Polls, 1979 – A Study of the General Election*, AEI Studies.

Lock, Andrew and Phil Harris (1996), 'Political Marketing – Vive la difference!', *European Journal of Marketing*, 30: 10–11, 21–31.

Lovelock, Christopher H. and Charles B. Weisberg (1977), *Public and Nonprofit Marketing: Cases and Readings*, Scientific Press.

Luck, D. (1969), 'Broadening the Concept of Marketing – Too Far,' *Journal of Marketing*, 33, 53–5 (July).

Mair, Peter (1989), 'Continuity, Change and the Vulnerability of Party', *West European Politics*, 12: 4, 169–87.

Mair, Peter (1994), 'Party Organisations: From Civil Society to the State', Chapter 1 in Richard S. Katz and Peter Mair (eds), *How Parties Organise: Change and Adaptation in Party Organisations in Western Democracies*, Sage.

Mair, Peter (1995), 'Political Parties, Popular Legitimacy and Public Privilege', in Jack Hayward (ed.), *The Crisis of Representation in Europe*, Cass.

Mair, Peter (ed.) (1990), *The West European Party System*, Oxford University Press.

Mancini, Paolo and David L. Swanson (1996), 'Politics, Media, and Modern Democracy: Introduction', Chapter 1 in David L. Swanson and Paolo Mancini (eds), *Politics, Media, and Modern Democracy. An International Study of Innovations in Electoral Campaigning and Their Consequences*, Praeger.

Mandelson, Peter (1988), 'Marketing Labour: Personal Reflections and Experience', *Contemporary Record*, 1: 4, 11–13 (Winter).

McGlone, Francis, Alison Park and Ceridwen Roberts (1996), 'Relative Values: Kinship and Friendship', Chapter 3 in Jowell *et al.* (eds), *British Social Attitudes: The 13th Report*, Dartmouth.

McLean, Iain (1987), *Public Choice: An Introduction*, Basil Blackwell.

McSmith, Andy (1998), 'Old Activists Reign as New Recruits Ditch Labour', *Observer* (18 October).

Moon, Nick (1999), *Opinion Polls: History, Theory and Practice*, Manchester University Press.

Moynihan, Dan and Brian Titley (1995), *Advanced Business*, Oxford University Press.

Muller-Rommel, Ferdinand (1990), 'New Political Movements and "New Politics" Parties in Western Europe', Chapter 11 in Russell J. Dalton and Manfred

Knechler (eds), *Challenging the Political Order: New Social Movements in Western Democracies*, Polity.

Newman, Bruce I. (1994), *The Marketing of the President: Political Marketing as Campaign Strategy*, Sage.

Newman, Bruce I. (1999), *The Mass Marketing of Politics*, Sage.

Newman, Bruce I. (ed.) (1999), *The Handbook of Political Marketing*, Sage.

Newton, Kenneth (1992), 'Caring and Competence: The Long, Long Campaign,' Chapter 5 in King *et al.* (eds), *Britain at the Polls 1992*, Chatham House.

Nicholson, Emma (1996), *Secret Society: Inside – and Outside – The Conservative Party*, Indigo.

Niffenegger, P. B. (1989), 'Strategies for Success from the Political Marketers', *Journal of Consumer Marketing*, 6: 1, 45–61.

Norman, Archie (1998), 'Power to Party Members', *The House Magazine* (30 March).

Norman, Archie (1999a), Letter about the Conservative Party, Correspondence with author (20 May).

Norman, Archie (1999b), Letter about Conservative Central Office Staff, Correspondence with author (23 May).

Norman, Phillip (1998), 'Bill and Seb's Excellent Adventure', *Sunday Times Magazine* (6 September).

Norris, Pippa (1997a), *Electoral Change Since 1945*, Blackwell.

Norris, Pippa (1997b), 'Anatomy of a Labour Landslide,' *Parliamentary Affairs*, 50: 4, 509–32

Norris, Pippa (1998a), 'The Battle for the Campaign Agenda', Chapter 5 in Anthony King (ed.), *New Labour Triumphs: Britain at the Polls*, Chatham House.

Norris, Pippa (1998b), 'New Labour, New Politicians? Changes in the Political Attitudes of Labour MPs 1992–1997', *Paper presented at the Political Studies Association Conference*, University of Keele (7–9 April).

Norton, Philip (1992), 'The Conservative Party from Thatcher to Major', Chapter 2 in King *et al.* (eds), *Britain at the Polls 1992*, Chatham House.

Norton, Philip (1998), 'The Conservative Party: "In Office but Not in Power"', Chapter 4 in Anthony King (ed.), *New Labour Triumphs: Britain at the Polls*, Chatham House.

O'Cass, Aron (1996), 'Political marketing and the marketing concept', *European Journal of Marketing*, 30: 10–11, 45–61.

O'Leary, Ray and Ian Iredale (1976), 'The Marketing Concept: Quo Vadis?', *European Journal of Marketing*, 10: 3, 146–57.

O'Shaughnessy, Nicholas J. (1990), *The Phenomenon of Political Marketing*, Macmillan.

O'Shaughnessy, Nicholas J. (1999), 'Political Marketing and Political Propaganda', Paper presented at the Political Marketing Conference, Bournemouth University (15–16 September).

Palmer, Alasdair (1998), 'Now New Labour Backs What the Tabloid Savages', *Daily Telegraph* (3 May).

Panebianco, Angelo (1988), *Political Parties: Organisation and Power*, Cambridge University Press.

Parkinson, Cecil (1986), 'The Conservative Campaign', Chapter 5 in Ivor Crewe and Martin Harrop (eds), *Political Communications: The General Election Campaign of 1983*, Cambridge University Press.

Payne, Adrian F. (1988), 'Developing a Marketing-Oriented Organisation', *Business Horizons*, 31: 3, 46–53.

Pearce, Malcolm and Geoffrey Stewart (1992), *British Political History 1867–1995*, Routledge.

Peele, Gillian (1990), 'British Political Parties in the 1980s,' Chapter 10 in Anthony Seldon (ed.), *UK Political Parties Since 1945*, Philip Allan.

Peele, Gillian (1998), 'Towards New Conservatives? Organisational Reform and the Conservative Party', *Political Quarterly*, 69: 2, 141–7 (April–June).

Poguntke, Thomas (1996), 'Anti-Party Sentiment – Conceptual Thoughts and Empirical Evidence: Explorations into a Minefield', *European Journal of Political Research*, 29: 3, 319–44.

Poguntke, Thomas and Susan E. Scarrow (1996), 'The Politics of Anti-party Sentiment: Introduction,' *European Journal of Political Research*, 29: 3, 257–62.

Powell, Chris (1998), 'The Role of Labour's Advertising in the 1997 General Election', Chapter 4 in Ivor Crewe, Brian Gosschalk and John Bartle (eds), *Political Communications: Why Labour won the General Election of 1997*, Frank Cass.

Punnett, R. M. (1992), *Selecting the Party Leader: Britain in Comparative Perspective* Harvester Wheatsheaf.

Rathbone, Tim (1982), 'Political Communications in the 1979 General Election Campaign by One Who Was In It', Chapter 5 in Robert M. Worcester and Martin Harrop (eds), *Political Communications: The General Election Campaign of 1979*, George Allen and Unwin.

Reid, David M. (1988), 'Marketing the Political Product', *European Journal of Marketing*, 22: 9, 34–47.

Robertson, David (1979), *A Theory of Party Competition*, John Wiley and Sons.

Rohrschneider, Robert (1993), 'Impact of Social Movements on European Party Systems', *Annals of the American Academy of Political and Social Sciences*, 528 (July).

Rose, Richard (1967), *Influencing Voters: A Study of Campaign Rationality*, Faber and Faber.

Rose, Richard (1997), 'The New Labour Government: On the Crest of a Wave', *Parliamentary Affairs*, 50: 4, 750–6.

Rose, Richard and Ian McAllister (1986), *Voters Begin to Choose: From Closed-Class to Open Elections in Britain*, Sage.

Rose, Richard and Ian McAllister (1990), *The Loyalties of Voters: A Lifetime Learning Model*, Sage.

Rosenbaum, Martin (1997), *From Soapbox to Soundbite: Party Political Campaigning in Britain since 1945*, Macmillan.

Rothschild, Michael (1979), 'Marketing Communications in Non Business Situations – or Why it's So Hard to Sell Brotherhood like Soap', *Journal of Marketing*, 43, 11–20 (Spring).

Sackman, Adrian I. (1996), The Learning Curve Towards New Labour: Neil Kinnock's Corporate Party 1983–92', *European Journal of Marketing*, 30: 10–11, 147–58.

Sainsbury, Diane (1990), 'Party Strategies and Party-voter Linkages', *European Journal of Political Research*, 18, 1–7.

Sanders, David (1992), 'Why the Conservative Party Won – Again', Chapter 6 in King *et al.* (eds), *Britain at the Polls 1992*, Chatham House.

Sanders, David (1998), 'The New Electoral Battleground,' Chapter 8 in Anthony King (ed.), *New Labour Triumphs: Britain at the Polls*, Chatham House.

Scammell, Margaret (1994), 'The Phenomenon of Political Marketing: The Thatcher Contribution', *Contemporary Record*, 8: 1, 23–43 (Summer).

Scammell, Margaret (1995), *Designer Politics: How Elections are Won*, St. Martin's.

Scammell, Margaret (1996), 'The Odd Couple: Marketing and Maggie', *European Journal of Marketing*, 30: 10–11, 122–34.

Scammell, Margaret (1997), 'The Model Professionals? Political Marketing US-Style and the Prospects of Americanisation', Paper presented at the Academy of Marketing Conference, Manchester Metropolitan University (July).

Scammell, Margaret (1999), 'Political Marketing: Lessons for Political Science', *Political Studies*, 47: 4, 718–39.

Scarrow, Susan E. (1996), 'Politicians against Parties: Anti-party Arguments as Weapons for Change in Germany', *European Journal of Political Research*, 29: 3, 297–317.

Scarrow, Susan E. (1998), 'Democracy Within – and Without – Parties: Britian in Comparative Perspective', Paper presented at the EPOP (Elections, Public Opinion and Parties) Conference, University of Manchester (11–13 September).

Schlesinger, Joseph A. (1984), 'On the Theory of Party Organisation', *Journal of Politics*, 46, 369–400.

Schlesinger, Joseph A. (1994), *Political Parties and the Winning of Office*, University of Michigan.

Scrivens, Ellie and Morgan Witzel (1990), 'Editorial', *European Journal of Marketing*, 24: 7, 5–14.

Seyd, Patrick (1998), 'Tony Blair and New Labour', Chapter Three in Anthony King (ed.), *New Labour Triumphs: Britain at the Polls*, Chatham House.

Seyd, Patrick (1999), 'New Parties/New Politics? A Case Study of the British Labour Party', *Party Politics*, 5: 3, 383–405.

Seyd, Patrick and Paul Whiteley (1992), *Labour's Grass Roots: The Politics of Party Membership*, Clarendon.

Seymour-Ure, Colin (1974), *The Political Impact of Mass Media*, Constable.

Shama, Avraham (1976), 'The Marketing of Political Candidates', *Journal of the Academy of Marketing Science*, 4: 4, 764–77.

Shapiro, Benson (1973), 'Marketing for Non-Profit Organisations', *Harvard Business Review*, 51, 123–32 (September–October).

Sharkey, John (1989), 'Saatchi's and the 1987 election', Chapter 7 in Ivor Crewe and Martin Harrop (eds), *Political Communications: The General Election Campaign of 1987*, Cambridge University Press.

Shaw, Eric (1993), 'Towards Renewal? The British Labour Party's Policy Review', *West European Politics*, 16: 1, 112–32 (January).

Shaw, Eric (1994), *The Labour Party Since 1979: Crisis and Transformation*, Routledge.

Short, Clare (1996), 'Interview', *New Statesman* (9 August), pp. 24–7.

Shrimsley, Robert (1999), 'Labour Alarm at Member Slump', *Daily Telegraph* (3 September).

Smith, Gareth and John Saunders (1990), 'The Application of Marketing to British Politics', *Journal of Marketing Management*, 5: 3, 295–306 (Spring).

Smith, Martin J. (1992), 'The Labour Party in Opposition', 'A Return to Revisionism?', and 'Continuity and Change in the Labour Party policy', Chapters 1, 2 and 3 in M. J. Smith and J. Spear (eds), *The Changing Labour Party*, Routledge.

Sopel, John (1995), *Tony Blair: The Moderniser*, Bantam.

Sparrow, Andrew (2000), 'Hague Offers "Grey Voters" £60 million Deal', *Daily Telegraph*. (29 May).

Sparrow, Nick and John Turner (1999), 'Defining a New Politics: The Development of New Market Research Techniques in the Formulation of Strategic Decision-Making within Political Parties', *Paper presented at the Political Marketing Conference*, Bournemouth University (15–16 September).

Strafford, John and Martin Ball (2000), Interview between John Strafford and Martin Ball, Campaign for Conservative Democracy group and the author (11 April).

Strom, Kaare (1990), 'A Behavioural Theory of Competitive Political Parties', *American Journal of Political Science*, 34: 2, 565–98 (May).

Swanson, David L. and Paolo Mancini (1996), 'Patterns of Modern Electoral Campaigning and Their Consequences', Chapter 13 in David L. Swanson and Paolo Mancini (eds), *Politics, Media, and Modern Democracy. An International Study of Innovations in Electoral Campaigning and Their Consequences*, Praeger.

Sylvester, Rachel and Alice Thomson (1998), 'The Asda Boss Now Selling William Hague', *Daily Telegraph* (15 August).

Tebbit, Norman (1989), 'The Conservative Campaign', Chapter 4 in Ivor Crewe and Martin Harrop (eds), *Political Communications: The General Election Campaign of 1987*, Cambridge University Press.

Thatcher, Margaret (1993), *The Downing Street Years*, HarperCollins.

Trustrum, L. (1989), 'Marketing Concept: Concept and Function', *European Journal of Marketing*, 23: 3, 48–56.

Tucker, W. T. (1974), 'Future Directions in Marketing Theory', *Journal of Marketing*, 38: 2, 30–5 (April).

Von der Hart, Hein W. C. (1990), 'Government Organisations and their Customers in the Netherlands: Strategy, Tactics and Operations', *European Journal of Marketing*, 24: 7, 31–42.

Wainwright, Hilary (1987), *Labour: A Tale of Two Parties*, Hogarth.

Wakeham, John (Lord) (1995), 'The Conservative Campaign: Against the Odds', Chapter 1 in Ivor Crewe and Brian Gosschalk (eds), *Political Communications: The General Election Campaign of 1992*, Cambridge University Press.

Walsh, Kieron (1994), 'Marketing and Public Sector Management', *European Journal of Marketing*, 28: 3, 63–71.

Walter, David (1999), 'Media Relationships Into the Future', Paper presented at the Political Marketing Conference, Bournemouth University (15–16 September).

Ward, Lucy (1999), 'Ministers spending millions on secret polls', *Guardian* (3 September).

Ware, Alan (1996), *Political Parties and Party Systems*, Oxford University Press.

Ware, Alan (ed.) (1987), *Political Parties: Electoral Change and Structural Response*, Basil Blackwell.

Webb, Paul (1992a), 'Election Campaigning, Organisational Transformation and the Professionalisation of the British Labour Party', *European Journal and Political Research*, 21, 267–88.

Webb, Paul (1992b), 'Britain: The 1987 campaign', Chapter 3 in Shaun Bowler and David M. Farrell (eds), *Electoral Strategies and Political Marketing*, Macmillan.

Webb, Paul (1994), 'Party Organisational Change in Britain: The Iron Law of Centralisation?', Chapter 5 in Richard S. Katz and Peter Mair (eds), *How Parties Organise: Change and Adaptation in Party Organisations in Western Democracies*, Sage.

Webb, Paul (1995), 'Are British Political Parties in Decline?', *Party Politics*, 1: 3, 299–322.

Webb, Paul (1996), 'Apartisanship and Anti-Party Sentiment in the United Kingdom: Correlates and Constraints', *European Journal of Political Research*, 29: 3, 365–82.

Webb, P. and D. Farrell (1999), 'Party Members and Ideological Change' Chapter 3, in Geoffrey Evans and Pippa Norris (eds), *Critical Elections: British Parties and Voters in Long-term Perspective*, Sage.

Webster Jr, F. E. (1988), 'The Rediscovery of the Marketing Concept', *Business Horizons*, 31: 3, 29–39.

Webster Jr, F. E. (1992), 'The Changing Role of Marketing in the Corporation', *Journal of Marketing*, 56, 1–17 (October).

Wensley, R. (1990), 'The Voice of the Consumer? Speculations on the Limits to the Marketing Analogy', *European Journal of Marketing*, 24: 7, 49–60.

Whiteley, Paul (1983), *The Labour Party in Crisis*, Methuen.

Whiteley, Paul (1997), 'The Conservative Campaign', *Parliamentary Affairs*, 50: 4, 540–52.

Whiteley, Paul (1998), 'New Labour: New Grass-Roots', Distinguished Speaker Presentation, Keele University (22 October).

Whiteley, Paul and Patrick Seyd (1998), 'New Labour – New Grass Roots Party?', Paper presented at the Political Studies Association Conference, University of Keele (April).

Whiteley, Paul, Patrick Seyd and Jeremy Richardson (1994), *True Blues: The Politics of Conservative Party Membership* Clarendon.

Whyte, J. (1988), 'Organisation, Person and Idea Marketing Exchanges', in M. Thomas and N. Waite (eds), *The Marketing Digest*, Heinemann.

Willetts, David (1997), 'Interview', *New Statesman* (17 October), pp. 8–9.

Willetts, David (1998), 'Conservative Renewal', *Political Quarterly*, 69: 2, 110–17 (April–June).

Wilson, Mark and Robin Croft (1999), 'Think Global, Act Local? The Impact of Interna Marketing on Party Activists', Paper presented at the Political Marketing Conference, Bournemouth University (15–16 September).

Woodward, Shaun (1995), 'The Conservative Party's Strategy', Chapter 4 in Ivor Crewe and Brian Gosschalk (eds), *Political Communications: The General Election Campaign of 1992*, Cambridge University Press.

Worcester, Bob (1987), 'Trying the Food on the Dog', *New Statesman* (24 July), pp. 12–13.

Worcester, Robert M. (1998), 'The Media and the Polls: Pundits, Polls and Prognostications in British General Elections', Chapter 6 in Ivor Crewe, Brian Gosschalk and John Bartle (eds), *Political Communications: Why Labour won the General Election of 1997*, Frank Cass.

Worcester, Robert M. and Martin Harrop (eds) (1982), 'The Advertisers – Discussion' and 'The Politicians: Discussion', in Robert M. Worcester and Martin Harrop (eds), *Political Communications: The General Election Campaign of 1979*, George Allen and Unwin.

Wright, Johnny (1986), 'Advertising the Labour Party in 1983', Chapter 7 in Ivor Crewe and Martin Harrop (eds), *Political Communications: The General Election Campaign of 1983*, Cambridge University Press.

Wring, Dominic (1994–95), 'Political Marketing and Organisational Development: The Case of the Labour Party in Britain', *Research Paper in Management Studies 12*, Judge Institute of Management Studies, University of Cambridge.

Wring, Dominic (1996a), 'Political Marketing and Party Development in Britain: A 'Secret' History', *European Journal of Marketing*, 30: 10–11, 100–11.

Wring, Dominic (1996b), 'From Mass Propaganda to Political Marketing: The Transformation of Labour Party Election Campaigning', in Colin Rallings, David M. Farrell, David Denver and David Broughton (eds), *British Elections and Parties Year Book*, Frank Cass.

Wring, Dominic (1997a), 'Reconciling Marketing with Political Science: Theories of Political Marketing', in *Proceedings of the 1997 Academy of Marketing Conference*, Manchester Metropolitan University.

Wring, Dominic (1997b), 'Soundbites versus Socialism: the Changing campaign Philosophy of the British Labour Party', Paper presented to the International Association of Mass Communication Research Conference on Media and Politics, Catholic University of Brussels (27 February–1 March).

# Index